AF662187

INDIGENISATION

Key to Self-Sufficiency and Strategic Capability

GLOBAL DEFENCE INDUSTRIALISATION AND
RE-MODELING THE INDIAN PROGRAMME

INDIGENISATION

Key to Self-Sufficiency and Strategic Capability

GLOBAL DEFENCE INDUSTRIALISATION AND
RE-MODELING THE INDIAN PROGRAMME

RANJIT GHOSH

idsa

INSTITUTE FOR DEFENCE STUDIES & ANALYSES
NEW DELHI

PENTAGON PRESS

Indigenisation: Key to Self-Sufficiency and Strategic Capability

Ranjit Ghosh

First Published in 2016

Copyright © Institute for Defence Studies and Analyses, New Delhi

ISBN 978-81-8274-892-7

All rights reserved. No part of this publication may be reproduced, stored in a retrieval system, or transmitted, in any form or by any means, electronic, mechanical, photocopying, recording, or otherwise, without first obtaining written permission of the copyright owner.

Disclaimer: The views expressed in this book are those of the author and do not necessarily reflect those of the Institute for Defence Studies and Analyses, or the Government of India.

Published by

PENTAGON PRESS
206, Peacock Lane, Shahpur Jat,
New Delhi-110049
Phones: 011-64706243, 26491568
Telefax: 011-26490600
email: rajan@pentagonpress.in
website: www.pentagonpress.in

Branch
Flat No.213, Athena-2,
Clover Acropolis,
Viman Nagar,
Pune-411014
Email: pentagonpresspune@gmail.com

In association with
Institute for Defence Studies and Analyses
No. 1, Development Enclave,
New Delhi-110010
Phone: +91-11-26717983
Website: www.idsa.in

Printed at Aegean Offset Printers, Greater Noida, U.P.

Contents

Acknowledgements *ix*
List of Figures and Tables *xi*

1. Introduction 1
   1.1 Military Capability Development and Sustenance 1
   1.2 Evolution of Indian Defence Industry 4
   1.3 Current Realities of Indian Defence Industry 7
   1.4 Objective and Scope of the Research Work 10

2. Defence Industrialisation in India: The Journey Upto 2015 12
   2.1 Comprehensive National Power 12
   2.2 National Security and Military Capability Development 12
   2.3 Defence Planning in India 13
   2.4 Defence Research and Development (R&D) 13
   2.5 Ordnance Factories (OF's) 16
   2.6 Defence Public Sector Undertakings (DPSU's) 22
   2.7 Private Sector Participation 28
   2.8 Defence Offsets 32
   2.9 Sustenance Engineering and Maintenance Management Aspects: Drivers for Self Sufficiency and Strategic Capability of Imported and Indigenous Systems 33

3. Israeli Defence Industry and Takeaways for India 38
   3.1 Evolution and Growth 38
   3.2 Overview—Trends in Defence Industry Activities 40
   3.3 Government Support 41
   3.4 Procurements 41
   3.5 R&D 42
   3.6 Exports 43
   3.7 Privatisation 44

3.8 Private Sector 45
3.9 Lessons for India 45

4. South Korean Defence Industry's Lessons for India 51
4.1 Evolution and Growth 51
4.2 Overview-Trends in Defence Industry and Defence Reform - 2020 Plan 54
4.3 Government Support 55
4.4 Defence Acquisition Programme Administration (DAPA) 56
4.5 Procurements 58
4.6 R&D 58
4.7 Korea Institute for Defence Analyses (KIDA) 61
4.8 Exports 62
4.9 Private Sector 63
4.10 Lessons for India 64

5. Chinese Defence Industry's Transformational Aspects for India 69
5.1 Evolution and Growth 69
5.2 Overview and Trends 73
5.3 Government Strategic Objective Budgetary Support and Procurement 76
5.4 Indigenous Innovation and Technology Development Strategy 77
5.5 R&D 79
5.6 Exports 83
5.7 Private Sector 84
5.8 Major Reforms Programmes 84
5.9 Foreign Investments 85
5.10 Lessons for India 86

6. US Defence Industrialisation and Reforms: Lessons for India 99
6.1 Evolution and Growth 99
6.2 Overview and Trends 108
6.3 Defence Industrial Base 109
6.4 Sequestration 110
6.5 Procurements and Acquisition Process 110
6.6 Indigenous Innovation and Technology Development Strategy 111
6.7 R&D 112
6.8 Exports and Markets 115
6.9 Privatisation 116
6.10 Major Reforms Programmes 117
6.11 Foreign Investments 118
6.12 Lessons for India 118

7. Re-modeling Indian Defence Industry Apparatus for Accelerating Indigenisation, Self-Sufficiency and Strategic Capability 124

7.1 Introduction 124

7.2 Options Available For Re-modeling the Indian DITB 125

7.3 Remodeling Indian Defence Industry Apparatus 128

7.4 Way Ahead for India 153

7.5 Suggested Action Plan For *MAKE IN INDIA* in Defence Sector 160

Index 170

Acknowledgements

I am grateful to the Institute for Defence Studies and Analyses (IDSA) for providing me the opportunity and all the support in writing this book.

I am also grateful to Mr V.K. Misra, former Secretary, Defence (Finance), Ministry of Defence (MOD) and presently my Centre Guide for his able guidance. His rich experience of dealing with the myriad issues of Indian defence at the highest level and his vast knowledge of the subject has greatly benefited my work.

I am particularly thankful to the two external discussants, Lt Gen NB Singh (Former DGEME, IHQ of MOD (Army), Dr RK Tyagi (Former CMD HAL) and the two anonymous referees for their invaluable insights, suggestions and comments.

I would like to thank Brigadier (Retd) Rumel Dahiya, DDG, IDSA for his patience and support during the writing of this volume.

My gratitude goes out to Mr Amit Cowshish, former Financial Advisor (Acquisition), MOD, Group Captain (Retd) Vinay Kaushal, Commodore (Retd) Ajay Chabbra and Dr Laxman Kumar Behera, of the Defence Economics and Industry Centre of IDSA for providing their scholarly inputs and enriching my work.

Last, but not the least, I thank the members of IDSA fraternity, particularly Vivek, Vaijayanti, Pushkar and Mukesh for their help in finishing this task.

New Delhi
February 2016

RANJIT GHOSH

List of Figures and Tables

Figure 2.1:	Nominal Life-Cycle Cost (LCC) Distribution	15
Figure 4.1:	Republic Of Korea's (ROK's) Reorganised Defence Acquisition Process	57
Figure 4.2:	The Agency for Defence Development's (ADD's) Proposed New Organisational Structure	60
Figure 6.1:	US Department Of Defence (DOD) Total Obligation Authority (TOA) by Major Appropriations Categories 1948–2007	100
Figure 6.2:	US Defence Budget Allocations FY 2008 to FY 2015	108
Figure 6.3:	Total DOD's Research Development Test and Evaluation (RDT&E) Budget Increase Post 9/11	113
Table 1.1:	World's Top 10 Importers and Exporters of Major Arms 2010-14	8
Table 2.1	Performance of Ordnance Factory Board (OFB) in Meeting the Targets over the Period 2008-13	18
Table 2.2:	Share of DPSU's in Capital Acquisition	25
Table 2.3:	Value of Production of Defence PSUs (INR in Crores)	26
Table 2.4:	Profit after Tax of DPSUs (INR in Crores)	26
Table 2.5:	List of Licenses Issued to Indian Industry – System/Sub-system/Component Level Capability (As on Oct 31, 2015)	29
Table 7.1:	DRDO Major Projects Original and Revised Date of Completion and Sanctioned Cost up to June 30, 2014	136
Table 7.2:	OFB TOT Agreements 1999-2005 and Status of Indigenisation	139
Table 7.3:	DPSUs Order Book Position and Order Book to Turnover Multiple	142

CHAPTER 1

Introduction

"There is an urgent need to review the whole concept of Indigenisation and self-reliance and it is time to go beyond the idea of looking at indigenisation purely as import substitution of components, subassemblies, etc. within the country from raw materials. Today Indigenisation as a concept will need to involve capability development, increasing know-why, design and system integration, rather than having numerical targets."

—Excerpts from Kelkar Committee Report of the Government of India (2005)

1.1 Military Capability Development and Sustenance

A constant review, assessment and analysis of the changing nature of threats that a country faces from other nation states and non-state actors, the ever increasing capabilities and weapon acquisition programmes of the potential adversaries and the ongoing continuous research and emergence of new military technologies around the world, are a few of the key drivers that necessitate the Armed Forces to constantly plan and upgrade their military arsenals. The military hardware and software that gets either developed by a home grown Defence Industry and Technological Base (DITB) or which is procured by the nation from other foreign sources, is expected to provide its Armed Forces the desired combat edge and the technological superiority over its adversaries. Moreover, all militarily advanced nations endeavour to achieve this superiority over the entire spectrum of conflict, be it in the conventional, strategic or non-conventional domains of warfare[1].

For such military capability development programmes to be relevant in future, especially for those relating to the development or procurement of military equipment and weapon systems in a country, the individual projects within the capability development programme need to be innovative in planning, contemporary and revolutionary in design, comprehensive and yet flexible to accommodate the ever dynamic parameters at the development stage of the project itself. In cases where this is not feasible, the incorporation of such dynamic parametres need to be undertaken subsequently, either during the next independent development or during the next spiral development version of the product[2].

Further, once the military hardware/software is successfully developed or procured and operationalised by the Services, there is a need to optimally exploit and effectively sustain the military system throughout its entire life cycle. This is crucial because, a 24x7 high fleet availability, serviceability and mission reliability status, is paramount to ensure the operational readiness, battle worthiness and the eventual success of the Armed Forces at all times.

An ideal arrangement for sustaining military systems could be argued to be the one where, the Original Equipment Manufacturer (OEM) or the Production Agency (PA) itself perform the life cycle maintenance engineering and logistics management functions. The services rendered by such an agency can then be evaluated against pre-determined, contractually negotiated, performance indices and standards. However, such an arrangement when tried out by the Armed Forces in the US, Australia, Canada and the UK, met with little success and the Forces soon had to revert back to their in-house Maintenance, Repair and Overhaul (MRO) agencies, to effectively deliver the much needed support services. The reasons which limited the number of Performance-Based Life-Cycle Product Support (PBL) contracts in the US were attributed to numerous factors like "*No US statute requires PBL contracting, although the Office of the Under Secretary of Defence endorses it.* (The) *decision makers are reluctant to change from standard ways of operating, such as* (the) *cost-plus incentive fee contracts. US* Department of Defence (*DOD*) *and contractors lack experience in writing, negotiating and managing PBL contracts. Project management offices have a shortage of knowledgeable* (and) *experienced PBL staff*" and so on[3]. As far as India is concerned, such a concept is new and is yet to be tried out.

Alternatively, if the adoption of PBL is not contemplated in totality by the purchaser, the OEM/PA could be asked during the Request For Proposal (RFP) to identify the life cycle maintenance and logistics management requirements of the military system under acquisition. The OEM/PA could further be asked to state the sustenance engineering and the maintenance interventions that would be required to be undertaken, as envisaged by the seller, as also submit their respective scope of work with price quotes. This would enable the buyer to make informed decisions with regards to whether each of the individual maintenance, sustenance engineering and logistics management activities are to be undertaken either through PBL/Annual Maintenance Contract (AMC)/on a Long Term Product Support Agreement (LTPSA) with the OEM/PA or alternatively, by the in-house MRO and logistics agencies. The decision between the two alternatives would to a large extent depend on the economics of either of the proposals under consideration.

In essence, it would be mandatory on part of the acquisition managers to consider a life cycle view of the maintenance engineering and the logistics management aspects that pertain to a class of equipment or weapon system under acquisition and to address these aspects early—ideally during the Research, Development and Production phase of a development project or at the pre-acquisition stage in the case of an outright purchase. Moreover, while the military product is being exploited in its service life, there could arise a need to undertake modifications, retro-fitments and up-gradations to overcome operational and technological obsolescence. Such a resuscitation activity will not only save on the costs of fresh acquisition's but also provide for the existing systems to enhance their functional capabilities—which is so essentially required in a modern-day battlefield. Thus, the US laws define "*The term 'product support arrangement' means a contract ... or a non-contractual arrangement, within the Federal Government, for the performance of sustainment or logistics support required for major weapon systems, subsystems, or components. The term includes arrangements for PBL, sustainment support, contractor logistics support, life-cycle product support or weapon systems product support*"[4].

A comprehensive military equipment life cycle support should span from the womb (i.e. the identification of the need for acquisition of a military system) to the tomb (i.e. the disposal of that very military system after its full exploitation). It should ideally be delivered by a modern and vibrant—scientific, technological and industrial base that is autonomous in nature and indigenous in make i.e. home-grown within the country or, till such time the base develops and matures, the military needs are delivered with the assistance of a nations reliable strategic partners.

"Indigenisation is the key to self-sufficiency and strategic capability". This implies, the domestic industry must develop in-house capacities, resources and skill sets that will not only help manufacture or produce the country's civil and defence requirements but also assist the nation in creating a long term advantage by providing a competitive export business for such products.

Before proceeding further, it would be appropriate to briefly dwell upon and elucidate certain terms that have frequently been used, often interchangeably, throughout this piece of work. The word 'Research' is to acquire new knowledge in basic sciences and technologies. 'Development of lab prototypes' requires developing new materials, processes, methods and technologies for specific military applications with a view to produce lab prototypes or simulation models for the conduct of proof of concept tests in laboratories. 'Development of operational weapon components' involves developing the component part as per the desired performance requirement of the product by prototyping through repeated demonstrations and validations up to getting it right. 'Development of an operational weapon system' involves developing it as per the desired performance requirement of the system by prototyping through architectural designing, engineering optimisation, manufacturing technologies and processes and, the integration to build and thereafter refine the system prototype's performance to near operational level. 'Production' is undertaken after trial evaluation of a successful prototyping and the introduction of Pre-production or Limited Series Production (LSP) models. 'Testing and Evaluation (T&E)' is undertaken to ensure systems achieve their stated performance standards. 'Quality certification' is provided either by an in-house or an external agency and ensures conformance to specifications and standards. 'Long term product support' requirements include MRO, modifications, retro-fitments and upgrades.

1.2 Evolution of Indian Defence Industry

Post-independence, from 1947 and up to the Sino-Indian and Indo-Pak wars in the early sixties, the near absence of a DITB in India had compelled large scale import of capital equipment for defence. Such equipment was mostly procured from off the shelf and from militarily advanced countries like the UK, France and Sweden. The trend since has continued, barring a few contracts post-1971 with the erstwhile Soviet Union, which allowed for Indigenous Manufacture (IM) under licensed production agreements. Technology transfer then was limited in scope and did not extend to design and development. Thus, the induction and pace of imbibing new technologies by the Indian defence industry remained slow. Coupled to this were comparatively low levels of investment in defence by both the government and the private sectors, the technology embargos and control regimes of the industrially advanced countries, a minimum Transfer of Technology (TOT) in licensed production and its poor absorption by the recipients i.e. the Ordnance Factories (OF's) and the Defence Public Sector Undertakings (DPSU's). Moreover, there was neither any incentive for the industry to progress the pace of indigenisation in terms of its content nor any mechanism by the government to monitor and verify the same in terms of the timelines, as and when these were stipulated in a few contracts. To make things worse, the government accentuated the problem by keeping the Indian private industry out of the defence sector's manufacturing and production activities for a considerable period of time, as compared to other militarily advanced countries thereby, further increasing the dependency on foreign sources and imports.

With the liberalisation of the Indian economy in 1991, the private company's tried entering the defence sector, initially in the form of sub-contractors in the ancillary industries. Yet, "*it wasn't until 2001 that India opened the defence (manufacturing) sector to private local firms and allowed some foreign participation, but only up to 26 per cent in defence Joint Ventures* (JV's). *(However), most foreign equipment manufacturers didn't want to part with their proprietary technology with such low equity participation*"[5]. Notwithstanding, this brought about a shift from the traditional buyer-seller relationship to that of coproduction, co-development and joint Research and Development (R&D). The Indian Government at all the meetings of the bilateral Defence Groups made this a standard demand and a small group of industry were formed to associate with each of the major supplier countries. Whenever technology was to be obtained, the insistence was on deeper depth of technology and including the design technology which could enable incorporation of design changes in locally produced systems to suit Indian requirements. As a result, since then, there's been at least an increase in the focus on indigenisation with the domestic defence industry constantly enhancing its capabilities through appropriate JV's and technology tie-ups.

In 2001, the Production and Research agencies endeavours were synergised with the requirements of the three Services through the creation of the 'Production Board' and the 'R&D Board', each chaired by their respective secretaries besides the formulation of each Service's Long Term Perspective Plans (LTPP) from 2002 onwards. Offsets were introduced for high value projects since 2005. Government, in 2011, announced a Defence Production Policy (DPrP), which considered self-reliance in defence manufacturing a vital, strategic and economic imperative. In 2012, HQ Integrated Defence Staff (IDS) promulgated the Services 'Long Term Integrated Perspective Plan' (LTIPP) 2012-27 and thereafter published 'The Technology Perspective and Capability Roadmap (TPCR)-2013'. The latter intended to provide the industry with a detailed perspective of what the Armed Forces are looking for, so that they could plan the necessary R&D efforts and investments for infrastructure up-gradation.

The Ministry of Defence (MOD) since 2002 has been promulgating the Defence Procurement Procedure (DPP). This document has undergone several revisions to promote indigenisation. The latest version was promulgated in 2013. DPP-2013 aims to balance the competing requirements of expediting capital procurement and developing an indigenous defence sector. It asserts conforming to transparency and accountability while laying a strong emphasis on promoting indigenisation and creating a level playing field for the Indian Industry. Further, none of the earlier editions have been as straight and comprehensive as the provisions announced in DPP-2013. The most important of these is the laying down of a hierarchy of acquisition programmes. Accordingly, a "*higher preference has now been accorded to the Buy (Indian), Buy and Make (Indian) and Make categorisation's*" over the 'Buy (Global)' category[6]. This, will make the Indian companies the prime players, thereby, giving them the first opportunity to meet the requirement of any defence procurement.

Historically, ever since Independence, the country's political leadership, bureaucracy, scientific community, industry (public, private, civil and defence) and the Armed Forces have been completely aware that the defence sector needs to achieve self-reliance, if not, self-sufficiency in the earliest timeframe feasible and yet, the growth trajectory of both the Indian defence industry and its technological base, in the last sixty-nine years, have been sub-optimal. The consistency has manifested in India's defence equipment's import to indigenous production ratio hovering around the 70:30 or now the 65:35 mark[7]. Consequently, India's Armed Forces ever since 2011 have become the leading importer of arms for four consecutive years[8]. New acquisitions—developments or procurements—include aircrafts, submarines, helicopters, tanks, long range guns, Unarmed Aerial Vehicles (UAV's) and missile systems, some of which are coming with Maintenance Transfer of Technology (MTOT) to include MRO while modernisation is looking at the operational and technological upgrades to overcome obsolescence.

What is Indigenisation, Self-Reliance and Self-Sufficiency ? For a lay man in short, "*The capability to design, develop and manufacture equipment within the country, using our own skills and resources, constitutes indigenisation. The capability to maintain and repair these, as well as (the) equipment sourced from abroad, makes us self-reliant. Not depending on* (the) foreign suppliers for anything, makes us self-sufficient"[9].

1.3 Current Realities of Indian Defence Industry

The requirement of a capable and responsive DITB is much more pronounced in India today. The opportunities inherent for public and private industry participation for self-reliance in defence encompasses both new acquisitions as well as modernisation/up-gradation and MRO activities pertaining to the existing inventories of the armed forces. As the Indian defence minister in his Republic Day 2015 Press Information Bureau (PIB) release mentioned "*There is a big opportunity in the defence sector for both (the) domestic and foreign investors. We have the third largest armed forces in the world with an annual budget of about US $ 38 billion and 40 per cent of this is used for capital acquisition. In the next seven to eight years, we would be investing more than US $ 130 billion in modernisation of our armed forces and with the present policy of MAKE IN INDIA, the onus is now on the industry to make the best use of this opportunity for the benefit of both business as well as the nation. Besides, under offset, more than INR 25,000 crore* (or INR 250 billion i.e. US $ 4.17 billion) *obligations are to be discharged in (the) next seven to eight years*"[10]. Thus, there are growing prospects for the Indian public and private players for enhancing their own capacity, qualitatively and quantitatively. There are challenges that will need to be reviewed by the stakeholders and strategised in a collaborative manner.

In 2016,it is extremely hard to comprehend as to how a country like India, even after developing a vast DITB in the long period of 69 years since independence, still finds itself dependent on foreign sources to meet 65 to 70 per cent of its defence needs. Moreover, this is at a time when the nation is striving to be a regional power and is the world's second fastest growing economy[11]. In the recent past, it has successfully test fired the Agni V Inter Continental Ballistic Missile (ICBM) and launched the Mars mission in space to join an elite club of industrially advanced and developed nations, besides maintaining its track record of indigenously excelling in high end technologies of space, nuclear, Information Technology (IT) and so on. Consequently, it is proud in having a large pool of technical manpower and scientific talent.

Further, with the third largest Armed Forces in the world (led by the US and China) and constantly being irked by two of its not so inimical neighbours, India's military needs are inevitably going to be plenty[12]. Accordingly, India since the first defence budget of 1950 has been spending around two per cent of its GDP on defence and at present is the ninth ranked defence spender in the world[13]. The spending in absolute terms has mostly increased in successive years and in the defence budget of "FY 2014-15 had stood at INR 2,290 billion (1.78 per cent of GDP and 12.76 per cent of the total Central Government Expenditure (CGE))[14]. This outlay was an increase of 12.43 per cent over the previous FY Revised Estimates (RE) and nearly 66 per cent over FY 2002-03. Further, the Indian finance minister raised the defence budget for FY 2015-16 by 7.5 per cent from INR 2.29 trillion to INR 2.46 trillion and for FY 2016-17 to INR 3.40 trillion (US $ 52.2 billion). This expenditure, besides its other constituents, is also for making up the existing deficiencies of equipment, replacing the old military hardware, where required and, for the sustenance of an ageing fleet. As a result, India is seen by the world as a huge market with a potential for high volume of sales. India on its part has obliged the big suppliers and the countries which develop and sell military hardware and thereby earned the dubious distinction of being the world's leading arms importer (Table 1.1) for four consecutive years since 2011 while featuring no where in the top 10 exporters of the world[15].

Table 1.1: World's Top 10 Importers and Exporters of Major Arms 2010-14

Ser	*Importer*	*Percentage of Global Share*	*Exporter*	*Percentage of Global Share*
1	India	15	USA	31
2	Saudi Arabia	5	Russia	27
3	China	5	China	5
4	UAE	4	Germany	5
5	Pakistan	4	France	5
6	Australia	4	UK	4
7	Turkey	3	Spain	3
8	USA	3	Italy	3
9	South Korea	3	Ukraine	3
10	Singapore	3	Israel	2
11	Others	51	Others	12
	Total	100		100

Source: Adapted by the author from "*SIPRI Yearbook 2015 - Recent trends in arms transfers*".

What is not understood is that despite a perennial demand for military hardware by the Indian Armed Forces, which wonderfully lends itself to the economy of scales (an essential pre-requisite for a profitable business model) the country repeatedly depends on imports to make up its defence requirements. This is when the nation for the very same purpose has a vast DITB that comprises of 52 defence laboratories and establishments, nine DPSUs, 39 OFs and a small yet ever growing private sector (about 20 major firms besides 1000 Micro, Small and Medium Scale Enterprises i.e. MSMEs). To coordinate their efforts is a huge bureaucracy in the MOD besides the political leadership that provides the necessary direction. Despite all this, we have a large import bill for military hardware which ideally should be procured ex indigenous sources. Critics who are fully aware of the poor state of India's DITB argue that the imposition of a diktat by the government for a "Buy Indian" procurement only for a majority of the military hardware could be counter-productive and pre-mature at this moment. Yet, the Indian defence planners, need not be dissuaded by such arguments and need to remain optimistic to steer and manoeuver the course towards this inescapable reality. This in turn would require a re-assessment of the requisite machinery and apparatus.

Nevertheless, a recent study by Britain's MOD has predicted that, India's defence expenditure is expected to accelerate over the next 30 years and rival that of the US and China. India and China are likely to spend far more on defence than any other country accounting for almost half of the world's total defence spending by 2045. "India's *defence budget could see it occupying a 'second tier' by then. Additionally, China, India and the US are likely to lead in defence-related R&D—further enhancing their military capabilities*". In the field of technology, the analysis indicates that "*China and India are likely to attain global leadership in select technical disciplines, achieving parity with the West in a number of niche areas as soon as 2015 and more widely by 2045*[16] "India is likely to be among the top three military powers in the world by 2045, along with the US and China, with a projected defence outlay of US $ 654 billion. Although, India's military-industrial acumen is unlikely to surpass the technological sophistication of the US by 2045, it may, along with China, rival it in terms of size. It is also likely to surpass Japan, Australia and South Korea (which will be ahead of other regional military powers) by developing sizeable and technically advanced armed forces, including ocean-going navies, capable of delivering an enduring maritime presence both regionally and further afield, according to the study titled 'Global Strategic Trends—Out to 2045'.

The above prophecy seems far from true, especially when considering the lagging science and technological base, a near absence of design and development capability, inadequate infrastructure and capacities, scarce resource allocations, inadequate private sector investments and the unnecessary bureaucratic control over the Indian DITB. However notwithstanding, if one is optimistic to undertake a review with a view to re-strategise the defence industry apparatus, the prophecy can but come true.

1.4 Objective and Scope of the Research Work

The best way to re-model the Indian DITB would probably be first to review the current state of defence industrialisation in India. This could be followed by a study of the defence industrialisation process that has been adopted by the militarily developed and developing nations to analyse, orient and adapt their best practices to the Indian DITB. The book after an introductory chapter thus reviews the journey of defence industrialisation in India up to 2015. Next, it reviews two fast-upcoming defence industries of Israel and South Korea to draw important takeaway's for India. This is followed by analysing the international practices that have been adopted by the defence industry of two leading military nations i.e. the US and China. Such an analysis further brings out valuable defence industry experiences and vital lessons for defence planners. The entire analysis also reveals that there is a requirement to re-assess, re-align and re-model the Indian defence industry apparatus in line with the vision of accelerating indigenisation, self-sufficiency and strategic capability, as pertaining to military systems. The book in its concluding chapter suggests three plausible options for remodeling the Indian programme, discusses in detail the pragmatic feasible model and recommends the way ahead besides suggesting an action plan for *MAKE IN INDIA* in the defence sector.

NOTES

1. John Aquila and David Ronfeldt "*In Athena's Camp:Preparing for Conflict in the Information Age*", Chapter I, pp.1-20 available at https://www.rand.org/content/dam/rand/pubs/monograph_reports/MR880/MR880.ch1.pdf (Accessed March 08, 2015).
2. "*Spiral Development Methodology*" available at http://www.qmetry.com/spiral.html (Accessed March 08, 2015).
3. Jane Feitler "*PBL 2012 Shows Performance-Based Logistics Moving to the Next Level*" available at https://www.gartner.com/ doc/ 2093616/pbl—shows-performance based-logistics (Accessed March 09, 2015).
4. US DOD's "Life-cycle management and product support" available at http://

uscode.house.gov/view.xhtml?req= (title:1 0% 20 sec tion:2337%20edition:prelim) (Accessed March 10, 2015).

5. "*Foreign-Investment Reform to Reshape India's Defence Industry*" *The Wall Street Journal*, June 26,2014 available at http:// www.wsj.com/articles/foreign-investment-reform-to-reshape-indias-defense-industry-1403821290 (Accessed March 10, 2015).
6. "*MOD Promulgates Defence Procurement Procedure - 2013*" Ministry of Defence (MoD) June 01, 2013 available at http://pib.nic.in/ newsite/mbErel.aspx?relid=96362 (Accessed March 11, 2015).
7. Rahul Bedi "*Indian defence imports total $17.25 bn over past 5 years*" IHS *Jane's Defence Weekly* November 30, 2014 available at http://www.janes.com/article/46508/indian-defence-imports-total-17-25bn-over-past-5-years (Accessed March 11, 2015).
8. "*SIPRI Yearbook 2015 - Recent trends in arms transfers*" available at http://www.sipri.org/research/armaments/transfers/ measuring/ copy_of_at-images/top-10-arms-importers_2010-14/image (Accessed March 12, 2015).
9. G Raj Narayan "*Indigenisation - the only way forward*" *Indian Defence Review*, May 29, 2015 available at http://www. Indian defencereview.com/indigenisation-the-only-way-forward/ (Accessed March 12, 2015).
10. Press Information Bureau Government of India January 28, 2015 "*Make in India - Defence Sector Special Feature Ministry of Defence / Republic Day 2015*" available at http://pib.nic.in/newsite/mbErel.aspx?relid=114990 (Accessed March 13, 2015).
11. "*India still second fastest growing economy:Chidambaram*" *The Hindu*, July 27, 2013 available at http://www.thehindu.com/ business/Economy/india-still-second-fastest-growing-economy-chidambaram/article4959820.ece (Accessed March 13, 2015).
12. "The 10 Biggest Armed Forces in the World" available at http://www.therichest.com/rich-list/the-biggest/the-10-biggest-armed-forces-in-the-world/ (Accessed March 13, 2015).
13. "*India ninth biggest military buyer in world*" *Times of India*, April 15, 2015 available at available at http://timesofindia. India times.com/india/ India-ninth-biggest-military-buyer-in-world/articleshow/33757926.cms (Accessed March 13, 2015).
14. "*Indian Defence Resource Allocation*" Defence Procurement and Acquisition News, July 17, 2014 available at http://www. defproac. com/?p=1106 (Accessed March 13, 2015).
15. *SIPRI Yearbook 2015 - Recent trends in arms transfers*" available at http://www.sipri.org/research/armaments/ transfers/ measuring/copy_of_at-images/top-10-arms-importers_2010-14/image (Accessed March 13, 2015).
16. '*India's defence spending to rival US, China in next 30 years' Financial Express* September 26, 2014 available at http://www. Financial expression/news and "*Can India Emerge As Top Global Military Power*" available at http://www. Businessinsider .in/articles (Accessed March 13, 2015).

CHAPTER 2

Defence Industrialisation in India: The Journey Upto 2015

2.1 Comprehensive National Power

An extremely important constituent for achieving 'comprehensive national power' is the growth of the country's DITB and how rapidly the same can attain a state of self-sufficiency to deliver military products on its own. This is important because self-sufficiency in defence is a vital imperative to achieve strategic autonomy and manoeuver strategic alliances and partnerships. Yet, in India, the goal of achieving self-sufficiency in defence—be it in the field of design, research, development, prototyping, engineering, manufacturing, system integration, production, testing, evaluation and quality certification, or in the subsequent long term product support requirements—has continued to remain elusive. The reasons for this could be many. However, the growth of a country's DITB is the direct consequence of its Armed Forces defence capability plans which by themselves stem from the National security imperatives.

2.2 National Security and Military Capability Development

The national security paradigms identified by a state help evolve the national security objectives and formulate the National Security Strategy (NSS). Further, the NSS is used to develop a long term military strategy and its military objectives as also, provide the planning guidelines for developing the military capability for implementing that military strategy. The planning of military capability development is undertaken in terms of force levels, force structure development, military R&D and infrastructure project development besides strategic budgeting which imparts the military capability, training, human resource etc. In the US, post the first gulf war, the NSS debate led to numerous formal government efforts, including the National Defence Panel (NDP) (1997) and the five Quadrennial Defence Reviews (QDR) (1997, 2001, 2005–06, 2010-11 and 2014-15)[1]. In India, we are yet to formulate a NSS document.

2.3 Defence Planning in India

In the Indian context, the Group of Ministers (GOM) Report in 2001 had observed that "*the defence planning process is greatly handicapped by the absence of a national security doctrine and* (the) *commitment of funds beyond a year. It also suffers from a lack of inter-Service prioritisation as well as the requisite flexibility*"[2]. Thus it was then suggested that there is a need to set up a Defence Planning Board (DPB) under the chairmanship of the Defence Minister"[3]. However the suggestion is yet to be implemented.

Next, in this chapter, let us review the journey of defence industrialisation in India upto the year 2015 to arrive at the current state of the four important constituents of the Indian DITB viz. the state of its Defence R&D and Defence Production Agencies i.e. the DRDO and the OF's, DPSU's and the Indian Private sector. Such a review will help identify their strengths and weaknesses in India's effort to achieve the goal of self-sufficiency in the defence sector.

2.4 Defence Research and Development (R&D)

2.4.1 Defence R&D Apparatus and Budget

Defence R&D activities in India have progressed without a clear vision, focus, planning and coordination as also not followed the global trends and success stories. R&D, be it for the civil or the military industry, is a long-term investment and undertaken to seed new innovations for driving economic growth. "*The Indian defence R&D machinery, comprises primarily of 52 scientific laboratories and establishments under the DRDO which maintains a strong partnership with 40 premier academic institutions, 15 national S&T agencies, 50 PSU's including the nine DPSU's, 39 OFs and 1000 plus private-sector industries*"[4].

In absolute terms, the DRDO's 2014-15 budget estimate of INR 15,282 crore (US $ 2.2 billion) is a mere three per cent of the DOD's US $ 63.5

billion R&D budget (for FY 2015)[5]. Considering the importance of higher investment on defence R&D, the Standing Committee on Defence, in a report presented to the Parliament in 1995 had suggested that the allocation to DRDO be progressively increased to 10 per cent of the defence budget by 2000. The Committee then, had taken note of the Self-Reliance Review Committee's plan (of achieving 70 per cent self-reliance by 2005) which itself was linked to a higher budgetary allocation for the DRDO[6]. However, the DRDO's budget was never raised to the 10 per cent mark during the recommended period, peaking to a much lower level of 6.74 per cent, and that too much later, i.e. in 2008-09. Since then, there has been a gradual decline, indicating the low priority accorded to the DRDO and to defence R&D, in the annual defence spending.

2.4.2 Collaborative R&D

Whenever joint R&D and production arrangements are planned to be established, the endeavour should be to first list out and then distribute either sides responsibilities (i.e. of the foreign partner and of the Indian entities) with regards to the systems/sub-systems and components of the programme. All systems should eventually fall within the scope of the work shares of either parties. There would also be the requirement of formulating appropriate management structures (of each side) and define their responsibilities with respect to the individual tasks and objectives. The GOM report in 2001 had recommended that such collaborative R&D ventures with the private sector should be institutionalised to instil a spirit of competitiveness and result orientation in R&D in India[7]. Now, with the *MAKE IN INDIA* initiative launched in 2014, the collaborative R&D ventures are likely to go beyond the Indian frontiers and would be with the best in class private companies worldwide. Further, as far as the product development activities are concerned, it has been observed ever since the late 1990s/early twenty first century, that there has been a growing trend towards the formation of global innovation networks. These networks "*integrate the dispersed engineering, product de-velopment and R&D across the national boundaries*"[8]. Their rapid rise has led to far-reaching structural changes to the geography of innovation and production, especially in the high-technology sectors and sooner that India integrates with such innovation networks the better it will be for the country.

2.4.3 R&D Investment

The R&D investment in India needs to be channelised into those pre-selected areas of science which are either being denied or are expected to be increasingly employed in the future systems and products[9]. The DRDO in the past has been undertaking R&D in areas which either does not concern the user or are not endorsed by them. Also, knowing that the Life Cycle Costs (LCC) of operations and maintenance constitute 60 to 80 per cent of the total LCC, the R&D scientists and engineers from the conceptual stage need to try and attain the minimum LCC of weapons systems and their Major Unit Assemblies (MUA's) that are to be developed indigenously[10].

Figure 2.1: Nominal Life-cycle Cost Distribution

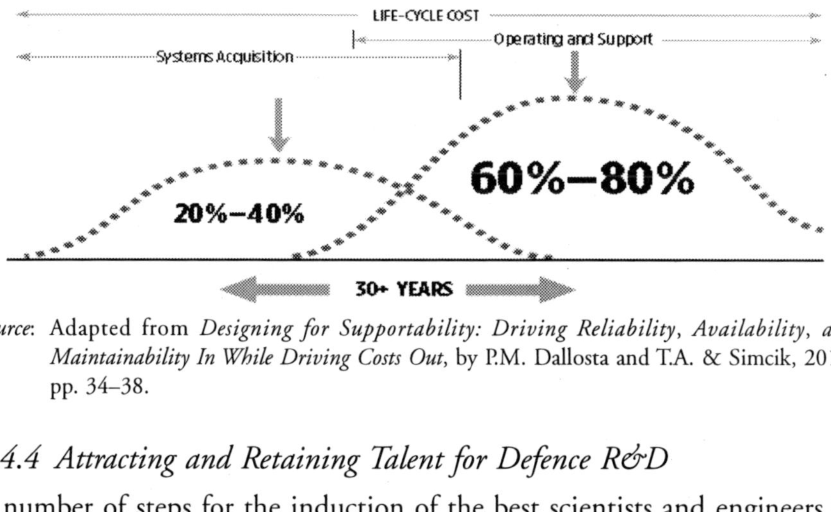

Source: Adapted from *Designing for Supportability: Driving Reliability, Availability, and Maintainability In While Driving Costs Out*, by P.M. Dallosta and T.A. & Simcik, 2012, pp. 34–38.

2.4.4 Attracting and Retaining Talent for Defence R&D

A number of steps for the induction of the best scientists and engineers in the country and their long-term retention have been initiated to address the critical manpower concerns in DRDO. Higher compensation and performance linked incentives were also recommended by the Rama Rao Committee to incentivise high calibre scientists to work in the DRDO. The DRDO's 2006 annual awards scheme consists of a total of 17 awards with remunerations ranging from INR 20,000 to INR 10 lakhs for individual, group, team and institutional awards[11]. These need to be reviewed and enhanced based on the inflation index as 10 years have passed since it was last reviewed. DRDO's scientist's, technicians and project teams delivering future path breaking innovations could be provided a higher level of recognition and compensated adequately with a sizable monetary award.

2.4.5 Implementing Rama Rao Committee R&D Recommendations

The creation of a Defence Technology Commission (DTC) under the Raksha

Mantri with the participation of key top level functionaries in the Government needs to be worked out and implemented. Also the Board of Research in Advanced Defence Sciences (BRADS) needs to be created. However, unlike as suggested by the Rama Rao Committee to replace the DRDO's existing grants-in aid programme, there is a need to have a supplementary programme to augment the process by being handled by another agency. As brought out in an earlier paper by the author, this could be "*from either the Department of Science and Technology (DST)/Centre for Scientific and Industrial Research (CSIR)/Indian Space Research Organisation (ISRO) or any other separately nominated agency. The DRDO with its 46 labs and four Test and Evaluation (T&E) centres can best be compared with the US DOD's Research Development Test and Evaluation (RDT&E's) 80 R&D labs and 26 T&E centres. As far as the functioning of Defence Advanced Research Projects Agency (DARPA) goes, it needs to be remembered that DARPA unlike the DRDO enjoys enormous freedom to award R&D contracts to any agency without having to go through a protracted bureaucratic approval processes. It must also be appreciated that 85 per cent to 90 per cent of DARPA's projects fail to meet their full objectives and this is well understood and accepted by the US government. Moreover, it need not be reiterated that a significant reason for the delay in most DRDO programmes is also the restriction of operating with the government processes and regulations which by themselves are extremely time consuming*"[12]. Notwithstanding, as suggested by the Rama Rao Committee its funding can be pegged at around 10 per cent of the DRDO budget to undertake 'radical innovations' in several cutting-edge technologies like those undertaken by the highly acclaimed DARPA of the US.

2.5 Ordnance Factories (OF's)

2.5.1 OF's Apparatus

The OFB, is a manufacturing organisation engaged in the manufacturing of defence products based on the TOT from the OEM or the DRDO. The OFB has 39 OF's and employs around 93,500 personnel besides two new factories coming up at Nalanda and Korwa[13]. The first OF, the Gun Powder Factory, was established in 1787 at Ishapore while the Gun and Shell Factory, set up in 1801 at Cossipore, made the first production by any OF in India. The OF's are an integrated industrial base for indigenous production of defence equipment and ammunition. Army is the principal client of the OFB accounting for about 75 to 80 per cent of the production. However, supply from the factories constitute only 48 per cent of the army's total requirement[14]. They also produce certain requirements of Paramilitary and Police Forces for arms, ammunition, clothing and equipment. The OF's try to improve their capacity utilisation by obtaining additional orders through continued efforts in diversification to non-defence customers and exports.

2.5.2 OF Management

The Department of Defence Production (DDP) of the MOD is the administrative and controlling authority of OF's. It takes major decisions pertaining to OFs' vendor development, product development/improvement and commercial interests[15]. At the next level is the OFB headed by a Director General (DG) who is also the chairman of the board. He is supported by eight members in the rank of additional secretaries, from the finance, personnel, planning and material management, projects and engineering, technical services, material and components, weapons, vehicles and equipment, ammunition and explosives, armoured vehicles (Avadi), ordnance equipment (Kanpur). The OF's are placed under five clusters or operating groups pertaining to ammunition, weapons, materials, armoured vehicles and ordnance equipment wherein, each of the five divisions consist of five to 10 factories. The OFB performs executive functions of laying down the policies and procedures on the functioning of the factories, monitoring receipts of orders from buyers, determining annual target for production and controls the overall budget of the organisation. At the lowest level are the factories which are normally headed by a senior general manager responsible for the day-to-day functioning of the factory. The factories are more or less independent in their functioning in terms of certain financial powers delegated to them and are also not fully accountable to the board or its chairman.

2.5.3 OF Capacity Utilisation

The OFB's production targets for the factories are planned on the basis of the requirements projected by the Armed Forces and the capacity of the factories for production[16]. The OFB plans the production on the basis of the firm orders placed by the Armed Forces. The capacity of the feeder factories and of the assembling factories (that assemble the final product for issue), together provide an assessment to the OFB on its capacity to meet the requirements of the Forces. The production targets are then fixed by the OFB in consultation with the Defence forces and communicated to the factories. The performance of the OFB in meeting the targets over the period 2008-13 is shown in Table 2.1. In 2012-13, the OFB could meet the targets of only 39 per cent of the items required by the Armed Forces.

Table 2.1 Performance of OFB in Meeting the Targets over the Period 2008-13

Year	*Number of Items*			*Percentage of Shortfall*
	Targets	*Production*	*Shortfall*	
2008-09	419	296	123	29
2009-10	434	300	134	31
2010-11	639	416	223	35
2011-12	547	195	352	64
2012-13	529	205	324	61

Source: Report No. 35 of 2014—Union Government (Defence Services).

The shortfall was due to the inability to source quality components in time from both local vendors and sister OF's (categorised under 'Inter-Factory Demands' (IFD's)) besides, where the clients reduced the demand during the year by short-closing indents. Such shortfalls need to be avoided by ensuring advance planning by all. As regards OFB, while it had fixed a capacity utilisation of 80 per cent in the factories the actual utilisation averaged to only 74 per cent during the last five years (FY 2010-15). This calls for either diversifying their business or downsizing the workforce.

2.5.4 OF's Production, Value of Issue (VOI/Turnover) and Indigenisation

The turnover during FY 2014 was INR 11,123 crore and is projected to increase to INR 11,900 crore for FY 2015. The VOI (turnover) per employee in OFB has gone up from 6.4 in FY 2008 to 11.9 in FY 2014 thereby, recording an increase of about 86 per cent over a six year period. The overall production has increased by associating the private sector industries as vendors. By March 31, 2014, about 5,600 vendors had been registered with the OFB. Almost 77 per cent of the supplies of the OFB went to the Indian Army[17]. The OF's also produce ammunition for the Navy and the Air Force and take up indigenous development of naval armaments. The OFB in FY 2013-14 recorded 85.3 per cent indigenisation in terms of Value Of Production (VOP). However, there is a need to indigenise the critical assemblies and systems.

2.5.5 OF's Transfer of Technology and Self-Reliance

The OF's with every licensed manufacture of equipment and major weapon system have regularly received and absorbed technologies that were acquired through the import route. As a result, they have upgraded their infrastructure with the induction of the state-of-the art technologies to meet the futuristic requirements. Along with the DRDO, the OFB has initiated a number of R&D projects to improve self-reliance in specific arms and ammunition as required by the Forces. On the basis of the LTIPP and the procurement policy of the Users, the OFB has broadly identified technology areas for future acquisition and for absorption in the OF's[18]. This needs to be a continuous process to achieve tangible results.

2.5.6 OF's In-house R&D Effort

The OF's manufacture defence products based on the TOT from the OEM or DRDO. However, they are also responsible for the indigenisation of the product being manufactured under TOT. Historically, the factories are not mandated to undertake any major R&D activities. Therefore, development of new products through in-house R&D is relatively a new concept in OFB. However, the OFB is paying special emphasis to in-house R&D and has developed quite a few products through it. The share of the R&D expenditure to the total revenue expenditure is however negligible and ranged between 0.267 per cent to 0.400 per cent between FY 2009 to FY 2013[19]. At INR 48 crore in 2012-13, R&D accounted for only 0.40 *per cent* of the total revenue expenditure of OFB. However, there have been a few success stories in OFB's R&D expenditure. For instance, the OFB through a collaborative effort developed the 155 mm artillery gun which was successfully trial evaluated in February 2013 following which, the Army placed an indent of 114 guns.

The Standing Committee on Defence in December 2014 had expressed concern about the R&D work undertaken in OF's. The "*Expenditure on R&D is minimal i.e. less than even 17 of Value Of Issues (VOI) in the last five years. With regard to the strategies/initiatives for R&D enhancement, the committee was informed that in 2003, OFB adopted a policy of in-house R&D resulting in formation of 11 Ordnance Development Centres (ODCs) in diverse technical fields.* (The) *OFB has decided to increasingly play the role of* (a) *lead integrator of defence equipment. Accordingly, OFB has initiated action to jointly work with major DPSUs. Reputed institutes like Indian Institute of Technologies (IITs) for R&D indigenisation. Adequate funds are available to OF's to carry out the development of arms and ammunitions with indigenous technology. However, it* (was) *regretted* (that) *no substantial R&D work is being undertaken at the OF's*"[20].

2.5.7 OF's Orders by Services and Delays in Execution

In March 2000, an indent was placed on the OFB for the delivery of 124 Main Battle Tank (MBT) Arjun from 2000 to 2006. The Heavy Vehicle Factory (HVF) was asked to produce 15 MBT under LSP by 2004. The bulk production of (balance) 109 MBT were to commence after the field trials. The OFB could not produce on time, the quantity indented. "*The OFB was still short of the indent by two MBTs which were under production and three MBTs were under inspection in December 2013. The delays in the production led to cost escalation by more than 2.5 times: from INR 17 crore per MBT to INR 44 crore*"[21]. It was also the tardiness in the creation of infrastructural facilities, in the production of critical assemblies (i.e. the hull and the turret) and in the sourcing of major assemblies etc. at the OF's, which led to delays in meeting the indent.

As far as T-90 tanks are concerned, the OFB, in November 2004, had received the indent for the manufacture of 300 indigenous T-90 tanks which were scheduled for supply during 2006 to 2010. Out of the indented 300, only 167 could be delivered up to the end of FY 2013[22]. The reasons for the delay were many and included, translation of TOT design documents took almost six years, development of production facilities took seven more years than the internal target date while the total cost of the project increased to INR 95 crore, the TOT documents in respect of some critical assemblies were not transferred by the Russian manufacturer ROE even after a lapse of 12 years up to July 2013. An important component was the gun system (including the barrel) for which the design had not been received even up to May 2014.

2.5.8 OF's Delay in Creation and Augmentation of Facilities

The OFB has a number of ongoing sanctioned projects for the creation and augmentation of its capacity for meeting the Armed Forces requirements. "*The total sanctioned cost of such ongoing projects* (in FY 2013) *was INR 4,571 crore*"[23]. The Standing Committee on Defence in 2014 had noted that there had been very long gestation periods in the case of such projects. "*For example, the project for the creation of capacity for the manufacturing of MBT Arjun @ 30 numbers per annum ...resulted in a time overrun of 10 years..., the creation of capacity for manufacturing T-90 tanks @ 100 numbers per annum sanctioned in 2003 led to* (the) *tanks* (being) *manufactured from Semi-Knocked Down (SKD) kits from 2009-10* (only). *Besides these, many projects which started in 2010, such as* (the) *creation of capacity for manufacturing of T-72 variants @*

50 numbers per annum, (the) *augmentation of capacity for manufacturing of armoured vehicle's engines from 350 to 750 per annum, the augmentation of capacity for manufacturing of spares for overhauling of T-72 &T-90 tanks have not attained 50 per cent completion even after a lapse of four to five years*"[24].

All-out efforts need to be made to streamline the project execution. Besides this, in the past too, OFB has had problems in meeting the target for manufacturing T-90 tanks, BMP-II's and Pinaka Rocket's due to various constraints as delayed product support from the OEM, discontinuity in production line due to non-availability of indents and also certain issues involving the modification of the design. These problems could have been envisaged at the planning stage and suitable remedial measures initiated to minimise the delays encountered at the time of execution.

2.5.9 OF's Quality of Products Manufactured

Again the Standing Committee on Defence in 2014 brought out the concerns about the quality of products manufactured by the OF's as sometimes defective ammunition reached the hands of the Army. The Committee enquired about the quality check(s) conducted for the products developed by the OF's and whether there was any second party inspection also. The Ministry then had replied that the "*Products manufactured by the OF's are 100 per cent inspected by the factories. Subsequent to it, a sample inspection is done by* (the) *Directorate General of Quality Assurance (DGQA) on behalf of the User as a Second Party Inspection. On an average, 21 laboratory tests are conducted by* (the)*OF & DGQA and four per cent rounds of every lot proof fired by* (the)*DGQA before acceptance and issue to* (the) *Indian Army*". With regard to quality assurance, the representatives of MOD had submitted "*We provide quality assurance to all stores which are supplied by the OFs, DPSUs and trade firms. DGQA establishments* (being) *co-located with the OFs provide intimate quality assurance cover to the products manufactured by OFs. ...DGQA is ensuring that everything is manufactured as per the process schedule. In case there are any problems ..... during the manufacture, DGQA carries out process audit of that particular process which is giving a defective product.*"

Excellent quality is essential in achieving indigenisation and self-reliance in respect of the different high-end technology systems and sub-systems. In spite of the remedial measures suggested by the OFB and DGQA, if the lacunae continue to persist, then the accountability needs to be fixed. To make OFB directly responsible for the quality issues, the MOD had earlier asked the OF's to move towards the process of self-certification. Although OFB has started self-certification of their products, the items, as of now, have been restricted to low-tech items like all clothing and general stores. At present, there is no time frame stipulated for covering the entire product range. The MOD, in consultation with the OFB, should lay down the precise time frame, by when all non-lethal items supplied, including those overhauled by the OF's, will be self-certified by the OF's.

2.5.10 OF's Exports

The MOD has allowed OFB to venture into direct exports business since 1989. The intention of the decision was that international exposure will make the factories quality and price conscious, allow the factories to take advantage of the spare capacity, besides generate the much needed revenue. To provide a competitive edge in the international market, the OFB was instructed to resort to "strategic pricing" covering the full material costs and a part of the labour and overheads costs[25]. Despite these initiatives, exports have not really gone up over the years.

2.6 Defence Public Sector Undertakings (DPSU's)

2.6.1 Highlights of the Nine DPSUs

Hindustan Aeronautics Limited (HAL) is the largest DPSU established in 1964 and has 20 production divisions. So far HAL has produced 15 types of aircrafts from in-house R&D and 14 types under license production[26]. It has established 10 R&D centers and one facility management division.

Bharat Electronics Limited (BEL) was established in 1964 with nine Strategic Business Units (SBUs) spread across the country. It is a technology driven company with a well-established R&D structure, on which it spends six to eight per cent of its annual turnover[27]. The company has a long association with DRDO laboratories, national laboratories and reputed academic institutions like IITs, Indian Institute of Science (IISc) etc., to adapt indigenous technologies into its products or jointly develop products for the defence Forces. BEL on an average is introducing around 10 new products every year and ranks 69th among the top 100 companies in the world in defence revenue as published by 'Defence News', USA. The indigenisation level of the products of the company is about 85 per cent of its turnover.

Bharat Earthmovers Limited (BEML) established in 1964 has four manufacturing complexes with nine production units located around Bangalore and engaged in the design, manufacturing, marketing and after sales service of defence & aerospace products besides its other verticals. R&D of defence equipment is taken up at the Kolar Gold Fields (KGF) and Bangalore complexes. The company spends around three per cent of its turnover towards R&D, which has resulted in the development of new products. The new/upgraded products have contributed to over 25 per cent of the total turnover in the last five years[28]. The indigenisation level in case of defence products, viz., PMS bridge, aircraft weapon loader, 50T trailer, etc. is 100 per cent and for High Mobility Vehicle (HMV) it is over 90 per cent.

Bharat Dynamics Limited (BDL) was incorporated in the year 1970 under the MOD. At present, BDL has a order book position of around INR 18,000 crore[29]. It has in-house Design & Engineering (D&E) division for up gradation of products and development of related test equipment. BDL has been nominated as the Lead Integrator for the Medium Range Surface to Air Missile (MR SAM) and Akash Surface to Air Missile (SAM) for the Indian Army and for the Long Range Surface to Air Missile (LR SAM) Missile Integrator of the Indian Navy being developed jointly by the DRDO and M/s. Israel Aircraft Industry (IAI), Israel. Besides increasing existing capacities, BDL is also establishing new manufacturing facilities to meet the growing demands of Anti-Tank Guided Missiles (ATGMs) and SAMs. Indigenisation of products like Konkurs-M, Invar ATGM and Milan-2T is up to 90 per cent, 80 per cent and 71 per cent respectively. INR 100 crore has been earmarked for FY 2015 on modernisation.

Mishra Dhatu Nigam Limited (MIDHANI) was established in 1973 as a DPSU to achieve self-reliance in the manufacture of a wide range of Super alloys, Titanium alloys, Special Purpose Steels etc. for the critical sectors, with technical knowhow from foreign collaborators. MIDHANI has so far developed, manufactured and supplied more than 105 grades of high performance alloys in different shapes, sizes, forms towards programmes of national importance in the defence, space and atomic energy sectors.

Mazagon Dock Limited (MDL) was incorporated as a Defence PSU in 1960 and is a leading Shipyard amongst all DPSU Shipyards engaged in construction of warships and submarines. The yard is presently constructing missile destroyers and Scorpene submarines and is thus helping the nation to achieve self-reliance in warship construction for the Indian Navy[30]. MDL has also been shortlisted to build frigates of P17A class which are follow on ships of Shivalik class ships. MDL has also been earmarked to build future submarines under Project 75-I.

Garden Reach Shipbuilders and Engineers Ltd (GRSE), since September, 2006 has kept pace with India's expanding maritime interests and is recognised as a leading shipbuilding yard. GRSE is building Anti-Submarine Warfare (ASW) corvettes for the Indian Navy. The First of Class ASW corvette (INS Kamorta) was delivered by GRSE in July 2014. The first ever Warship exported by India is an Offshore Patrol Vessel built by GRSE for the Government of Mauritius. GRSE has a R&D policy duly approved by its Board.

Goa Shipyard Ltd. (GSL) established in 1957 undertakes R&D of its product range and new shipbuilding projects based on in-house design. GSL's indigenously developed designs of patrol vessels have saved the country considerable foreign exchange by avoiding import of ship designs. To meet the country's defence requirements as well as anticipated demand in the international market, in-house R&D for new platforms, On-board Patrol Vehicle (OPV), ASW shallow water craft and interceptor craft is in progress.

Hindustan Shipyard Ltd. (HSL) 'Scindia Shipyard Limited' setup in 1941 was renamed HSL in 1952 when the Government of India acquired its two thirds holdings. It has developed in-house designs for tugs, cargo vessels under standard flexible design and concept design for survey vessels, etc. Recently the design department has been revamped with 40 licenses of Aveva and 35 licenses of Autocad-14[31]. During FY 2014, training for this state-of-the art software has progressed satisfactorily and the licenses are being used.

2.6.2 DPSU's Diversification of Business from Defence Sector

HAL has diversified into the manufacture of structures and assemblies for aerospace launch vehicles, satellites, industrial and marine gas turbine engines and is a major partner for the space programme's of ISRO[32]. BEML has diversified its business by successfully manufacturing railway coaches and wagons for the Indian Railways and defence forces besides assembling state-of-the-art stainless steel metro coaches for Delhi Metro Rail Corporation (DMRC) under technical collaboration with M/s Rotem of South Korea. GRSE builds ultra-modern commercial vessels which include small harbour crafts, fast and powerful patrol vessels, tanker fleet and the new generation hovercraft.

Consequently, from the budgetary perspective the DPSU's share in the capital acquisition of Armed Forces has dropped over the years as seen in Table 2.2[33].

Table 2.2: Share of DPSU's in Capital Acquisition

Year	*Value of Defence Sales By DPSUs (Rs. Cr)*	*India's Capital Acquisition (Rs. Cr)*	*Share of DPSUs in Capital Acquisition (%)*
1999-00	6276	10219	61
2000-01	5365	10502	38
2001-02	5552	14430	38
2002-03	6152	12939	48
2003-04	6925	14584	47
2004-05	7874	27209	29
2005-06	69116	25491	36
2006-07	11095	26900	41

Sources: Annual Reports of DPSU's and Report of Standing Committee on Defence.

Diversification of product range by defence State Owned Enterprises (SOE's) is not a recent phenomenon and is being practiced by most advanced countries and must be encouraged. China's Civil-Military Integration (CMI) strategy is actually nothing but the diversification of China's Military Industrial Complex (MIC) into expanding the product range to encompass civil applications and markets.

2.6.3 DPSU's Disinvestment

Important provisions of the new industrial policy of 1991 included, 20 per cent of the shares of selected profit making PSU's will be sold to financial institutions, mutual funds etc.(the institutions will hold the shares for a specified period after which they will be permitted to sell the shares in the share market), the government will provide more autonomy and not interfere in the day to day functioning of PSU's (instead these units will be controlled by the government through Memorandum of Understanding (MOU) reached between these units and the government) and unviable PSU's will be closed down[34].

Disinvestment is the dilution of the stake of the government in a public enterprise. If dilution is less than 50 per cent the government retains management even though disinvestment takes place. It is not privatised. But if the dilution is more than 50 percent there is transfer of ownership and management. It will be called privatisation.

2.6.4 DPSU's Value of Production (VOP) and Profit after Tax (PAT)

The VOP of DPSUs and OF's and the PAT of DPSUs are shown in Table 2.3 and Table 2.4 respectively.

Table 2.3: Value of Production of Defence PSUs (INR in Crores)

Name of DPSU	*2011-12*	*2012-13*	*2013-14*	*2014-15 (upto Dec. 2014)*
HAL	12693	14202	15867	9915
BEL	5794	6290	6127	4026
BEWL	4077	3360	3165	1671
BDL	993	1177	1804	1298
GRSE	1294	1529	1611	863
GSL	676	507	509	387
HSL	564	484	453	160
MDL	2524	2291	2865	2028
MIDHANI	496	537	572	403
OFB	12391	11975	11123	7138
Total	41502	42352	44096	27889

Source: Government of India Ministry of Defence "Annual Report 2014-15".

Table 2.4: Profit after Tax of DPSUs (INR in Crores)

Name of DPSU	*2011-12*	*2012-13*	*2013-14*	*2014-15 (upto Dec. 2014)*
HAL	2539	2997	2693	1238
BEL	830	890	932	440
BEWL	57	-80	5	-178
BDL	235	288	346	244
GRSE	108	132	121	24
GSL	83	16	-61	6
HSL	-86	-55	-46	-96
MDL	494	413	398	226
MIDHANI	68	83	83	42
Total	4328	4684	4471	1946

Source: Government of India Ministry of Defence "Annual Report 2014-15".

2.6.5 DPSU's In-house R&D Effort

Most DPSU's are drawing up a three/five year R&D plan and intend getting into tie-ups with reputed academic institutions like IITs, IISc, Welding Research Institute (WRI), etc. for carrying out hands-on R&D projects. On comparative terms, the spending by the Indian DPSU's do not match anywhere near its global defence industry counterparts. For instance, the French company, Thales, spends 20 per cent of its revenues on R&D as against eight per cent spent by BEL, which arguably is the most innovative defence enterprise for electronics in India. The lack of in-house R&D in most of the enterprises makes them perpetually dependent on either the DRDO or the foreign companies for obtaining the technology for production. In the case of the OFs, the largest and the oldest MOD run organisation in India, their in-house developed products contribute only 7.5 per cent to their total turnover[35].

2.6.6 DPSU's Offset Absorption Roadmap

"*Offset opportunities are fast emerging in the services industries like forging, TIG/MIG welding, overhauling, precision engineering etc. for which specialised steel is required. This makes MIDHANI an essential driver for offset absorption and the resultant strengthening of indigenous manufacturing capability*"[36]. In the light of the substantial offset opportunities and consequent expansion, there is likely to be a significant increase in MIDHANI's current revenues. Also, MDL's existing production lines seem blocked for a considerable number of years with domestic as well as foreign OEMs preferring government shipyards as MDL to discharge their future offset obligation.

2.6.7 DPSU's Exports

The volume of defence exports by DPSU's is meagre by world standards. The low exports by DPSUs is attributable to a number of factors, such as the overflowing order books, quality of product offered, marketing strategy, etc. amongst others. As far as the latter is concerned, DPSUs, especially the shipyards are way behind. HAL has achieved export sales of INR 257 crore up to the end of December 2014. The export turnover of BEL for FY 2015 (up to December 2014) is US $ 30.44 million[37]. These need to grow in future to bring down the domestic products costs.

2.7 Private Sector Participation

2.7.1 Governments Industrialisation Approach and Private Sector in Defence Production

At the time of Independence, the Indian leadership had aimed to achieve self-sufficiency in all realms of production. To realise this, the Industry Policy Resolution 1948 and the Industries Development & Regulation (IDR) Act, 1951, had emphasised on the 'core' industries (as defence, atomic energy, railways, power, heavy engineering etc.), to be under the category of public sector, reserved for development by the central government[38]. The decision primarily was due to the poor development of the private sector and the weak R&D base. The 1962 debacle made the policy makers realise that defence had been neglected and attaining self-sufficiency in the defence sector was far-sighted. It required a shift of focus from the earlier self-sufficiency model adopted to the self-reliance model wherein, self-reliance in its true sense does not preclude accessing external sources for technology and systems, or external assistance in any stage of the production cycle. Consequently, most defence acquisitions thereafter, up to the mid-90's, were either outright purchases or under license production/TOT. The DPSUs/OFs could thus gain expertise only in production—of assembling the Completely Knock Down (CKD) and/ or the Semi Knock Down (SKD) Kits that were imported from the OEM. The real TOT aimed at enhancing indigenous design and development was conspicuously absent in all these deals.

The lessons of licensed production and consequent over-dependence on the Soviet Union drove India's defence industrialisation approach towards indigenous design. From mid-1980's India increased its defence R&D budget to allow DRDO to get into high-profile defence projects. Post economic liberalisation by India in 1991, the manufacture of components, assemblies and sub-assemblies was thrown open to the private sector which mostly supplied these items to the OFs/DPSUs. Since indigenous efforts were not adequate to meet the armed forces requirements, focus shifted towards co-development and co-production in partnership with foreign firms. Thus "*in 1998, India and Russia signed an inter-governmental agreement to jointly produce* (the) *Brahmos supersonic cruise missile. This was a JV in which India had a 50.5 per cent share and Russia the rest—the equity structure so designed to enable the JV to operate like a private entity for fast decision making*"[39]. The GOM Report – 2001 in the aftermath of the armed conflict between India and Pakistan in 1999, suggested changes in the acquisition procedures as also for enabling a greater participation of the private sector in defence production. Accordingly, the Government in 2001, opened defence production to 100 per cent Indian private sector participation and permitted Foreign Direct Investment (FDI) of up to 26 per cent both, however were subject to industrial licensing conditions to be set by the Ministry of Commerce and Industry[40].

2.7.2 Industrial Licensing (IL) for Private Sector in Defence Production

The Department of Industrial Policy and Promotion (DIPP) next notified detailed guidelines for the issuance of license for the production of arms and ammunition[41]. Thus, the role of the Private Sector shifted to that of being partners in the manufacture of complete advanced equipment/systems. The DIPP since 2002 and up to the end of 2014, had issued 240 Letters of Intents (LOIs)/Industrial Licenses (ILs), for the manufacture of a wide range of defence items to 144 private companies[42] (307 ILs to 182 private Indian companies up to Oct 31, 2015). 49 licensed companies (50 covering 79 IL's up to Oct 31, 2015) have reported commencement of production. Long pending issues are being constantly addressed. Restriction of annual capacity in IL for the defence sector has been removed and initial validity of IL granted under the IDR Act increased from three years to seven years with a provision to further extend it by three years on a case-to-case basis. The Licensee now is allowed to sell defence items to Government entities under the control of Ministry of Home Affairs (MHA), PSUs, State Governments and other Defence Licensee companies without the approval of DDP. Further, with regard to the issue of grant of IL for MRO activities in the defence sector, it has been decided along with the approval of the competent authority in DDP that MRO activities in the defence sector may be treated as 'services' and should not be subjected to IL under IDR Act unless, it actually involves the manufacturing of components/sub-assemblies which are licensable and that the product should remain the property of the same customer after MRO operation[43].

Table 2.5: List of Licenses Issued to Indian Industry – System/Sub-system/ Component Level Capability (As on Oct 31, 2015)

System/Sub-system/Components	*Industry Licenses*
Armoured Vehicle/Arms Ammunitions	34
Underwater Equipment/Underwater Ammunitions	11
Ground Equipment/Ground Launch System	19
Night Vision/Sensor based Systems/Optical Goods/Display systems	37

(*Contd.*)

System/Sub-system/Components	*Industry Licenses*
Radar/Electronics Systems/Radio/Avionics/Airborne Guidance and Control System/Simulators	88
Bulletproof Jacket/Ballistic Protection	14
Network-Centric/Electronic Warfare System/Combat Management System	29
Rocket, Missiles, Torpedo Tubes/Air Defence Gun/UAV's System and Sub-systems	51
Warship/Submarines	9
Ship, Submarine, Maritime Equipments	11
Aircraft Engine/Airframe/Aircraft systems and Sub-systems	38

Source: Lecture by Shri AK Gupta Secretary Defence Production at IDSA on "Make in India: The Way Ahead for Indigenous Defence Production in India" on December 07, 2015

2.7.3 Defence Products for Private Sector in Defence Production

DDP initially in June 2014 had finalised and forwarded to DIPP a Defence Products List for licensing purposes under the IDR Act, 1951[44]. The list covered electronic, aerospace and defence equipment under four major categories including parts thereof pertaining to all types of armoured fighting vehicles, air and spacecraft's, warships, arms ammunition and allied equipment. Items not included in the list did not require IL for defence purposes. Moreover, dual use items, other than those specifically mentioned in the list also did not require IL. Subsequently, the category-wise list (Category A and Category B) from the security angle was finalised by the Standing Committee on Private Sector Participation in Defence Production. This was in accordance with the requirement in the Security Manual prepared earlier where, the categorisation was to be done by the DDP and forwarded to DIPP with their comments on the Category A, B or C items. As per the new list comprising of 16 serials, only the parts/components of equipment's, castings, forgings, test equipment's have been removed, as not considered strategic and sensitive from the security point of view. Therefore, in the new lists, no item will be categorised as Category C and licensable defence items will be categorised into Category A and Category B only[45]. This will consequently reduce the entry barriers for the industry, particularly for the small and medium segment.

2.7.4 Security Manual for Private Sector Defence Industries

DDP has prepared a Security Manual for private sector defence industries which provides for the physical documentation and IT security for the companies[46]. It clarifies the security architecture required to be put in place by the industry while manufacturing defence equipment. These security guidelines are to be adopted and followed by the Indian Licensed Industries after they are granted IL to undertake the manufacture of a defence item. For compliance, security manual has been divided into three parts; Category A, B & C. Depending on the products or weapons or the equipment, the companies will be required to comply with the security protocol. Category-A products are highly classified and sensitive from the security angle and the manufacturing of these items require the highest level of security; Category-B include semi-finished products, sub-assemblies, sub-systems of main weapons/ equipment's/platforms and some finished products of lesser degree of sensitivity. Category-C include products which do not involve use of any classified/secret information and are very generic in nature. The products in this category will normally not be specifically designed or modified for military use and therefore will require only a very minimal level of security. With the issue of the Security Manual, the requirement of affidavit from the applicants has been done away with.

2.7.5 Other Major Initiatives by Indian Government to Attract Domestic Private Sector Companies in Defence Production

To ensure a level-playing field, the anomalies in excise duty/custom duty have been removed and all Indian industries (public and private) which are now subjected to the same kind of excise and custom duty levies[47]. The Exchange Rate Variation (ERV) protection has been allowed on foreign exchange component to all Indian companies, including private companies in all the categories of capital acquisitions, so as to create a level playing field between the Indian and foreign industry.

Outsourcing and Vendor Development Guidelines for DPSUs and OFB mandate each DPSU and OFB to have short-term and long-term outsourcing and vendor development plans, including for the development of vendors for import substitution, to gradually increase the outsourcing from the private sector including from the Small and Medium Enterprises (SMEs). Preference is accorded to 'Buy (Indian)', 'Buy & Make (Indian)' and 'Make' categories of acquisition over the 'Buy (Global)' category, thereby, giving preference to the Indian industry in defence procurement.

2.7.6 Raksha Udyog Ratnas (RURs)/Industry Champions

The MOD, to encourage the production of major defence items in the private industry, articulated certain guidelines in DPP 2006 for the identification of a number of industry leaders in the private sector, which would be called RURs/Industry Champions[48]. The objective of the guidelines was to create and nurture a number of private companies who would then assume the responsibility of Tier-I companies and perform the role of system integrators and producers of major weapon platforms and systems for the armed forces. The guidelines further stipulated that the industry Champions would be, 'treated at par with the DPSUs which are selected by the Government, for receiving technology and undertaking licence production through TOT from overseas sources.' In addition, a provision was made in the DPP that the RURs would be eligible to bid for "Make" projects under which the MOD would share 80 per cent of the finances for the developmental work.

Following the promulgation of RUR guidelines, an expert committee was constituted in May-2006 under the chairmanship of a former secretary of defence production, Mr Prabir Sengupta and its Report submitted to the MOD in June-2007. The Report however, has not been implemented, due to the opposition from the labour unions (associated with the DPSU's) and the manner in which the selection was carried out[49]. It was reported that the Committee could only recommend a handful of companies totalling 13 in all, against a "large number" of companies who had expressed interest to be accredited as RURs. The MOD, so far has however not ruled out the RUR option. The Parliamentary Standing Committee on Defence "*strongly desire(d) that the Government should take expeditious steps to select and notify RURs at the earliest so that the misgivings among the defence industries are removed and they gear themselves up for effective participation in the national effort for self-reliance*"[50]. This aspect requires a re-look and promulgation at the earliest.

2.8 Defence Offsets

25 Defence offset contracts are under implementation with offset obligations of approximately INR 29,274 Crore (US $ 4.87 billion). The offset obligations of these offset contracts extend from 2008-22. Another 45 cases worth US $ 8-10 billion are under different contracting stages. The OEMs now can inform the name of the Indian Offset Partners (IOPs) and the components for offset discharge just one year prior to the year of offset discharge unlike the earlier requirement where it was required to be prescribed for the entire period of the contract and at the time of signing of the contract. Even for previously signed contracts, the procedure to change the IOPs and the components has

been simplified. One of the major demands of the industry has been to re-instate the provision of services for discharge of offsets. This has also been considered and some of the services have been restored for the discharge of offsets with certain conditions and limitations.

2.9 Sustenance Engineering and Maintenance Management Aspects: Drivers for Self Sufficiency and Strategic Capability of Imported and Indigenous Systems

2.9.1 Sustained Optimal Serviceability Status is Inescapable

To achieve combat readiness of Military Forces at all times, it is imperative that the full serviceability of critical platforms, mounted equipment in form of sensors, decision support systems and weapons, and other support systems are maintained optimally at all times. Therefore, the deciding factor for a favourable outcome will be the overall mission reliability and sustainability of weapons and equipment systems for the duration of combat. A sustained optimal serviceability status of critical military systems is paramount for India and needs to be achieved.

2.9.2 Performance Based Logistics (PBL)

The cost of acquisition of a system accounts for only 20 to 25 per cent of the total Life Cycle or Ownership cost. Therefore, it is imperative that a holistic life cycle management approach is adopted for acquisition of all high value large population systems. Moreover, to ensure combat readiness, a high level of serviceability is critical. The US first introduced this concept in 2001 for the acquisition of major weapon systems like the F-18 and F-14. The US was followed by the British and then the Australians in adopting PBL.

NOTES

1. Catherine Dale "*National Security Strategy: Mandates, Execution to Date, and Issues for Congress*" CRS Report for Congress Prepared for Members and Committees of Congress, p. 6 available at https://www.fas.org/sgp/crs/natsec/R43174.pdf (Accessed March 13, 2015).
2. "*Report* of the *Group of Ministers* on National Security", p. 98 available at http://www.vifindia.org/sites/default/files/ GoM%20 Report %20on%20National%20Security.pdf (Accessed March 13, 2015).
3. Narendra Singh Sisodia and Amit Cowshish"*Defence Planning, Programming and Budgeting*", p. 109 of IDSA book titled "*Core Concerns in Indian Defence and the Imperatives for Reforms*" available at http://www.idsa.in/book/CoreConcerns in Indian Defence _vmisra (Accessed March 16, 2015).

4. Mohanty, Deba R, "*A Dismal Show amid Pockets of Excellence: The State of Defence Innovation in India*", p.4, IGCC Defence Innovation Brief January 2015 available at http:// igcc.ucsd.edu/research/technology-and-security/defense-innovation/in India, (Accessed March 16, 2015).
5. "*US Department of Defence FY 2015 President's Budget March 2014*", p. 6. Office of the Under Secretary of Defence (Comptroller) available at http://comptroller.defense.gov/Portals/ 45/Documents/defbudget/fy2015/fy2015_Budget_ Request_ Overview_Book.pdf. (Accessed March 17, 2015).
6. Standing Committee on Defence, 10th Lok Sabha, "*Demand for Grants (1995-96), 4th Report (Lok Sabha Secretariat: New Delhi, 1995),*" p. 24 and Standing Committee on Defence, 10th Lok Sabha, "*Defence Research and Development: Major Projects, 5th Report (Lok Sabha Secretariat: New Delhi, 1995),*" p. 6. available at http://www.worldcat.org/title/eighth-report-standing-committee-on-defence-1995-96-tenth-lok-sabha-ministry-of-defence/oclc/ 51379274 (Accessed March 18, 2015).
7. "*Report* of the *Group of Ministers* on National Security" pp.110-111 available at http:// www.vifindia.org/sites/default/files/ GoM%20Report %20on%20National%20Security.pdf (Accessed March 18, 2015).
8. Cheung, Tai Ming "*The Chinese Defence Economy's Long March from Imitation to Innovation*" available at http://igcc.ucsd. edu/ assets/001/500868.pdf (Accessed March 19, 2015).
9. Ranjit Ghosh "*Defence Research and Development: International Approaches for Analysing the Indian Programme*", p. 36, IDSA Occasional Paper No. 41 available at http://www.idsa.in/ occasionalpapers/OP_ DefenceResearchand Developmen_ RanjitGhosh_ 140815 (Accessed March 19, 2015).
10. Capt Gary Jones, USAF, Edward White, Lt Col Erin T. Ryan, USAF, and Lt Col Jonathan D. Ritschel, USAF "*Investigation Into the Ratio of Operating and Support Costs to Life-Cycle Costs for DoD Weapon Systems Defence*" ARJ, January 2014, 21(1), p. 450. A Publication of the Defence Acquisition University available at http://www.dau.mil/publications/ DefenseARJ/ ARJ/ARJ68/ ARJ 68_Jones.pdf (Accessed March 19, 2015).
11. About Defence Research & Development Organisation (DRDO)"*DRDO Awards* "available at http://www.drdo.gov.in/ drdo/ English/index.jsp?pg=policies.jsp (Accessed March 20, 2015).
12. Ranjit Ghosh "*Defence Research and Development: International Approaches for Analysing the Indian Programme*", p. 36. IDSA Occasional Paper No. 41 available at http://www.idsa.in/ occasionalpapers/OP_ DefenceResearchand Developmen_ RanjitGhosh_ 140815 (Accessed March 20, 2015).
13. "*Governmentof India MOD Annual Report 2013-14*", p. 62 available at http://mod.nic.in/ writereaddata/AnnualReport2013-14-ENG.pdf, (Accessed March 20, 2015).
14. "Report No. 35 of 2014- Union Government (Defence Services)", Performance of Ordnance Factory Board (OFB), p. 126 available at http://www.saiindia.gov.in/english/ home/ our_products/Audit_Report/Government_Wise/union_audit/recent_ reports/union_ compliance/2014/Defence/Report_35/chap_8.pdf (Accessed March 23, 2015).
15. Laxman Kumar Behera, "*India's Ordnance Factories: A Performance Analysis*" pp.64-65*IDSA Journal of Defence Studies available at* http://www.idsa.in/journalofdefencestudies (Accessed March 23, 2015).
16. "Report No. 35 of 2014- Union Government (Defence Services)", Performance of Ordnance Factory Board (OFB) pp.114-115 available at http://www.saiindia.gov.in/english/ home/ our_products/Audit_Report/Government_Wise/union_audit/recent_ reports/union_ compli a nce/2014/Defence/Report_35/chap_8.pdf (Accessed November 10, 2015) and

"*Government of India MOD Annual Report 2013-14*", p. 63 available at http://mod.nic.in/writereaddata/AnnualReport20 (Accessed March 23, 2015).

17. "*Government of India MOD Annual Report 2014-15*", p. 58 available at http://mod.nic.in/writereaddata/AR1415.pdf (Accessed March 24, 2015).
18. "*Government of India MOD Annual Report 2013-14*", p. 63 available at http://mod.nic.in/writereaddata/AnnualReport2013-14-ENG. pdf (Accessed March 25, 2015).
19. "Report No. 35 of 2014- Union Government (Defence Services)" Performance of Ordnance Factory Board (OFB), p. 128 available at http://www.saiindia.gov.in/english/ home/ our_products/Audit_Report/Government_Wise/union_audit/recent_reports/ union_ compliance/2014/Defence/ Report_35/ chap_8.pdf (Accessed March 25, 2015).
20. "*Ministry of Defence Demands For Grants (2014-15) for Ordnance Factories and DRDO*", p. 43 presented by the Standing Committee on Defence to Lok Sabha on December 22, 2014 and available at http://164.100.47.134/lsscommittee/ Defence/ 16_Defence_5.pdf (Accessed March 26, 2015).
21. "Report No. 35 of 2014- Union Government (Defence Services)" Performance of Ordnance Factory Board (OFB) pp. 158-159 available at http://www.saiindia.gov.in/english/ home/ our_products/Audit_Report/Government_Wise/union_ audit/recent_ reports/ union_ compliance/2014/Defence/Report_35/chap_8.pdf (Accessed March 27, 2015).
22. Report No. 35 of 2014- Union Government (Defence Services)" Performance of Ordnance Factory Board (OFB) pp. 165-168 available at http://www.saiindia.gov.in/english/ home/ our_products/Audit_Report/Government_Wise/union_audit/recent_ reports/ union_ compliance/2014/Defence/Report_35/chap_8.pdf (Accessed March 27, 2015).
23. "Government *of India MOD Annual Report 2013-14*", p. 63 available at http://mod.nic.in/writereaddata/AnnualReport2013-14-ENG.pdf (Accessed March 30, 2015).
24. "*Ministry of Defence Demands For Grants (2014-15) for Ordnance Factories and DRDO*", p. 42 presented by the Standing Committee on Defence to Lok Sabha on December 22, 2014 and available at http://164.100.47.134/lsscommittee/ Defence/ 16_Defence_5.pdf (Accessed March 30, 2015).
25. Laxman Kumar Behera, "*India's Ordnance Factories: A Performance Analysis*" p.74IDSA *Journal of Defence Studies available at* http://www.idsa.in/journalofdefencestudies (Accessed March 31, 2015).
26. Government of India Ministry of Defence "Annual Report 2014-15", p. 59 available at http://mod.nic.in/writereaddata/ AR 1415.pdf (Accessed March 31, 2015).
27. Government of India Ministry of Defence "Annual Report 2013-14" p.67 available at http:/ /mod.nic.in/ writereaddata/ Annual Report2013-14-ENG.pdf (Accessed April 01, 2015).
28. Government of India Ministry of Defence "Annual Report 2013-14" p.69 available at http:/ /mod.nic.in/ writereaddata/ Annual Report2013-14-ENG.pdf (Accessed April 06, 2015).
29. Government of India Ministry of Defence "Annual Report 2014-15", p. 61 available at http://mod.nic.in/writereaddata/ AR1415 .pdf (Accessed April 07, 2015).
30. Government of India Ministry of Defence "Annual Report 2013-14" p.71 available at http:/ /mod.nic.in/ writereaddata/ Annual Report2013-14-ENG.pdf (Accessed April 08, 2015).
31. Government of India Ministry of Defence "Annual Report 2013-14" p.74 available at http:/ /mod.nic.in/ writereaddata/ Annual Report2013-14-ENG.pdf (Accessed April 09, 2015).
32. "*Defence-Undertakings- Facts about India*", p. 1available at http://www.facts-about-india.com/ defence-undertakings.php (Accessed April 10, 2015).
33. Laxman Kumar Behera, "India's Defence Public Sector Undertakings: A Performance Analysis" p.122 *IDSA Journal of Defence Studies* 3(4). October 2009 available at www.idsa.in/ sites/default/files/jds_3_4_lkbehera.pdf (Accessed April 10, 2015).

34. Sri Santosh Koner and Professor Jaydeb Sarkhel "Disinvestment of Public Sector in India: Concept and Different Issues", p. 1 available at http://www.iosrjournals.org/iosr-jef/papers/vol3-issue6/E0364852.pdf (Accessed April 13, 2015).
35. "*Defence Innovation in India: The Fault Lines*" p.31 IDSA Occasional Paper No. 32 by Laxman Kumar Behera available at http://www.idsa.in/occasionalpapers/DefenceInnovationsinIndia_lkbehera.html (Accessed November 13, 2015).
36. Aviotech Defence Advisory & Investments"Summary of Performance of Unlisted Defence Public Sector Undertakings (DPSUs) for FY11 and FY10", p. 8 available at http://www.aviotech.com/pdf/Summaryof_performanceof_unlisted_DPSUs.pdf (Accessed November 14, 2015).
37. Government of India Ministry of Defence "*Annual Report 2014-15*" pp.59-60 available at http://mod.nic.in/ writereaddata/ Annual Report2013-14-ENG.pdf (Accessed November 15, 2015).
38. "*The Industrial Policy Resolution 1948*" available at http://www.yourarticlelibrary.com/industries/the-industrial-policy-of-1948-of-india-categories/23439/and the "*Industries (Development & Regulation) Act, 1951*" available athttp://dipp.nic.in/English/ Policies/Industries_act1951.pdf (Accessed November 15, 2015).
39. Laxman Kumar Behera, "*Indian Defence Industry issues of Self Reliance*" *p.42 available at*http://www.idsa.in/monograph/ IndianDefenceIndustry (Accessed November 16, 2015).
40. Government of India, Ministry of Commerce and Industry, Department of Industrial Policy and Promotion, "*Press Note No 4 (2001 series) Revision of existing sectoral guidelines and equity cap on Foreign Direct Investment (FDI), including investment by Non Resident Indians (NRIs) and Overseas Corporate Bodies (OCBs)*" available athttp://dipp.nic.in/English/policy/changes/ press4 _01.htm (Accessed April 16, 2015).
41. Government of India, Ministry of Commerce and Industry, Department of Industrial Policy and Promotion, "*Press Note No 2 (2002 series) Guidelines for licensing production of Arms and Ammunition*" available at http://dipp.nic.in/English/policy/changes/ press2_ 0 2.htm (Accessed April 17, 2015).
42. Government of India Ministry of Defence "*Annual Report 2014-15*" p.54 available at http://mod.nic.in/ writereaddata/ Annual Report2013-14-ENG.pdf (Accessed April 17, 2015).
43. Government of India Ministry of Defence Department of Defence Production Office Memorandum" *Requirement of Industrial License for Maintenance Repair and Overhaul (MRO) activities*" available at http://www.ddpmod.gov.in/showfile.php?lid=153 v (Accessed April 20, 2015).
44. Government of India, Ministry of Commerce and Industry, Department of Industrial Policy and Promotion, "*Press Note No 3 (2014 series) List of Items requiring Industrial License*" available at http://dipp.nic.in/English/acts_rules/Press_ Notes/ pn3_2014 .pdf (Accessed April 20, 2015).
45. Government of India Ministry of Defence Department of Defence Production Office Memorandum" *Policy Issue: Categorisation of Revised Defence Products List into Category A, B and C from Security Angle*" available at http://www. Ddp mod.gov.in/ showfile.php? lid=157 (Accessed April 21, 2015).
46. Government of India Ministry of Defence Department Of Defence Production "*Security Manual for Licensed Defence Industries June 2014*" available athttp://www.ddpmod.gov.in/showfile.php?lid=151 (Accessed April 21, 2015).
47. Government of India Ministry of Defence, "*Private Sector Participation in Defence Production*" Press Information Bureau release July 24, 2015 available at http://pib.nic.in/newsite/PrintRelease.aspx?relid=123696 (Accessed April 22, 2015).

48. Ministry of Defence, *Defence Procurement Procedure (Capital Procurements) 2006*, New Delhi: Government of India, 2006 available at http://cgda.nic.in/pdf/dpp2006.pdf (Accessed April 22, 2015).
49. Laxman Kumar Behera, "*Enhancing Private Sector Participation In India's Defence Production*" Defence & Security Analysis 27(3), p. 256, September 2011 *available at* http://www.idsa.in/journalofdefencestudies (Accessed April 23, 2015).
50. Government of India, Ministry of Defence, Standing Committee on Defence (2009-10), "*Action Taken by the Government on the recommendations contained in the Thirty-third Report of the Committee (Fourteenth Lok Sabha) on Indigenisation of Defence Production – Public–Private Partnership, New Delhi: Lok Sabha Secretariat, 2008–2009*" available at http://www.performance.gov.in/sites/default/files/departments/defense-prod/Standing%20 Committee %20 Reports%202009-10.pdf (Accessed April 23, 2015).

CHAPTER 3

Israeli Defence Industry and Takeaways for India

3.1 Evolution and Growth

The Israeli defence industry's evolution and growth is explained by Sharon Sadeh as the result of a mix of imported technology and Israeli innovation. He goes on to add that "*the industry evolved through several stages, starting with small arms production and maintenance of more complex weapons, followed by licensed production and JVs, adoption and upgrading of licensed systems, and local production and design of components. The French arms embargo of 1967 and the aftermath of the 1973 war served as a catalyst for the next phase, i.e. independent design and the production of major weapons systems and platforms. This rapid progress backfired during the 1990s, as the industry shrank and focused on the production of niche systems and components due to a sharp fall in domestic and foreign sales*"[1].

In the 1930's, many military workshops operated underground and supplied military hardware to the Israeli freedom fighters. By 1933, the largest of such group of factories became the Israel Military Industries (IMI)[2]. During the 1940's and 1950's, several defence industries expanded to support the Israeli war of independence in 1948-49 and, the Sinai War of 1956. Post-independence, the government realised that Israel due to its hostile neighbourhood would continue to face frequent conflicts. Moreover, the tripartite declaration of 1950 by UK, France and the USA (to limit the arms supplies to the belligerents in the region) evoked serious concerns as to whether the needs of self-defence could be met based on imports alone. Israel, thus wanted to develop a self-sufficient defence manufacturing industry to meet the requirements of its armed forces[3]. Many industries were consolidated under a single management and incorporated into the military, besides the IMI. During this period, Israel Aircraft Industries (IAI) and Rafael were also formed. From the mid-1950's to1967, France became the primary and often the only source of defence imports and provided advance armaments.

In 1967, during the six day war with the Arabs, France ceased its supplies to Israel and imposed a unilateral arms embargo. This ultimately led to an expansion of Israel's defence industry, especially of the aerospace and electronics sectors, for which France had supplied most of the equipment. Consequently, funds meant for French companies were diverted to the domestic companies following which, Israel in the next three years (by end 1970) quadrupled its output[4]. Additional investments in 1970's expanded the industry further and brought in private companies. During the next 15 to 20 years, the self-sufficiency doctrine saw Israel develop its own fighter aircraft (Kfir), MBT (Chariot), missile boat and varied types of missiles. By 1981, the defence sector accounted for 25 per cent of the total labour force as compared to 10 per cent in the 1960's[5].

However, the severe domestic economic crisis in the mid-1980's, reduced Israel's defence budget and forced the DIB to reform. The 'Lavie' programme for developing a new fighter aircraft was cancelled in 1987 and was a result of the ready availability of US alternate arms to the Israeli Defence Force (IDF). This, changed the traditional role of the defence industry from that of a chief weapons developer and supplier to that of merely one upgrading Israeli made systems and supplying force multiplier systems—i.e. weapons that would guarantee qualitative technological superiority in the battlefield and which was not available from other sources. Further, the drop in foreign orders consequent to the collapse of the Soviet Union and the end of contracts with foreign customers, adversely affected the defence industry[6]. The three major SOE's or conglomerates – IAI, IMI and Rafael advanced defence systems, funded by the defence budget reported huge losses between 1989 and 1995. The finance ministry convinced the government that there was a need to downsize the defence SOE's as these, despite the government bailout and subsidies, remained inefficient due to their labour structure which could neither diversify nor layoff the surplus employees due to their strong unions while the workers were being paid irrespective of profits. Israel's defence SOE's were thus forced to undertake massive layoffs from 43,700 in 1985 to about 23,000 in 1997[7]. The DIB consequently had to re-align its focus to develop original and unique technological force multiplier solutions as retro fitment products and systems upgrades than as hither to fore producing complete platforms. Since the local demand was insufficient, domestic companies relied on exports to generate their revenues.

The US aid to Israel since the 1970's has provided its defence industry an opportunity (through collaboration on US imports and by supporting the industry penetrate the world's export markets). Close ties with the US has led to producing innovative solutions in UAV's, light assault weapons and missile detection systems. These have largely been funded by the US through an annual Foreign Military Financing (FMF) aid of about US $1.8 billion annually, for the purchase of US made defence equipment by Israel. After the peace accord with Egypt in 1979, Israel's reliance on imports from the US (out of the FMF aid) increased sharply[8]. The IDF and the ministry of finance have since become habituated to these US grants, including the stipulation that Israel buys US products, and they now perceive it as an indispensable part of the Israeli defence budget. Israel is the single largest recipient of US aid and was funded about US $ 68 billion between 1950 and 2009[9]. In the latter half of the last decade (2001-10) US military aid financed over 18 per cent of the Israeli defence budget. However, the impact of the US FMF has been that, the Israeli government has brought less from the domestic suppliers and more from the US. It is expected that between FY 2009 and 2018, Israel will receive almost three billion dollars annually as FMF and can spend more than a quarter of this on domestic procurement—a huge impetus for the DIB of Israel. No other military aid recipient of the US (as Egypt or Pakistan) is allowed this benefit[10].

3.2 Overview—Trends in Defence Industry Activities

In 2013, Israel's defence industry comprised of around 150 companies and employed 30,000 people. The three SOE's IAI, IMI and Rafael accounted for 70 per cent of the Defence Industrial Base (DIB) while the remaining comprised of one large privately owned company (Elbit is the largest and overall ranks second amongst all industries behind IMI), several medium enterprises and many small private companies that provide niche capabilities to the major contractors. In addition, the IDF's have a "division of technology and logistics" which runs large refurbishment and maintenance centres. Israel focuses on high technology systems, subsystems, integration and upgrades to existing platforms besides the development and manufacture of unmanned systems. Israel today does not produce its own major defence systems and concentrates on being the supplier-of-choice to other companies especially in the US besides, providing localisation and system integration capabilities[11]. Israel's core capabilities have evolved from its continued reliance on the US for major military platforms. Since the 1980's, Israeli capabilities have evolved in niche areas and often been designed to be integrated into US platforms meant for the export market.

3.3 Government Support

Israel's defence budget has grown at approximately the same rate as its Gross Domestic Product (GDP). The recent defence forecasts and spending on an average have been around 7.5 per cent of its GDP[12]. Political support has however not always been extended to increased defence budgets which, since the 1980's, have steadily reduced as a proportion of the overall spending. Due to the annual disagreements between the ministry of defence and the ministry of finance, the two ministries are developing a framework that would see the defence budget drawn up on a multiyear basis and remove it from the annual planning cycle[13].

3.4 Procurements

The Procurement and Production Directorate (PPD) of the MOD is responsible for military procurement and also oversees the manufacture and development of indigenous weapon systems.

Israel's ministry of industry, trade and labour, in March 2007, amended the 'Mandatory Industrial Cooperation (MIC)' regulation. The new rules impose a mandatory requirement for government corporations and public agencies to ask for industrial cooperation when their purchase of foreign goods or services exceeds the threshold of Israeli Shekels (ILS) 25 million (or US $ 5 million) and includes provisions for offset investment in Israel worth 50 per cent of the contract value as an "Industrial Cooperation Undertaking (ICU)"[14]. This also applies to related follow-on contracts worth US $ 5,00,000 or more[15]. The goal of the policy is to develop new markets and industrial and trade cooperation. In addition, to direct R&D grants for industry, job creation, international cooperation in industrial R&D, encouragement of technological entrepreneurship and development of future technologies by increasing academic industrial interaction and cooperation.

The Industrial Cooperation Authority (ICA) requires a minimum of 20 per cent subcontracting for any foreign project/product purchased. Preference is given to Israeli products over imported ones provided the cost of the former does not exceed more than 15 per cent of the latter[16]. An Israeli product is one whose Israeli content exceeds 35 per cent. A minimum of 35 per cent offsets are applied to defence contracts with acquisition minimum value of US $ 5 million.

3.5 R&D

Israel, because of its knowledgeable human capital, has since the very beginning been emphasising on improving its education system, building necessary Science and Technology (S&T) infrastructure and developing its military-related R&D facilities. In 1958, the military R&D units in the MOD, were organised into a separate unit called Rafael advanced defence systems (or the armaments development authority). This today has developed into Israel's, central organisation for defence systems production, technology and research[17]. Also, given Israel's security compulsions and its reliance on airpower, Bedek was established in the early 1950s and has developed into the IAI. This, like the HAL in India has had significant success in terms of development of indigenous aircrafts, UAV's and air defence systems. Rafael designs, develops and manufactures a wide range of high technology defence systems for air, land, sea and space applications. To improve Rafael's efficiency, the SOE was made into a limited company in the early part of this century and since then, with a huge export component, has improved its profitability and sales. It invests in defence related R&D and almost 10 per cent of its revenue is re-invested into research[18]. It has also formed partnerships with the civilian companies to develop the commercial applications of its advanced technologies, over which it holds the patent rights. It has partnerships with Israeli companies and international aerospace companies, especially in the US and developing countries like India (sale of mobile air defence missiles lately). Over last 10 years Rafael, has been both, a prime contractor and a sub-contractor on major defence systems. Rafael thus handles complex projects, from initial development, through to prototyping, production and acceptance tests. It provides customer service and support, upgrade of existing systems and offers turnkey projects involving the transfer of either technologies or the complete production facilities.

Israel identifies and develops its R&D talent in many ways. The 'talpiot' is an elite unit which recruits only the best young Israeli's across the country's schools and combines their military service with an education in science and engineering that rivals degrees from leading institutions as Massachusetts Institute of Technology (MIT)[19]. It is believed that a start-up which involves a member from talpiot is said to guarantee business investments from the U.S. and other foreign firms which are aware of the skill capabilities and technological prowess of the alumni from these units.

The IDF and the MOD's Directorate of Defence R&D (MAFAT) works on R&D with the arms industry (including SOE's and research centres)[20]. On a case to case basis, the General Staff creates a Special Project Office (SPO) to manage major R&D or procurement projects and as a lobbying group to defend arms projects against critics. State owned IAI Ltd is involved in research, design, development, integration, testing, upgrade, support and service of land, sea, air and space systems, equipment and technologies. Elbit Systems operates a number of subsidiaries in areas of aerospace, land and naval systems, C4ISR, advance electro-optic, space technologies, EW, ELINT, data links and military communication systems. Elbit also focuses on upgrades and development of new technologies for defence and homeland security applications. Rafael develops, manufactures and supports a range of systems and components for missiles, weapons systems, electronic systems and ordnance[21]. Rafael is involved in the development of commercial applications and technology transfers. The company has a central role in the nation's defence R&D effort and in the subsequent production of weapons and equipment's embodying cutting edge technologies. The Elisra group designs, develops, manufactures, integrates and supports advanced systems solutions for air, sea and land systems. IMI provides land based combat systems through land systems division. The rocket systems division designs, develops and manufactures solid rocket weapon systems and the advanced systems division provides precision attack systems. IMI is also Israel's sole producer of small arms and heavy ammunition.

3.6 Exports

The Industry base provides much of Israeli military's requirements although the revenues are sourced through exports. Overall 70 per cent of military industrial output of Israel is directed towards export markets which include European nations (notably UAV technologies), US and India. Israel is also eyeing an increase in export sales to Vietnam, Azerbaijan, Brazil and Poland. Collectively, the five major companies, IAI, IMI, Rafael, Elbit and Elisra account for 90 per cent of current export contracts[22]. Israel looks to the US for 95 per cent of its imported material while the European Union makes up the remaining five per cent. Israel for the period from 2010 to 2014 was ranked 10th in the list of the world's top arms exporters and accounted for two per cent of the global share[23].

Israeli defence companies in the past have adopted a number of approaches to access the European markets. In 1997, Rafael established the Euro-spike consortium with Germany's Diehl munition systems and Rheinmetall defence electronics to market the Spike family of anti-tank missiles and in the next six years succeeded in getting orders from Finland, Netherland, Poland and Romania to declare the transformation of Euro spike into a JV by 2004[24]. Elbit's JV with French group Thales UAV tactical systems (U-Tacs) secured a UK contract with a large share for the Israeli company. Similarly, aiming for the European aerospace markets IAI, Rafael armament development authority and Elbit systems in 2005 formed Aeronautics and Space Industries of Israel (ASII).

A rift was also created between Israel and the US in June 2004 when the IAI had intended to provide spares for the Harpy anti-radar reconnaissance UAV's earlier sold to China in 1991[25]. The US suspected the sale was to upgrade the system. The result of the disagreement led to a decline in Israel's export to China. The US successfully put pressure on Israel to cancel another contract of 1.2 billion US $ for the sale of IAI's Phalcon airborne early warning systems to China, which eventually led to a claim for compensation. All this ultimately led to the setting up of the Israeli defence export control division.

Many Israeli companies have overlapping areas of capabilities (as UAV's, armour, C4I systems) and are often in competition with each other in the export markets. Hence consolidation amongst the Israeli defence sector makes a business sense.

3.7 Privatisation

Economic problems in Israel during the period 1985-92 led to a reduced defence spending. This in turn had an intense impact on Israel's state owned defence industries. The procurements from the local defence industries decreased by around 50 per cent and the employees strength was reduced by about 35 per cent by end 1992[26]. The fiscal contraction most affected the IMI while all the three leading SOE's experienced economic challenges that prompted restructuring. To overcome some of the problems, the government provided continued support to all the three companies with a conspicuous annual funding of US $ three billion to IMI for over a decade up to 2010. These problems made the Israeli Government think ever since 2000 for privatisation of the three companies. The options considered include part privatisation of IMI (earmarked for privatisation since 2005) or IAI, next a merger of IMI and the more stable Rafael (may be in the longer run) and last but not the least, a likely amalgamation or super merger of all the three into a giant diversified defence group behemoth (however concentration may prove damaging to competition). The contention against privatisation has been employee opposition via unions and the issue of fiscal deficit incurred by IMI. In December 2013, a privatisation programme was formally announced under which IMI will lose 950 workers out of its payroll of 3000 workers, vacate its premises for the development of a residential area and receive assured annual order from the MOD worth US $ 142 million. However, core capabilities that are essential to national securities will remain in the hands of the state in a new company called IMI systems.

3.8 Private Sector

The private companies gradually developed the expertise required for competing with the defence SOE's and by 1990's started attracting a larger portion of MOD orders. This was facilitated by the introduction of a "Compulsory Tender Law" that required the MOD (and all other governmental branches) to introduce competition into the bidding process of services and products[27]. This effectively ended MOD's preferential stand towards state-owned firms and imposed problems to it as it became a buyer, owner and regulator. Privately owned industries emerged as strong and viable competitors, both domestically and internationally. While restructuring, consolidation and privatisation of the state owned sector, the private sector, despite their commercial and financial benefits, were kept off. Some years later, the private industry accounting 30 per cent of the DIB started a process of mergers, consolidation and acquisitions from mid-1990's onwards. Elbit Systems and El-Op Electro-Optics merged in July 2000, while the Koor group consolidated including Tadiran Electronic Systems, Tadiran Spectralink and BVR, under the umbrella of Elisra Electronic Systems.

3.9 Lessons for India

Israel adopted a dual-policy approach to defence procurement. It brought most weapons from abroad and concurrently invested heavily in establishing a sophisticated defence industry, that would tailor weapons systems to its requirements and also develop only those new ones, not available elsewhere, by creating advanced defence oriented R&D facilities. Consequently, initially Israel allocated resources to defence R&D over housing and infrastructure, to establish an independent military industrial base. For this, a comprehensive knowledge base was established in universities and government laboratories through the global network and by applying reverse engineering, industrial espionage and smuggling of specialists and equipment through covert operations. For example, the Kfir fighter plane was based on plans of the French Mirage III, acquired clandestinely through a Swiss source in the 1960's[28].

Factors that facilitated the development of Israel's arms industry included a population which is highly educated and can work in the technology sector; weapon development activity undertaken in close cooperation with the IDF, irrespective of its commitment to purchasing the equipment; continuous government support to military R&D funding—approximately 7.5 per cent of Israel's military spending is dedicated to R&D; Israel's cordial relationship with Western Europe and USA encouraging the sharing of technology; US providing significant military aid (FMF)—more than 18 per cent of Israel's defence budget coming from FMF and 26 per cent of this aid can be used to buy Israel made weapons—This provides the financial capacity for Israel to focus on building domestic arms technology; Frequent rejection of Israel's requests for weapons and technologies, recurrent arms sanctions and intensified re-armament of Arab nations during the 1960's convinced Israeli leadership to develop a broadly based indigenous arms production capability[29].

A liberal export policy coupled with combat proven systems secured Israel's defence industry's position in the world markets. Israel offered quick operational solutions with a considerably faster development process[30]. "*The high national priority on defence efforts, the quality of minds involved in the (defence) industry, the fact that the end user was often part of the design and production team, (and) bringing to bear practical experience and specific requirements*", all aided the process. The increase in exports in the 1980's subsidised R&D costs of new weapons and cut domestic R&D budget.

Israel depends upon a human capital intensive growth strategy and this is evident from its education structure and facilities that provide quality education. Israel's R&D expenditure is 4.2 per cent of its GDP and is the highest amongst all nations in terms of percentage of GDP[31]. The importance

Israel places on S&T is exemplified by its high density of scientists and technicians as a proportion of its population. The infrastructural investment is fuelled by foreign aid and investment, and is exceptional. Israel's defence allocation in real terms has consistently increased over the last decade. This is despite the fact that its military expenditure as a per cent of GDP shows a decline from 9.6 per cent to 6.5 per cent over the last decade[32]. The decline is more because of a substantial increase in its GDP and even with a reduced military expenditure of 6.5 per cent of GDP, Israel ranks in the top 10 countries of the world. However, since 2008, Israel has stopped receiving bilateral foreign aid, usually called Economic Support Fund (ESF). Given the expansion of the hi-tech sector, supported by US military co-operation and aid, Israel has leapfrogged into the realm of a developed country from its status, for over six decades, as an emerging economy. Israel has also joined the Organisation for Economic Co-operation and Development (OECD) thereby, transiting to the status of a developed economy.

Israel employs an exceptionally creative set of scientists and engineers in the high-tech industries especially in the military production sector, because nearly 75 per cent of the arms are to be exported. Hence, the defence sector has been getting a major impetus towards the creation and development of new technologies in the international arms market. Also, Israel operates a conscription army in which all teenagers at the age of 18 have to join the IDF. The structure of the IDF is unique in the way in which skills learnt during army service are transferable to civilian life and Israel reaps some of the richest rewards.

Defence exports from Israel succeeded after graduating from a modest beginning with small arms and ammunition to more sophisticated systems and equipment's incorporating advanced technologies; initially by targeting the sub-markets of developing nations and then successfully penetrating markets of industrially advanced countries; in the post-cold war era, many instances of export activity involved making collaborative frameworks that involved industrial cooperation with domestic companies in target countries for upgrading the customers military equipment and finally to improve their position in the overseas markets, Israeli defence companies either got into permanent JVs with foreign defence companies to serve the requirements of the home market of developing/developed countries as also to enable them enhance their sales to third parties world-wide[33]. Israel's case study clearly provides an insight into the role that exports can play in balancing out local demand fluctuations and generate the revenues to sustain the defence industry when the domestic demand recedes.

Israeli defence industry's faster system development process and the offering of innovative operational solutions were the result of direct contact, continuous communication and close teamwork between IDF end users, developers (engineers and technicians) and the producers.

Israel's experience shows the possible transitional steps to make SOE's competitive and included setting up accounting and costing systems besides other organisational adjustments. Comprehensive restructuring included closing plants, laying off workers to make companies leaner, efficient and prepared to compete in the global arms market. Management's focus shifted to profitability and cash flow considerations which improved their financial situation and consequently allowed diversification and expansion into new areas and products besides increasing partnerships with foreign defence companies. The crisis showed disadvantages of SOE's to both the companies and the government and the need for early privatisation despite reluctance of labour unions and political pressures. The SOE's consequently accelerated their growth through internal restructuring and setting up joint ventures while the defence private sector adopted a process of local consolidation through mergers and acquisitions. The consolidation process generated synergetic effects that strengthened industrial capabilities and expanded market opportunities thus allowing rapid industrial growth.

The special relationship with the US gave Israel many distinct advantages. There were buybacks by American arms manufacturers selling military equipment to Israel and JVs of Israeli and American defence companies for development, production and marketing of new weapon systems. "There were various models of co-operation: division of labour in development and production; co-opting US firms into production of military systems developed in Israel, joint marketing to third parties and others[34].

Israeli experience shows export is essential for defence industry to keep its critical mass because the local market is too small to support it.

NOTES

1. Sadeh Sharon "*Israel's Beleaguered Defence Industry*" *Journal of Middle East Review of International Affairs* 5(1) p.67 available at http://www.rubincenter.org/2001/03/sadeh-2001-03-05/ (Accessed April 24, 2015).
2. "*Israel – Defence Industry*" IHS Jane's World Defence Industry 2014 p.25.
3. Lifshitz Yaakov "*Defence Industries in Israel*" The Global Arms Trade: A Handbook Edited

by Andrew T H Tan p.266 available at http://www.gbv.de/dms/zbw/59370763X.pdf (Accessed April 26, 2015).

4. "*Israel – Defence Industry*" IHS Jane's World Defence Industry 2014 p.25.
5. "*Israel – Defence Industry*" IHS Jane's World Defence Industry 2014 p.25.
6. Sadeh Sharon "*Israel's Beleaguered Defence Industry*" *Journal of Middle East Review of International Affairs* 5(1) p.71 available at http://www.rubincenter.org/2001/03/sadeh-2001-03-05/ (Accessed April 28, 2015).
7. Sadeh Sharon "*Israel's Beleaguered Defence Industry*" *Journal of Middle East Review of International Affairs* 5(1) p.72 available athttp://www.rubincenter.org/2001/03/sadeh-2001-03-05/ (Accessed April 30, 2015).
8. Sadeh Sharon "*Israel's Beleaguered Defence Industry*" *Journal of Middle East Review of International Affairs* 5(1) p.69 available at http://www.rubincenter.org/2001/03/sadeh-2001-03-05/ (Accessed May 01, 2015).
9. "*Israel – Defence Industry*" IHS Jane's World Defence Industry 2013 p.16.
10. Broude Mark, Deger Saadet and Sen Somnath "*Defence, innovation and development: the case of Israel*" p.41. Journal of Innovation Economics and Management 2013/2 Edited by *De* Boeck Supérieur available at http://www.cairn.info/revue-journal-of-innovation-economics-2013-2-page-37.htm (Accessed May 05, 2015).
11. "*Israel – Defence Industry*" IHS Jane's World Defence Industry 2013 p.16.
12. "*Israel – Defence Industry*" IHS Jane's World Defence Industry 2013 p.16.
13. "*Israel – Defence Industry*" IHS Jane's World Defence Industry 2013 p.16
14. "*Israel – Defence Industry*" IHS Jane's World Defence Industry 2013 p.18.
15. "The Israeli arms industry" SIPRI Yearbook 2011 Armaments, Disarmaments and International Security p.239 available at http://www.sipri.org/yearbook/2011/files/SIPRIYB11summary.pdf. (Accessed May 09, 2015).
16. "*Israel – Defence Industry*" IHS Jane's World Defence Industry 2013 p.18.
17. Broude Mark, Deger Saadet and Sen Somnath "*Defence, innovation and development: the case of Israel*" *Journal of Innovation Economics and Management* 2013/2 p.42. edited by De Boeck Supérieur available at http://www.cairn.info/revue-journal-of-innovation-economics-2013-2-page-37.htm (Accessed May 11, 2015).
18. Broude Mark, Deger Saadet and Sen Somnath "*Defence, innovation and development: the case of Israel*" *Journal of Innovation Economics and Management* 2013/2 p.43. edited byDe Boeck Supérieur available at http://www.cairn.info/revue-journal-of-innovation-economics-2013-2-page-37.htm (Accessed May 15, 2015).
19. Broude Mark, Deger Saadet and Sen Somnath "*Defence, innovation and development: the case of Israel*" *Journal of Innovation Economics and Management* 2013/2 p.49. edited by De Boeck Supérieur available at http://www.cairn.info/revue-journal-of-innovation-economics-2013-2-page-37.htm (Accessed May 19, 2015).
20. "*Israel – Defence Industry*" IHS Jane's World Defence Industry 2013 p.16.
21. "*Israel – Defence Industry*" IHS Jane's World Defence Industry 2013 p.17.
22. "*Israel – Defence Industry*" IHS Jane's World Defence Industry 2013 p.17
23. Becker Sam "*10 Countries That Export the Most Weapons*" *available at* http://www.cheatsheet.com/business/the-worlds-10-largest-arms-exporters.html/?a=viewall (Accessed May 20, 2015).
24. "*Israel – Defence Industry*" IHS Jane's World Defence Industry 2013 p.17
25. "*Israel – Defence Industry*" IHS Jane's World Defence Industry 2013 p.17
26. "*Israel – Defence Industry*" IHS Jane's World Defence Industry 2013 p.18
27. "*Israel – Defence Industry*" IHS Jane's World Defence Industry 2014 p.24.

28. Sadeh Sharon "*Israel's Beleaguered Defence Industry*" *Journal of Middle East Review of International Affairs* 5(1) p.73 available at http://www.rubincenter.org/2001/03/sadeh-2001-03-05/ (Accessed May 21, 2015).
29. Sadeh Sharon "*Israel's Beleaguered Defence Industry*" *Journal of Middle East Review of International Affairs* 5(1) p.65 available at http://www.rubincenter.org/2001/03/sadeh-2001-03-05/ (Accessed May 23, 2015).
30. "*The Israeli arms industry*" SIPRI Yearbook 2011 Armaments, Disarmaments and International Security pp.236-237 available at http://www.sipri.org/yearbook/2011/files/SIPRIYB11summary.pdf. (Accessed May 23, 2015).
31. Sadeh Sharon "*Israel's Beleaguered Defence Industry*" *Journal of Middle East Review of International Affairs* 5(1) p.66 available at http://www.rubincenter.org/2001/03/sadeh-2001-03-05/ (Accessed May 25, 2015).
32. "*2014 R&D MagazineGlobal Funding Forecast*" Dec 2013 available at http://www.battelle.org/docs/tpp/2014_global_ rd_ funding_forecast.pdf , (Accessed May 27, 2015).
33. Broude Mark, Deger Saadet and Sen Somnath "*Defence, innovation and development: the case of Israel*" *Journal of Innovation Economics & Management* 2013/2 p.40 edited byDe Boeck Supérieur available at http://www.cairn.info/revue-journal-of-innovation-economics-2013-2-page-37.htm (Accessed May 29, 2015).
34. Lifshitz Yaakov, "*Defence Industries in Israel*" The Global Arms Trade: A Handbook Editor Andrew T H Tan p.269 available at http://www.gbv.de/dms/zbw/59370763X.pdf (Accessed May 29, 2015).
35. Lifshitz Yaakov "*Defence Industries in Israel*" The Global Arms Trade: A Handbook Editor Andrew T H Tan p.274 available at http://www.gbv.de/dms/zbw/59370763X.pdf (Accessed June 01, 2015).

CHAPTER 4

South Korean Defence Industry's Lessons for India

4.1 Evolution and Growth

South Korea in-spite of a traumatic experience of the Korean War from 1950-53 did not build a DIB after the war. This was due to the Republic of Korea's (ROK's) continuing security partnership with the US and also the need to develop the country's economy after the war. However, an attack by the North Korean commandos on the presidential mansion in Seoul in January 1968 and an announcement next year of the gradual disengagement of the US from Asia, changed that decision. The latter, led to a reduction of the US troops and the weakening of the US security commitment to South Korea. The two events convinced South Korea to create its own DIB. Up to the mid-1960, Korea had completely depended on the military aid and equipment provided by the US. Thus in 1969, Korea did not have an industrial structure to undertake large-scale defence industrialisation and began with the production of ammunition and small arms. This itself was undertaken with the help of the US technical data packages and the manufacturing license agreements[1].

Notwithstanding, the government right from the beginning (i.e. from the early 1970's), was instrumental in driving the country's defence industrialisation process. It designated certain industries as defence contractors and provided them the financial and economic benefits. The defence contractors, were mostly major subsidiaries of large family-owned business conglomerates, called *chaebols*, who primarily engaged in the civil sector. For defence production, the *chaebols* and specialised in specific weapon systems as combat vehicles, aircrafts, surface combatants, guided munitions and so on[2].

In 1971, the Ministry of National Defence (MND) set up an integrated 'Defence Procurement Agency' (DPA). The DPA handled the initial specification work which included the procurement of defence materials for the Korean military forces, management of the sources of supply, acquisition of price information, cost management, offset negotiation and military specification and standardisation besides, the construction of military facilities and payments to contractors[3].

In 1971, to promote defence R&D in the country and as a part of the industrialisation process, the government set up an 'Agency for Defence Development' (ADD). Consequently, the state was to conduct R&D while the industry was to perform the production activities. In 1972, the national defence objectives were published for the first time and brought forth the ROK's security goals. The command and control changes kept ROK armed forces under the overall US command while a combined ROK–US headquarters was established. A more developed arms industry was planned and the procurement system was to be restructured. The government extended further support when the national assembly enacted a special law[4]. "*The Special Law on the Promotion of the Defence Industry was enacted in 1974 to provide a legal foundation for the enhancement of the defence industrial sector through a wide range of incentives such as preferential financial arrangements, tax and tariff reduction, concession of plant sites, and other administrative support*"[5]. In fact, "*three government decrees put the indigenous South Korean defence industry into motion: A 1973 law on defence Industry, a 1974 force improvement plan for build-up of ROK's armed forces and, a 1975 defence tax law to finance the development of the defence industry*"[6].

South Korea, thereafter, adopted a massive and yet a systematic defence industrialisation process from 1974 onwards. Commencing from ammunition and small arms production, it next set up a heavy-chemical industry, especially for the defence. Thereafter, the machinery, electronics and shipbuilding industries were selected to take part in the defence industry's production process. These industries were recognised as strategic industrial sectors, whose growth would contribute to the country's economic development. The industries chosen by the government, within each sector of the economy, were already established big business conglomerates, which were by then engaged in civil production. After having been recognised as strategic industries for the defence sector, the selected industries were required to engage in military production, in parallel with their activities in the civilian sector. Moreover, "*during the 1970's, chaebols were required by law, to devote 70 per cent of their industrial capacity to production of defence material*"[7]. South Korea's military equipment production throughout the 1970's and 1980's was based on US technology and was highly dependent on the technological assistance provided by the US. Defence material, were acquired through reverse engineering, licensed production or direct imports. Thus, the modernisation of ROK's armed forces during this period remained dependent on the US support. This was despite the political tradition of seeking a self-reliant defence posture. Consequently, domestic defence technologies to a great extent remained based on what the country had managed to reverse-engineer[8].

ROK's defence policy during the 1980's focused beyond the licensed production of US-designed conventional weapons to that of implementing the Government's vision of military modernisation and self-reliance, including its command and control. From 1977 to 1984, contractors focused on product development through modification, re-design, and re-production via reverse engineering. From the early 1990's, the focus was to enhance indigenisation activities by accelerating the pace of domestic defence R&D. Government support was available through the implementation of the offset policies when arms were being procured from abroad and, it led to significant improvements in the country's technological sophistication. Coupled with this, the constant improvements in the R&D sector resulted in South Korea developing and producing its own weapons systems, although this was by also including the technologies provided by foreign contractors. "*Key present-day military equipment, such as the K2 Main Battle Tank (MBT), the K21 Infantry Fighting Vehicle (IFV), the K9 Self-Propelled Howitzer and the T/FA-50 jet aircraft have all to a great extent been developed domestically*"[9].

By 1987, defence research had been systematically expanded into the social sciences field by the establishment of the Korea Institute for Defence Analyses (KIDA)[10]. At the end of the war in 1953, the ROK was lesser industrialised than North Korea, and remained so in the 1960s. However, by 1980 it was well ahead both in economic and industrial terms. "*By the late 1990s, South Korea's military modernisation had begun to assume many characteristics of the Revolution in Military Affairs (RMA) pioneered in the US and had begun to affect intense changes in the nation's defence industry and associated defence exports*"[11].

4.2 Overview-Trends in Defence Industry and Defence Reform - 2020 Plan

South Korea, since 2006, is implementing a Defence Reform - 2020 Plan (DRP). This is to be executed over 15 years. The reforms plan, hopes to achieve significant reduction in the size of the armed forces while at the same time intends to equip the forces with the state-of-the-art weapons systems. The new systems are to provide qualitative improvements as also enhanced operational capabilities for the conduct of future network-centric and Joint Warfare (JW) operations. South Korea, accordingly will acquire new destroyers, submarines, fighter aircrafts and missile defence systems. These are to be sourced preferably through indigenous development and production. "*The ROK military expects to deploy its first units of next-generation MBTs, fighter aircraft, multiple-rocket launchers, surface-to-air missile systems, submarines and naval surface combatants within the set time frame of the defence reform plan*"[12]. The DRP when initiated in 2006 considered the changing regional security environment including a rising China – the need to balance the relationship between Japan and China, and the desire to reduce the dependence on the US as a security provider, especially when considering that the transfer of wartime operational control was due in 2015 and, would also compel an independent yet strong defence posture. Since its announcement, there have been two attempts to revise the defence reform plan. The first revision in 2009 was in terms of a reduction in the plan's required budget. Then in 2011, as a fallout of the North Korean military aggression whereby a new plan was proposed. "*Although the revision has not yet been passed in the National Assembly, the new 307 (also known as the 11-30) plan is expected to complement and partly override the ongoing DRP, and extend the reform process to 2030*"[13]. Notwithstanding, there are significant challenges to the successful implementation of South Korea's defence reform.

Besides the reduction in troops, the reforms, plan to abolish the draft system and change to a volunteer-based professional military. The DRP also aims to shift the administrative control over the force improvement budget and the acquisition process from the military and the MND to the civil servants. DRP in 2005 called for a rapid increase in the share of civilian personnel in the MND, from 52 per cent to 71 per cent[14]. It considered this, a necessity to establish greater civilian oversight and influence over the ROK's defence policies. This was because many of the high-level bureaucrats in the ministry were either former or currently serving military officers, and most of the former ministers of national defence were serving in the armed forces as chairmen of the Joint Chiefs of Staff (JCS). Accordingly, the military's dominance over the defence industrial sector diminished. The creation of the Defence Acquisition Programme Administration (DAPA) in 2006 was the manifestation of this structural shift[15]. It reduced the influence of the MND and the military establishment over matters of acquisition, planning and implementation as the administrative control now rests with the civil servants at DAPA. Further, it also reduced the ADD's dominance in the defence R&D sector, as defence R&D activities are increasingly being delegated, by DAPA, to the contractors themselves.

4.3 Government Support

South Korea's defence industry has been supported by several government-led initiatives and policies that were mostly implemented since the 1990s. The ROK's procurement trends since the late-1990s also show a growing emphasis on acquiring domestically developed and manufactured products[16]. The DRP too has indirectly impacted the defence industrial development process. The ROK armed forces and the government's demands for improved and advanced weapons platforms have made the defence industry to move away from production through imitation and reverse engineering and rely more on indigenisation and in-house R&D. The emphasis on procuring equipment that is based on domestic R&D and production within the country is also mandated by the DRP 2020.

Defence contracts and contractors are designated by the government which then by law entitles the selected contractors to ample benefits and subsidies. Once a contract is awarded, the government provides guarantees that it will procure the products once manufactured and assembled[17]. The defence industry thus enjoys major incentives to maintain production, as the supply and demand is institutionally guaranteed by the Korean Government.

South Korea prefers defence industrial cooperation with other countries on a state-to-state level as against between defence contractors. South Korea over the next five years is expected to sharply increase its defence budget to 232.5 trillion Won (US $ 214.7 billion) for the fiscal period 2016-20. This, on an average will be a seven per cent increase during the cited period, when compared to its 2015-19 version. Out of this budget outlay, the costs for maintaining troops is set at 155.2 trillion Won (66.75 per cent) and the rest is to be used for the improvement of military capabilities. "*The budget injection* *of 8.7 trillion Won (US $ 8.03 billion) is based on the assessment that Pyongyang is believed to have reached a "significant" point in its efforts to master the technology to miniaturise nuclear warheads that fit atop missiles*"[18].

4.4 Defence Acquisition Programme Administration (DAPA)

The DAPA is a military procurement agency that replaced the former DPA on January 02, 2006. DAPA is responsible for managing and executing acquisitions of foreign and domestic defence material. It streamlines and consolidates eight organisations that are responsible for equipment procurement and the development of technology'. These organisations were earlier under the purview of the MND which exercised administrative control while the three military services had their own decentralised procurement offices.

The former DPA was managed by the military. However, DAPA is a civilian agency with military support. DAPA will continue to report to the Defence Minister who is a civilian. The new agency formed will ensure transparency in procurement as the closed decision-making process has been replaced by one which will be discussed and controlled by the Defence Acquisition Programme Executive Committee, which also involves external expert participation. Local agents need to register and be certified by the DAPA to supply their products and services to the MND.

ROK's Reorganised Defence Acquisition Process is shown in Figure 4.1. Since the establishment of DAPA, the efficiency of program management has improved due to the introduction of Integrated Project Team's (IPT). The time required for procurement administration has reduced due to the improvement of the procurement process and eventually accrued savings in the required budget. An IPT manages all the processes from the determination of requirements to the completion of the program, including planning and compilation of budget under the charge of the project manager[19]. Advanced countries have been administering the IPT system for the past several years. The JCS and the service branches provide the MND and DAPA with information on the Required Operational Capabilities (ROCs) of new equipment and the projected operational environment where these are to be deployed. For this, each service branch of ROK's armed forces has a combat development division for planning and communicating the requirements of new weapons systems. The JCS formulates the mid-term and long-term acquisition plans which describe the expected future capability requirements of the armed forces. The military also takes part in the testing and evaluation of prototype weapons systems on delivery by the producing contractor. This is carried out by the relevant service branch together with the JCS[20].

Figure 4.1: ROK's Reorganised Defence Acquisition Process

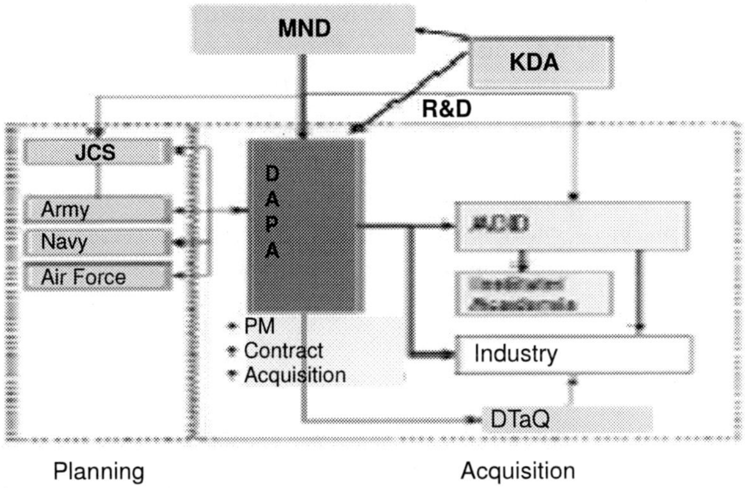

Key: JCS=Joint Chiefs of Staff; T&E=test and evaluation; DQAA=Defence Quality Assurance Agency; PMO=Procurement Management Office; DPA=Defense Procurement Agency; DTaQ=Defense Technology and Quality agency.

Source: The Republic of Korea: A Defence and Security Primer.

DAPA plays a major role in the acquisition process. It is the government's only institution conducting formal negotiations on the issues pertaining to the price, technology transfers, local production and offset packages[21]. It exercises authority over the budget allocations for acquisitions and whether a weapons system is to be procured domestically or from the foreign market. Yet another significant role of the DAPA is to promote the domestic industry and R&D whereby it will naturally favour the procurement of defence material developed and produced within South Korea[22]. The domestic competition for R&D and production contracts is also handled by DAPA. It selects the prime contractor based on the bidders' level of technological advancement and the estimated cost of production (i.e. the selection of a bidder for a contract is based on the twin criterion of providing the best technology at the lowest cost of production i.e. on a L1T1 criterion). R&D contracts have been increasingly awarded to industries other than the ADD to improve the capabilities of the industry and reduce the dominance of the ADD in the defence R&D sector.

4.5 Procurements

South Korea directs or channelises its offsets by influencing the source selection and reserving the right to nominate the local companies that will partner the foreign companies for their discharge of offset obligations. The source selection is influenced by stating upfront, in the RFP, the offsets that are required in the case of each acquisition. The required offsets are also divided into different categories (not more than six) with each category assigned a numerical weighted value. The categories there after become the basis for selecting the winner. At present, South Korea considers five categories of offsets with 'Category A' having the highest weighted value of '6' followed by 'Category B' of '4' and 'Category E' with lowest value of '1'. DAPA has also the provision of giving '10' points provided a foreign company agrees to provide state of the art technology that can be utilised in the R&D projects[23]. South Korea reserves the right to select the local companies, known as Korean Industry Participant (KIP), who would partner with the foreign companies for the discharge of offset obligations. In those cases where the foreign vendors are allowed to suggest KIP, DAPA has also the final say. By reserving the right to select the KIP, the DAPA ensures that the right kind of domestic industry players get the opportunity which is in the interest of the Korean industry.

4.6 R&D

In 1971, the government, under the MND, set up its defence R&D organisation called the 'Agency for Defence Development' (ADD). The ADD, as envisaged, enjoys near monopoly in the country's defence R&D sector. This is because "*The ADD's relative advantage over the industry's defence R&D sector is its access to the established research and test facilities, which include the 56 major laboratories where R&D and testing of weapons systems are conducted (21 of these, are dedicated for R&D work relating to missile technology and precision-guided munitions)*"[24].

South Korea, since 1971, has increasingly tried to produce defence equipment that is based on technologies acquired through its own R&D. Traditionally, the ADD was responsible for defence R&D. However, since 2006, the ADD is being asked to shift its focus onto R&D activities that relate to core defence technologies. These technologies are identified as crucial for national security and should therefore remain under the control of the government. Most other defence R&D efforts of systems engineering and integration, are increasingly being outsourced to the domestic defence industries, implying there is a growing division of labour in the defence R&D sector. Thus, industries since 2006 are increasingly getting into both production and R&D-related activities.

South Korea has also been increasing its defence expenditure on R&D. The defence R&D budget of about US $ 1.3 billion in 2009 increased to about US $ 2 billion by 2013 thereby, recording an increase of about 54 per cent in just four years[25]. South Korea now aims to further augment the investment in R&D from the current 6.5 percent of the total defence budget to 8.4 per cent by 2020 to further promote defence R&D[26]. Further, many former ADD researchers have been recruited by the R&D sections of the defence contractors. Despite, the role of the ADD having progressively reduced, it still maintains the most advanced defence R&D capabilities owing to its long-standing monopoly, access to advanced research facilities built and maintained over the years and its experience in the sector.

The ADD's budget in 2011 was around US $ 1 billion. Over 70 per cent of this was spent on R&D-related activities and excluded the administrative and technological support functions[27]. The ADD activities include, core technology R&D; defence systems R&D; and technological support to the industry and the armed forces. The second activity of defence systems R&D or general weapons systems R&D is being progressively undertaken by the defence contractors and thus the ADD's future R&D activities are likely to focus only on core, high-end technologies, to include strategic weapons systems as cruise and ballistic missiles and provide necessary assistance to the defence industries in the areas in which they intend taking over the responsibility[28]. The ADD's Proposed 'New Organisational Structure' is shown in Figure 4.2.

Figure 4.2: The ADD's Proposed New Organisational Structure

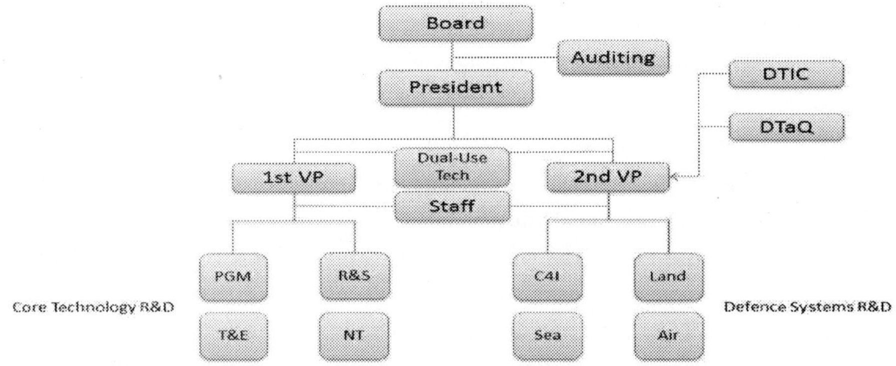

Key: VP=vice-president; PGM=precission-guided munititions; T&E=test and evaluation; R&S=radar and surveillance; NT=neo-technologies; C4I=command, control, communcations, computers and intelligence; DTIC=Defense Technology InnoCenter; DtaQ=Defense Technology and Quality (agency)

Source: The Republic of Korea: A Defence and Security Primer

The changing R&D work share between the defence contractors and the ADD is being incorporated in the ADD's evolving organisational transformation structure. The overall defence R&D activities of the agency will eventually be divided into two parallel structures between two executive vice-presidents—one predominantly concerned with the strategic and core technology R&D, including precision-guided munitions, radars and surveillance systems, neo-technologies as high-energetic materials and so on while the second dealing with the defence systems R&D category and thus becoming more of a support to the major defence contractors' research divisions[29].

The new organisational structure in addition incorporates the 'Defence Technology Innovation Centre' (DTIC) and the 'Defence Technology and Quality (DTaQ) agency'. These two institutions are directly linked to the activities under the second vice-president of ADD. The DTIC is a new department established within DAPA for planning and delegating R&D programmes either to industries or to the ADD. The DTaQ agency is not a part of DAPA but is practically directed by it, as the ADD. Thus, the various changes to ADD's organisational structure and its receding dominance in South Korea's defence R&D sector are largely the result of the directives and policies pursued by DAPA.

South Korea while acquiring weapons systems from foreign countries is seeking to obtain their technology transfers as well. The offset policy is one of the measures employed to achieve such transfers. In addition, South Korea is seeking joint ventures with countries other than the US to produce defence systems and undertake their development. ROK's defence private sector is also increasing their defence R&D activities and seeking both the acquisition and the development of core technologies besides exploring the foreign markets for their products. Both the state and the defence industry are striving to transform the defence sector into a more export-oriented industry. The industry besides sustaining its own production capacity for the domestic requirement is also looking at supplying to foreign countries and industries. The government too has pitched in by designating the defence industry as a new strategic industrial sector in South Korea and a potential contributor to national economic growth. This implies the defence industries are identified as economic assets besides being a tool for national security[30].

South Korea traditionally has strong political and military ties with the US. Consequently, the US is ROK's main supplier of defence material while Korea remains dependent on foreign suppliers for core technologies. ROK's advanced weapons systems are based on technologies developed outside South Korea, and predominantly in the US. However, South Korea is endeavouring to undertake joint defence industrial cooperation with nations other than the US. Such cooperation is expected to gain access to and develop more advanced defence technologies besides diversifying its supplier base, increase competitiveness in international arms market, increase external demand and facilitate export of defence material. Thus DAPA, South Korea's newly established procurement agency, favours joint cooperation to develop and produce weapons systems than directly procure equivalent material from foreign contractors. "*South Korea resembles Brazil, India and Singapore in this regard; they wish to strengthen the domestic defence technology industrial base by actively accessing attractive foreign defence technology and introducing it into their domestic defence industry, not least through direct military offset arrangements and bilateral defence technology collaboration. All four nations have high ambitions for developing their national defence industries*".

4.7 Korea Institute for Defence Analyses (KIDA)

The president is the final authority to approve acquisitions of defence material, especially direct acquisitions from foreign suppliers. The office of the president, the Blue House, is thus involved in the defence industrial sector, although from a relatively peripheral position. The National Assembly and its Committee on Defence approve the budget appropriations, including those necessary for defence procurements and the mid-term defence plans. Further, the National Assembly favours acquisitions through domestic R&D and production than through foreign suppliers[31].

KIDA is a defence research and analysis agency responsible to the MND. It does not involve directly in the defence industrial sector as DAPA and ADD of the MND do. However, it plays an important role in the evaluation of the force requirement programmes presented to the MND. It therefore, has a part in the defence industrial sector and the acquisition process as an advisory body which submits its analyses directly to the MND. KIDA has a centre for weapons systems studies, which is involved in the policy, strategic and financial planning concerning weapons systems. KIDA is thus primarily meant to strengthen the position of the MND vis-à-vis DAPA in the defence industrial sector in general, and the acquisition process in particular. In practice, the analyses and evaluations performed by KIDA are second opinions pertaining to acquisitions and force modernisation programmes that are provided to the MND and aim to complement the analyses conducted by DAPA[32].

4.8 Exports

South Korea's defence industrial strategy is also guided by the political ambition to increase the quantity and value of exports of defence material. DAPA has set a target of US $ 10 billion a year in arms exports by 2017[33]. South Korea's defence exports have gone from US $ 144 million in 2002 to US $ 3.6 billion in 2014, with an average annual gain of 31 per cent over the past five years. South Korea was the 13th biggest exporter of major arms in 2014, up from 30th eight years ago. Currently South Korea's arms production is mainly for domestic use, with just 12.8 per cent of output exported in 2013 and expected to grow to 18-20 percent in 2015[34]. South Korean defence material, when compared to other internationally leading defence suppliers, is mostly exported to nations with high economic growth rates, with significant ambitions for their individual defence industrial sectors and those having relatively unsophisticated levels of defence technological advancement. Turkey and Indonesia in recent years have emerged as the primary recipients of South Korean defence material. For example, Turkey was the first country other than ROK to acquire the K9 Self-Propelled Howitzer, produced by Samsung

Techwin, South Korea. Further, the K11 airburst multi-purpose combat rifle had also attracted foreign attention, and the UAE in 2010 bought 40 units[35]. Reports indicate that negotiations have also been held with a number of countries, including Jordan, Thailand and Indonesia, regarding the sale of K1A1 and K2 MBT's[36]. Other weapons systems for future exports include KSS-I attack submarines, T/FA-50 jet aircraft, K9 howitzers and, Low-cost Guided Imaging Rocket (LOGIR) missiles.

4.9 Private Sector

Most major defence industries are subsidiaries to a few big business conglomerates, also known as *chaebols*, whose main activities are in the civil sector. These are family-owned private enterprises which have traditionally been given strong government support[37]. Nine out of the 10 most prominent defence contractors/parent companies include Daewoo, Doosan, Hanwha, Hyundai, STX, Samsung and LG and each specialise in distinct military hardware. The organisational set-up of these defence industries allows them to use the parent company's civilian R&D and production capabilities for spin-on to the defence sector, and vice versa. Such a strategic placement of the defence industries has helped Korea in promoting the development of dual-use technologies and the diversification of production. In 2009 the government thus amended the law on the promotion of dual-use technology to enhance cooperation between the civilian and defence production sectors. Notwithstanding the above, ROK's defence industries have comparatively lagged in R&D and their ability to develop core technologies as thermal imaging sensors, flight control systems, engines and stealth technologies[38]. Consequently, Korea has relatively lagged in its capability to independently develop and produce advanced weapons systems and continued to rely heavily on foreign suppliers[39].

This is despite the fact that the South Korean defence contractors enjoy substantial government support. The support includes the policy of "buy Korean", which implies the procurement of domestically produced defence material will be prioritised over foreign direct acquisitions[40]. There is also the system of state subsidy to existing defence industries wherein, a large contract for a specific weapons system given to one contractor can be complemented by a smaller contract in the same technical area to another industry. In this way multiple and parallel competences are being upheld in the defence sector.

4.10 Lessons for India

"ROK's defence industry's dependence on US technology and Washington's subsequent supplier control regulations – prohibiting a recipient country from exporting US military equipment to a third party – placed severe limitations on the industry's continued defence-technological development. By end of 1980's, South Korea's defence industrial export potential was hamstrung by US regulations coupled with an increasingly competitive international arms market. In addition, although a DIB had been established, production remained limited to assembly of pre-manufactured equipment, co-production and licensed production agreements until end of 1980's"[41].

For today's modern technology driven Armed Forces, the defence Science and Technology (S&T) capacity of a nation determines the survival of its defence industry. In the case of ROK, the development of advanced weapons systems and capabilities for essential technologies remained at a relatively low pace due to three primary reasons. Firstly, the country's constant reliance on foreign nations for advanced weapon systems, secondly, the country's defence research activity heavily focused on systems development as against developing technologies, and lastly, the separation, between the ADD which managed the R&D and the defence industry which took on the assembly and production of the defence systems. To ensure defence S&T standards do not lag behind that of advanced nations, the national S&T policy must be driven and integrated with the requirements of R&D in the defence sector; the civilian resources should be employed in a strategic manner for which the cooperation between the civil and military sectors should be strengthened. Further, there is a need to delineate and define the distinct roles that the state research facilities and the defence industries have to perform towards building a modern R&D infrastructure and developing the essential technologies in-house. The MND has also proposed a vision of "securing world-class defence science and technology capabilities," for the ROK[42].

By exercising control over domestic defence acquisitions while at the same time having both export promotional and regulatory authorities situated under the same roof, DAPA is a special, if not unique, kind of organisation[43].

South Korea has developed a number of defence products through domestic R&D. These include advanced C4I systems, armoured vehicles, precision guidance missiles, UAVs, and naval and air assets. This was made possible due to an assertive government policy which encouraged domestic procurement of RMA-related assets and thus improved its industrial capabilities in the areas of information technology, heavy machinery and shipbuilding, mobile vehicles and aerospace technology[44]. A number of systems and a few upgrades were acquired through co-production or production through technology transfer, while licensed production was limited only to advanced systems. Consequently, for joint operation assets such as C4IRS, the software was mostly acquired through domestic R&D, while the hardware as AWACS and high altitude UAVs were purchased from abroad. In contrast, most air force assets are being acquired from abroad with the exception of the basic aircrafts KT-1 and KO-1 (through domestic R&D), fighter aircrafts T-50 and FA-50 (through co-production with Lockheed Martin), and advanced fighter aircrafts KF-16 (through licensed production). Further, a large number of defence items for the army and the navy are planned to be acquired through domestic R&D. The navy is planning to obtain the next generation destroyers (KDX II and III) through domestic R&D, with only Harpoon, LYNX and P-3C to be purchased from overseas[45].

The impressive performance of the DIB in South Korea is largely attributed to the government's policies over the years. In the formative years of defence industry in the 1970's, there was a heavy emphasis on acquisitions through domestic R&D. However, as domestic R&D acquisitions encountered problems, such as delayed delivery, cost overruns and performance defects, the government shifted its acquisition policy from domestic R&D to overseas direct acquisition, which in turn discouraged the domestic defence industry. In 1998, however, the government introduced a law for promotion of civilian-military dual use technology. This was to facilitate domestic R&D acquisitions, especially for RMA. In January 1999, the government amended its existing 'Special Law on the Defence Industry' to encourage participation in the defence industry by technologically more specialised firms. Then, more importantly, the government increased the investment in domestic R&D from four per cent of defence expenditure in 2003 to 6.7 per cent in 2007[46].

South Korea consequently has shown two noticeable trends. One is a trend towards the export of big ticket items such as aircrafts and naval vessels, which are closely related to RMA. The other is a trend towards the Koreanisation of defence articles. Having experienced enormous pressures from the US regarding the third country arms sales regulation in the 1980s and 1990, South Korea has been more actively pursuing production of defence articles through domestic R&D. For example, Samsung Techwin has been successful in developing and exporting the K-9 *Self-Propelled Howitzer* on an indigenous base while the production and export of KT-1 training aircraft is yet another success. South Korea has also been able to get away from the American restriction on export of KT-50 training aircraft by reaching an agreement with Lockheed Martin. Samsung Thales has also successfully exported RMA-related software through the upgrading of indigenous technology. In cumulative terms during 1998-2006, exports of military aircrafts and related services accounted for about 24 per cent of total military exports, followed by naval vessels (23 per cent), ammunition (21 per cent), and off-set based exports (14 per cent).

NOTES

1. Chung-in Moon and Jin-Young Lee "The *Revolution in Military Affairs and the Defence Industry in South Korea*", p. 117 available at http://securitychallenges.org.au/ArticlePDFs/vol4no4MoonandLee.pdf (Accessed June 04, 2015).
2. Kaan Korkmaz and John Rydqvist "The Republic of Korea : A Defence and Security Primer" pp. 13-14 available at http:// foi.se/ReportFiles/foir_3427.pdf (Accessed June 05, 2015).
3. "*Defence Industry (S Korea)*" *available* at http://www.globalsecurity.org/military/world/rok/industry.htm (Accessed June 05, 2015).
4. Kaan Korkmaz and John Rydqvist "*The Republic of Korea : A Defence and Security Primer*", p. 71 available at http://foi.se/ ReportFiles/foir_3427.pdf (Accessed June 08, 2015).
5. Chung-in Moon and Jin-Young Lee, "The *Revolution in Military Affairs and the Defence Industry in South Korea*", p. 120 available at http://securitychallenges.org.au/ArticlePDFs/vol4no4MoonandLee.pdf (Accessed June 08, 2015).
6. "*Defence Industry (S Korea)*" available at http://www.globalsecurity.org/military/world/rok/industry.htm (Accessed June 09, 2015).
7. Moon and Paek, "*Defence Innovation and Industrialisation in South Korea*", p. 2 available at https://escholarship.org/uc/item/ 29n4c3jv (Accessed June 09, 2015).
8. Kaan Korkmaz and John Rydqvist, "*The Republic of Korea: A Defence and Security Primer*", p. 72 available at http://foi.se/ ReportFiles/foir_3427.pdf (Accessed June 10, 2015).
9. Moon and Paek, "*Defence Innovation and Industrialisation in South Korea*", p. 11 available at https://escholarship.org/ uc / item/29n4c3jv (Accessed June 11, 2015).
10. Kaan Korkmaz and John Rydqvist, "*The Republic of Korea: A Defence and Security Primer*", p. 28 available at http://foi.se/ ReportFiles/foir_3427.pdf (Accessed June 11, 2015).
11. Chung-in Moon and Jin-Young Lee, "The *Revolution in Military Affairs and the Defence Industry in South Korea*", p. 117 available at http://securitychallenges.org.au/ArticlePDFs/vol4no4MoonandLee.pdf (Accessed June 12, 2015).
12. Kaan Korkmaz and John Rydqvist, "*The Republic of Korea : A Defence and Security Primer*", p. 53 available at http://foi.se/ ReportFiles/foir_3427.pdf (Accessed June 12, 2015).
13. Kaan Korkmaz and John Rydqvist, "*The Republic of Korea : A Defence and Security Primer* " p.12 available at http://foi.se / ReportFiles/foir_3427.pdf (Accessed June 15, 2015).
14. Kaan Korkmaz and John Rydqvist, "*The Republic of Korea: A Defence and Security Primer*", p. 53 available at http://foi.se/ ReportFiles/foir_3427.pdf (Accessed June 15, 2015).
15. Kaan Korkmaz and John Rydqvist, "*The Republic of Korea: A Defence and Security Primer*" p.74 available at http://foi.se/ ReportFiles/foir_3427.pdf (Accessed June 16, 2015).

16. Moon and Paek, "*Defence Innovation and Industrialisation in South Korea*", p. 2. available at https://escholarship.org/uc/item/ 29n4c3jv (Accessed June 19, 2015).
17. Moon and Paek, "*Defence Innovation and Industrialisation in South Korea*", p. 5 available at https://escholarship.org/uc/item/ 29n4c3jv (Accessed June 22, 2015).
18. Oh Seok-min, "*S. Korea to raise defence spending by 2020*" Yonhap news April 20, 2015 available at http://english.yonhapnews.co.kr/ sear ch1/2603000000.html?cid= AEN20150417009700315 (Accessed June 22, 2015).
19. "*Defence Industry (S Korea)*" available at http://www.globalsecurity.org/military/world/rok/ industry.htm (Accessed June 17, 2015 and Moon and Paek (2010) "*Defence Innovation and Industrialisation in South Korea*", p. 2.available at https:// escholar ship.org/uc/item/29n4c3jv (Accessed June 17, 2015).
20. Kaan Korkmaz and John Rydqvist, "*The Republic of Korea: A Defence and Security Primer*", p. 88 available at http://foi.se/ ReportFiles/foir_3427.pdf (Accessed June 18, 2015).
21. Kaan Korkmaz and John Rydqvist, "*The Republic of Korea: A Defence and Security Primer*", p. 83 available at http://foi.se/ ReportFiles/foir_3427.pdf (Accessed June 18, 2015).
22. *FWC Sector Competitiveness Studies-Study on the Impact of Emerging Defence Markets and Competitors on the Competitiveness of the European Defence Sector* "*The defence market and sector in South Korea*", p. 178. available at http://ec.europa.eu/enterprise/sectors/defence/ files/study_defence_final_report_en.pdf (Accessed June 19, 2015).
23. Defence Acquisition Programme Administration (DAPA), Republic of Korea, "*Defence Offset Programme Guidelines*", February 2014, p. 16.available at https://www.dapa.go.kr/common/ downLoad.action?siteId=dapa_eng&fileSeq=O_20645. (Accessed June 25, 2015).
24. Kaan Korkmaz and John Rydqvist, "*The Republic of Korea: A Defence and Security Primer*" p.84 available at http://foi.se/ ReportFiles/foir_3427.pdf (Accessed June 25, 2015).
25. Kaan Korkmaz and John Rydqvist, "*The Republic of Korea: A Defence and Security Primer*" p.74 available at http://foi.se/ ReportFiles/foir_3427.pdf (Accessed June 26, 2015).
26. Oh Seok-min, "S. Korea to raise defence spending by 2020" Yonhap news April 20, 2015 available at http://english. yonhapnews. co.kr/ search1/2603000000.html?cid= AEN20150417009700315 (Accessed June 26, 2015).
27. Kaan Korkmaz and John Rydqvist, "*The Republic of Korea: A Defence and Security Primer*" p.84 available at http://foi.se/ ReportFiles/foir_3427.pdf (Accessed June 29, 2015).
28. Kaan Korkmaz and John Rydqvist, "*The Republic of Korea: A Defence and Security Primer*" p.84 available at http://foi.se/ ReportFiles/foir_3427.pdf (Accessed June 29, 2015).
29. Kaan Korkmaz and John Rydqvist, "*The Republic of Korea: A Defence and Security Primer*" p.84 available at http://foi.se/ ReportFiles/foir_3427.pdf (Accessed June 30, 2015).
30. Kaan Korkmaz and John Rydqvist, "*The Republic of Korea: A Defence and Security Primer*" p.75 available at http://foi.se/ ReportFiles/foir_3427.pdf (Accessed July 01, 2015).
31. Moon and Paek (2010), "*Defence Innovation and Industrialisation in South Korea*", p. 20.available at https://escholarship.org/ uc/item/29n4c3jv (Accessed July 02, 2015).
32. Kaan Korkmaz and John Rydqvist, "*The Republic of Korea: A Defence and Security Primer*" p.88 available athttp://foi.se / ReportFiles/foir_3427.pdf (Accessed July 02, 2015).
33. Kaan Korkmaz and John Rydqvist, "*The Republic of Korea: A Defence and Security Primer*" p.92 available at http://foi.se/ ReportFiles/foir_3427.pdf (Accessed July 02, 2015).
34. Joyce Lee and Tony Munroe, "*South Korea seeks bigger role in global arms bazaar*" Reuters June 23, 2015 available at http://www.reuters.com/article/2015/04/22/us-southkorea-defence-exports-idUSKBN0ND0TW20150422 (Accessed July 02, 2015).
35. Global Security, "K9 *155mm Self-propelled Howitzer*", available at *http:// www.globalsecurity.org/military/world/rok/k9.htm* (Accessed July 03, 2015).

36. Jung, Sung-ki, "*Korea Emerges as Arms Development Powerhouse*", *The Korea Times*, June16, 2010 available at http:// koreatimes.co.kr/www/news/nation/2011/12/205_67771.html (Accessed July 03, 2015).
37. Stockholm International Peace Research Institute (2011), *SIPRI Yearbook 2011*, Armaments, Disarmament and International Security, p. 241.available at http://www.sipri.org/yearbook/ 2011 (Accessed July 03, 2015).
38. Moon and Paek, (2010) "*Defence Innovation and Industrialisation in South Korea*", p. 3-4.available at https://escholarship.org/ uc/item/29n4c3jv (Accessed July 06, 2015).
39. Stockholm International Peace Research Institute (2011), *SIPRI Yearbook 2011*, Armaments, Disarmament and International Security, p. 243. available at http://www.sipri.org/yearbook/ 2011 (Accessed July 07, 2015).
40. Moon and Paek (2010), "*Defense Innovation and Industrialization in South Korea*", p. 3-4.available at https://escholarship. Org /uc/item/29n4c3jv (Accessed July 07, 2015).
41. Kaan Korkmaz and John Rydqvist, "*The Republic of Korea: A Defence and Security Primer*" p.72 available at http://foi.se/ ReportFiles/foir_3427.pdf (Accessed July 08, 2015).
42. Paek Jae-ok, "*Defence science and technology of the ROK and desirable directions for relevant R&D policies*" published in *The Korean Journal of Defence Analysis* 22(2), June 2010, pp.197-215 available at http://210.101.116.28/ W_files/ kiss5/ 2p801310_pv.pdf (Accessed July 09, 2015).
43. Kaan Korkmaz and John Rydqvist, "*The Republic of Korea : A Defence and Security Primer*" p.83 available at http ://foi.se/ ReportFiles/foir_3427.pdf (Accessed July 09, 2015).
44. Chung-in Moon and Jin-Young Lee, "The *Revolution in Military Affairs and the Defence Industry in South Korea*", p. 127 available at http://securitychallenges.org.au/ArticlePDFs/ vol4no4MoonandLee.pdf (Accessed July 10, 2015).
45. Chung-in Moon and Jin-Young Lee, "The *Revolution in Military Affairs and the Defence Industry in South Korea*", p. 128 available at http://securitychallenges.org.au/ArticlePDFs/ vol4no4MoonandLee.pdf (Accessed July 10, 2015).
46. Chung-in Moon and Jin-Young Lee, "The *Revolution in Military Affairs and the Defence Industry in South Korea*", p. 131 available at http://securitychallenges.org.au/ArticlePDFs/ vol4no4MoonandLee.pdf (Accessed July 13, 2015).

CHAPTER 5

Chinese Defence Industry's Transformational Aspects for India

5.1 Evolution and Growth

China has a long history of defence equipment manufacturing. However, more recently, in the early twentieth century, the development of a DIB for the supply of modern arms to the Chinese armed forces was central to the self-strengthening movement pursued by the Qing Dynasty. Modern developments began in the early 1930's with the creation of a major Peoples Liberation Army (PLA) weapons manufacturing facility in Jiangxi province after the Japanese invaded Manchuria (North East China)[1]. Defence production activities remained the PLA's responsibility over the next three decades and deficiencies led to restructuring in the 1950's. The trend continued with the post-1949 defence-industrial model functioning under the State's control and adopting a bureaucratic structure. All kinds of arms production were to be executed by State Owned Enterprises (SOEs) while defence-related R&D was to be performed by research institutes or academic institutions which answered the State.

The restructuring in 1950's created six Ministries of Machine-Building which were responsible for production of material and military equipment related to nuclear, aviation, electronics, tanks and artillery, shipbuilding and space. Ever since then, there has been a substantial requirement of arms for the PLA. These ministries helped build platforms based on Soviet designs of the 1950's and 1960's. For example, between 1950's to 1997, China produced more than 14,000 military aircrafts and 50,000 aircraft engines, mostly for the PLA[2]. In 1953, USSR agreed to assist China in the construction of a

DIB and R&D infrastructure. Soviet technicians assisted in the modernisation of China's shipyards, streamlined Russian-supplied factories and provided blueprints for the weapons that these plants were to produce. In January 1955, China decided to develop nuclear weapons, and in 1956 to build ballistic missile delivery systems. In 1958, Moscow refused to support the development of nuclear powered attack submarines (SSN) and ballistic missile submarines (SSBN), following which Beijing undertook indigenous programmes for the submarines and solid-fuelled ballistic missiles to arm the SSBN. In the summer of 1959 Moscow withdrew its support of Beijing's nuclear weapons R&D, and in 1960 ended its assistance for both civil and military programmes[3].

After the Soviet defence-industry's support to China ended in 1960, Beijing continued to exploit the foreign sources of arms technology. This was mostly limited to reverse engineering of arms and components by copying foreign designs. "*China during this period was subjected to a Western arms embargo between the early 1950's and 1980's and, after 1960, was the target of what effectively constituted a Soviet arms embargo as well. Only towards the end of the Cold War* (1986-87), *China supplemented its efforts with selective purchases of technology and subsystems from other states. By late 1990's, most indigenously developed weapons systems in China were 15 to 20 years behind those of the West, comparable with 1970's and early 1980's-era technology and their quality control was consistently poor*"[4]. During this period, China took a long time in developing prototypes into production versions. For example, the J-10 fighter jet—China's fourth-generation-plus combat aircraft—took more than a decade to move from the start in 1988 to first flight prototype stage in 1996, and more than 20 years (eight prototypes and a dozen plus production-standard aircrafts) before it entered operational service with the PLA Air Force (PLAAF) (in 2008)[5]. Further, it is believed the J-10 fighter is based on technology derived from Israel's cancelled Lavi fighter-jet program. Also the Chinese military is mostly dissatisfied with the quality and capabilities of the weapon systems produced by the domestic arms factories and favours imported weapons platforms over local ones. Thus, despite China's four ongoing fighter aircraft programmes in production or development stages, i.e. the J-7, J-8 II, JH-7 and J-10, the PLA decided to buy several dozen Su-27 and advanced Su-30 strike aircrafts. Similarly, despite the Chinese shipyards building the 'Song' and several new types of destroyers, the PLA Navy (PLAN) procured Kilo-class submarines and several types of destroyers. In addition, China purchased precision-guided munitions, advanced air-to-air missiles, airborne warning and control aircraft and transport aircrafts besides, several hundred

S-300 and SA-15 surface-to-air missiles thereby, becoming one of the world's largest arms importers, between 1998 and 2005[6].

Many structural and organisational deficiencies impeded design, development and manufacture of advanced conventional arms and necessitated the requirement of introducing reforms. The inefficiencies included the large number of factories and their overcapacity in the aircraft, shipbuilding and arms industry besides the highly compartmentalised and non-horizontally integrated DIB which restricted the diffusion of advanced civilian technologies. Also, communication between R&D institutes (designing weapons) and factories (producing them), and amongst defence enterprises collaborating on weapons projects as also between the defence industry and the PLA, on requirements and specifications was limited. Further, the DIB functioned under a typical SOE management which was bureaucratic and risk averse. This discouraged innovation, impeded R&D growth and further added to program delays. Production management was centralised with most critical project decisions made by the chief engineer. Lower-level managers adopted standard procedures than applying their professional experiences. The play safe attitude, inhibited experimentation and innovation[7].

By mid-1990's, at least 70 per cent of China's state-run factories were operating at a loss, most defence firms were burdened with considerable debt, much of it owed to the state-run banks. The Arms factories were owed money by other loss making state-owned companies. "*In early 1990's, in order to 'corporatise' the DIB, the Chinese transformed the Military Industrial Complex (MIC) from a series of machine-building ministries into large SOE's*"[8]. For example, the ministry of aerospace was broken into the Aviation Industries of China (AVIC: aircraft) and the China Aerospace Corporation (CASC: missiles and space), while the ministry of atomic energy was converted into China National Nuclear Corporation (CNNC). At the same time, control of individual production facilities, research units and trading companies was transferred to these new corporations.

The progress of China's defence industry's modernisation was accelerated through the reforms post 1990 and is attributable to four main reasons[9]. First, the higher defence-budget allocation for military equipment increased the spending by defence enterprises on R&D and their production capabilities. Second, the gradual commercialisation of defence enterprises during China's economic transformation of 25 years improved R&D exposure to international markets both, through partnerships and competition with foreign firms. Third, the defence industry consistently in the 1990's had access to limited foreign military equipment and technical assistance, especially from Russia and Israel which assisted copying and producing weapon systems, integrating advanced technologies into production lines, and raising the technical expertise of personnel involved in defence production. Fourth, earlier, Beijing had avoided implementing the fundamental reforms of rationalisation and consolidation that was essential and now implemented to revitalise the defence industry.

In 1998, China's leadership adopted a new series of policies to revamp the defence procurement system and reform the defence enterprises. Specifically, China's leaders aimed to inject into the defence-industrial system the principles of "competition, evaluation, supervision and encouragement, known as the "Four Mechanisms". The aim of the ongoing reforms is to centralise and standardise the weapon procurement decisions while decentralising the operations of the defence-enterprises[10]. First, to change the weapon-procurement process, the central government policies included issuing formal procurement regulations, provisions to standardise the procurement process, accelerating the establishment of a competitive-bidding system for military contracts and so on. Secondly, to make the defence enterprise more efficient and raise their R&D and production capabilities, several new policies were adopted and included exposing the defence enterprises to competitive market pressures, introducing new mechanisms for quality assurance and quality control; making enterprises less reliant on state subsidies, downsizing, modernisation of some production complexes, enhanced partnerships with civilian universities and institutes for improving educational training relevant to military R&D and so on.

The establishment of the General Armament Department (GAD) in 1998 and its active involvement in weapons R&D allowed the military for the first time to occupy a central role in the defence industrial innovation system[11]. Coupled with this was the curtailment in authority and role of the Commission of Science, Technology, and Industry for National Defence (COSTIND) and its successor State Administration for Science, Technology and Industry for National Defence (SASTIND). From its inception, GAD's relationship with the defence industry mostly lacked trust. The defence industry's poor performance and inability to meet the PLA's needs led military chiefs in the 1990's and early 2000's to implement competitive bidding in the acquisition process by looking overseas for arms to meet some of its critical needs.

Another defence reform in July 1999 created 10 new Defence Industry Enterprise Groups (DIEGs). These DIEGs functioned as true conglomerates, integrating R&D, production and marketing. It also intended to encourage the new industry enterprise groups to compete with each other for PLA procurement contracts, which would pressurise them to be more efficient and technologically innovative. These new enterprise groups were given the authority to manage their own operations and take responsibility for their own profits and losses.

The defence firms played an important role in this relationship. Before the 1998 reforms, the defence enterprise groups were all state-owned, bureaucratic, monopolies with little independence from the central government[12]. The reforms transformed the conglomerates into profit-oriented, shareholding entities with operational autonomy while remaining entirely state owned. Moreover, each defence conglomerate was divided into two entities to promote limited competition within their industrial sectors. The arrangement ensured cooperation between the firms and the PLA through realistic commitments and extensive information sharing. Accordingly, revenues and profits for the entire defence industry have grown strongly since the early 2000's. The cooperation between the PLA and the defence industry is at multiple levels ranging from high-level strategic and doctrinal planning and policy-making at the centre to the factory floors around the country. PLA, civilian defence industry officials, and S&T experts have been cooperating on long-range S&T development plans since the early 2000's. This includes the drafting of the S&T development plans.

5.2 Overview and Trends

Over the years, Beijing has built and improved upon its huge MIC which at present is organised along 10 major conglomerates. These conglomerates are responsible for design, development, and manufacture of a wide range of military products ranging from nuclear warheads and their delivery systems, to fighter aircrafts, submarines, tanks, and radars among others. The noticeable feature of these products is their increasing technological sophistication that has surprised many advanced countries. The success of China's defence industry has been ascribed to the sustained policy and structural reforms undertaken by China's leadership.

The precise size of China's DIB varies from one estimate to another, largely because of opacity in official information system and the complex nature of

Chinese armed forces' involvement in defence production. According to authoritative source, *Jane's*, there are "at least 10,000 enterprises (state and privately owned companies) employing about 2.5 million people which have a PLA involvement of one sort or another, including the production of weapons for sale"[13]. Of these around 1,000 are SOE's, which employ around three million workers, including over 3,00,000 engineers and technicians[14]. These enterprises largely centre around 10 conglomerates with each one controlling several dozens of subsidiaries to more than 100[15]. A few large conglomerates are discussed.

The Aviation Industry Corporation (AVIC) of China is a single "ultra-large" corporate entity formed from the merger of AVIC I and AVIC II in November 2008. These had operated separately for over a decade. The merger was undertaken to improve business practices, streamline bureaucracy and increase production capacity. While employing nearly 4,50,000 people, the new entity is responsible for developing, manufacturing and marketing both military and commercial aircrafts, engines and airborne equipment. With nearly 200 subsidiary companies and 20 listed companies, AVIC is managed through 10 business units relating to defence, transport aircraft, aviation engines, helicopters, avionics, general aviation aircraft, aviation R&D, flight test, trade and logistics, and asset management. Its major products include JF-17 Thunder fighter; F-7 and F-8 combat aircraft; FBC-1, H-5 and H-6 bomber aircraft; trainer aircraft; turbo fan engines; weapon systems; military helicopters; and Unmanned Aerial Vehicles (UAVs)[16].

China State Shipbuilding Corporation (CSSC) is an "extra-large" conglomerate engaged in shipbuilding, ship-repair, shipboard equipment production, marine design and research[17]. With two headquarters in Beijing and Shanghai, CSSC controls over 60 enterprises. It has nine R&D institutes including the notable Marine Design and Research Institute of China (MARIC). Over the years, the corporation has evolved as one of the largest shipbuilders in the world with a wide spectrum of products, ranging from conventional oil tankers and bulk carriers to sophisticated and state-of-the-art vessels, as LNG carriers, chemical carriers, passenger freight ships, container ships, LPG carriers, large self-unloading ships, high speed ships and various civil ships and offshore engineering facilities. In defence, CSSC boasts of "remarkable capacity for building surface warships, submarines and auxiliary vessels. In recent past, it has built and delivered to PLA Navy a large number of ships, including those of 'new generations' as missile destroyers, missile frigates, and space instrumentation ships, among others, claims the official website. CSSC has the ultimate goal of becoming the largest shipbuilder by 2015. For this it is constructing two shipbuilding bases in Changxing Island of Shanghai and in Longxue, Guangzhou. With completion of these two bases, CSSC's shipbuilding capacity would increase from four million dwt (dead weight ton) to 14 million dwt by 2015[18].

China Shipbuilding Industry Corporation (CSIC) is another state-owned conglomerate in the ship-building and associated sector. It comprises of 46 industrial subsidiaries and 28 Scientific and Research Institutes, with a total workforce is 1,40,000, including 30,000 engineers for R&D. Its main activities include ship design, ship-building, ship-repairing and marine engineering. On the civil side, it has a wide range of products including tankers, chemical and product carriers, bulk carriers, containerships, ro-ro vessels, LPG, LNG and, engineering and offshore vessels. CSIC claims to have built and exported ships to "over 60 countries and regions around the world". Currently, the annual shipbuilding capacity of CSIC is five million dwt, claims the official website. On the defence side, the group claims to be the "largest manufacturer" of naval products, with the core capability to "design and build many different types of naval ships including submarines, missile destroyers and fleet replenishment vessels"[19].

China North Industries Group Corporation (CNGC) and China South Industries Group Corporation (CSGC) are China's two enterprises that are responsible for the ordnance sector. Among the two, CNGC is the largest producer of weapons. Also referred to as NORINCO (G), the group employs nearly 3,00,000 people, has 103 subsidiaries and 35 research institutes[20]. Besides, it has established over 100 JVs and has more than 20 overseas offices and 60 branches. The product profile of the enterprise include "tanks, armoured vehicles, artillery guns and shells, missiles, bombs, explosives, fuses and pyrotechnics, propellants, optical products, electronic and photo electronic products, information and control products, night vision equipment, anti-chemical devices, and simulation and training equipment etc. It also undertakes R&D of high-tech defence equipment in the fields of precision strike, amphibious operation, in-depth neutralisation, air defence, antimissile, information and night vision, high-efficient destroy and damage"[21].

China National Nuclear Corporation (CNNC) and China Nuclear Engineering and Construction Corporation (CNECC) are two enterprise groups that manage China's nuclear industry. CNNC manages the R&D,

production, and foreign cooperation related to nuclear power, nuclear materials, the generation of nuclear electricity, uranium exploration, nuclear instrumentation, and the application of nuclear technologies. CNECC on the other hand constructs nuclear power plants and defence infrastructure facilities. Its business areas include nuclear engineering, surveying, manufacturing, foreign trade, real estate and software development. It serves as the prime contractor for domestic nuclear power projects. Specifically, it manages the construction and engineering for China's nuclear power plants in Yagang, Lingao, Tiangang, and Qinshan.

China Aerospace Science and Technology Corporation (CASC) and China Aerospace Science and Industry Corporation (CASIC) oversee China's missile and aerospace sector. CASC develops and manufactures ballistic missiles and space launch vehicles. It also specialises in providing launch services for civilian commercial satellites." CASIC's primary focus is missile systems. Its business areas also include satellite R&D and delivery systems, and military and civilian applications of information technology.

China Electronics Technology Enterprise (CETC) was created in 2002. CETC represents Beijing's defence electronics industry. With its supervisory responsibility over 47 SOE's and the research institutes previously under the authority of the former Ministry of Industry Information, CETC's creation signified China's move towards a strong defence electronics and IT sector.

5.3 Government Strategic Objective Budgetary Support and Procurement

China's strategic objective for its DIB is benchmarked in its defence White Paper(s). These bring out China's defence planners intent. Beijing endeavours to achieve a capability to develop and produce advanced military systems on par with those of major industrialised nations by 2020. The last defence White Paper published in 2013 states the expectations out of its indigenous DIB. It states that China's armed forces are looking for military preparedness for winning local wars under conditions of informationisation meaning high intensity, information centric regional military conflict of short duration for which PLA will work to strengthen development of new and high-tech weaponry and equipment to build a modern military force structure with Chinese characteristics[22].

The first and foremost factor for the rapid progress in China's defence industrial capability is Beijing's sustained double-digit annual increase in its military spending in general and procurement spending in particular. In March 2015, China announced its official defence budget to about US $ 145 billion (approximately 890 billion Yuan)[23]. This represents a 10.1 per cent growth over the previous year's defence spending and nearly six fold increase over the 2011 defence procurement allocation of over US $ 25 billion[24]. Already, China is the second-biggest military spender in the world behind the US after having surpassed the UK in 2008. China's new budget for the PLA is four times that of its rising Asian rival, India. "*What is particularly striking about the growth in defence spending over the last two decades is that it has almost always outpaced GDP growth. Between 1998 and 2007, China's economy grew at an average annual rate of 12.5 per cent, while its defence spending increased at an average of 15.9 per cent per annum. Given that the economy is likely to grow by only seven per cent in 2015, and its defence spending is growing at double digits, the dis-connect between economic performance and defence spending is becoming more pronounced*"[25].

As per the official figures, as published by its state-owned press agency, *Xinhua*, the defence expenditure has witnessed a double digit growth rate for every successive year since 1978. From the defence industry point of view, a growing portion of the defence budget is allocated for procurement, giving a push for sophistication in research, design and production capabilities. Between 1990 and 2003, the official defence budget allocation for weapon acquisition grew from five billion RMB to 64.8 billion RMB (nearly 13 fold increase), and represented twice the growth rate of the total defence budget. The share of defence budget devoted to equipment thus increased from 16.3 per cent to over 34 per cent in 2003[26]. The expansion of China's state run DIB over the last decade since mid-2000s, has led to an average annual revenue growth of the 10 state owned corporations to about 20 per cent per year. "*The growth is essentially attributed to China's rapidly increasing defence budget and its priority to procure more from indigenous sources than from abroad less, in areas of continuing industrial weakness. Imported weapons systems are financed by separate currency allocations from the State Council and are not charged against the PLA budget*"[27]. "*Equipment imports from Russia range from US $ one billion to US $ three billion annually and equipment procured include advanced fighter aircraft, missile systems, submarines, and destroyers*"[28].

5.4 Indigenous Innovation and Technology Development Strategy

As per the Chinese leadership, the concept of "indigenous innovation", involves a way to promote original innovation by re-assembling existing technologies in different ways to produce new breakthroughs and absorbing and upgrading imported technologies. Thus, China's technological development strategy is a four-part process known as "Introduce, Digest, Absorb, and Re-innovate" (IDAR). It refers to the different steps required to turn foreign technology into a re-made domestic variant[29].

Further, for technology acquisition/introduction/pre-concept stage Chinese defence S&T system employs open source information collection and espionage activities to overcome the restrictions imposed on transfer of defence-related technology due to the various arms control regimes. For open source information collection, China has built a substantial infrastructure since the 1950s initially to support the construction of its strategic programme. Information collection is an element of the Information Analysis and Dissemination (IAD) system. Espionage could be industrial or cyber (computer network exploitation) espionage. China's industrial espionage efforts accelerated in the early 1990's as China took advantage of the economic chaos in Russia and the former Soviet republics to gain access to their defence industrial facilities and scientific and engineering personnel. This helped the aircraft, missiles, radar, fire-control, naval and manned space systems to advance by one or more generations.

For technology assimilation/digestion/concept refinement of foreign inputs, a S&T IAD system has been built with around 400 analysis and diffusion centers within the S&T system. However, classified intelligence collected by PLA intelligence agencies are only available for the military component of the IAD system. This is centralised under the China Defence S&T Information Centre (CDSTIC) which is affiliated to the GAD.

For technology absorption/transformation/engineering and manufacturing development, an assortment of approaches that include collaborative international JVs and illicit transfers and unauthorised reverse engineering is being used. Chinese authorities are investing heavily to build an extensive technology and engineering ecosystem to support efforts to combine the digested foreign and local technologies. This includes establishment of national engineering research centers, enterprise-based technology centers, state key laboratories, national technology transfer centers, high-technology service centers, and the recruitment of foreign technical experts through organisations such as the state administration of foreign expert's affairs. The development of China's first narrow-bodied jet air-liner, the C-919, is a prime example of the IDAR approach. Chinese aviation firms are mainly responsible for building the fuselage and other less technologically-advanced portions of the plane while Western companies are providing the engines, avionics, and other technologies that China lacks.

For technology exploitation/re-innovation/product or system development/transformation into actual output, the underdeveloped advanced manufacturing capabilities which are critical to precision production of high-technology products is a major handicap. Accordingly, the Chinese authorities have made development of civilian and defence-related advanced manufacturing capabilities a leading priority in their S&T and economic development plans. While these stress on the importance of developing indigenous S&T capabilities, China is making major progress by gaining access to foreign technologies and know-how. "*The high-end equipment manufacturing industry development plan calls for conducting secondary innovation based on the introduction and absorption of technologies, which is an oblique reference to the strategy of combining and integrating advanced foreign technology with domestic capabilities*"[30].

China's defense innovation system has been a mix of foreign imitation and autonomous innovation. Reliance on external sources has helped build the extensive conventional weapons establishment from the early 1950s, while the small specialised and strategic (nuclear, space, and ballistic missiles) arms complex was developed comparatively independently as it was denied external assistance. The two sectors were eventually consolidated in the 1980s and the defence economy has thereafter sought to pursue a twin-tracked imitation-innovation approach[31].

5.5 R&D

China has consistently increased its annual R&D investment which has ranged between 12 per cent to 20 per cent from the 1990's and has been able to reach the US $ 284 billion investment mark in 2014. The same kind of R&D intensity is likely to make it surpass the US by about 2022, when both the countries will invest close to US $ 600 billion in R&D[32]. China during the 12th FYP period (2011-15) is targeting to increase its R&D spending to 2.2 per cent of GDP by 2015 and endeavours to transit from a manufacturing economy to an innovation driven economy by 2020. Chinese leadership has the perspective to drive the innovation vision, as eight of the nine members of China's Politbureau Standing Committee (PSC) have engineering degrees[33].

China's allocation for military RDT&E is not available in the public domain. However, IHS Jane's estimates 2013 allocation to be US $ eight billion (This is more than six per cent of its total defence budget)[34]. This spending is further improved by the RDT&E policy directive to the state-run defence enterprises to spend at least three per cent of their annual revenues on R&D by 2020 and other additional governmental spending authorised to defence R&D agencies as the PLA and the SASTIND. It is also expected that several agencies and government departments invest in R&D as the CMI strategy encourages dual sector integration. In addition, there are inflows from China's promotion of foreign investments in the non-defence R&D sectors.

China in 2006 promulgated two separate National S&T programmes for the period 2006-20—for defence and its civilian counterpart. These are the development programmes of S&T for National Defence and the National S&T development programme for the civilian counterparts. In consonance with China's military modernisation plans and its efforts to indigenously manufacture products related to information warfare, the defence R&D programme prioritises the efforts required in the various associated defence areas. The focus of defence R&D programme is on basic and advanced defence technologies, early and advanced–stage applied R&D of next generation weapons and development of the dual-use high-end technologies and manufacturing for the defence sector. The civilian S&T plan also provides the details of the specific dual-use high-end technology projects that are underway with the defence industry and receiving priority state funding.

"*Since late 1990s, Chinese defence R&D apparatus has undergone a revamp and grown to conduct high-quality work. The key goals of the reforms include enhancing basic research capabilities, diversifying the managements funding from the state to the corporate sector, bringing defence R&D system closer to the rest of the national innovation system, and maintaining close linkages with* (the) *universities and civilian research institutes*"[35]. Further, China's 10 defence conglomerates own a large part of the R&D apparatus and invest heavily in innovation activities. Their collaboration with the foreign firms and accessing of foreign markets has helped bring in external knowledge and technology. Seven universities affiliated to SASTIND are the principal source of human talent for the defence economy. The talent recruited by defence S&T establishment is of a higher quality than the rest of the national R&D system. Much of China's defence technological development over the last two decades is attributed to the import and absorption of technologies and knowledge from abroad, especially from Russia. China acquired more than US $ 30 billion of weapons and defence technologies from Russia between 1992 and

2009, involving mostly aviation and naval sectors. However, this also led to distrust because of Chinese efforts to illegally reverse engineer Russian weapons. "*China regularly produces near-replicas of foreign weapons systems based at least in part on Russian, Ukrainian, French, Israeli or U.S. designs but aspires to be more indigenously innovative. To the extent that this risk-averse approach to technology development remains profitable, it is likely to continue in both commercial and defence sectors and stymie efforts aimed at the acceptance of greater risks (both financial and technological) in developing indigenous and more advanced innovative capabilities*"[36]. Further, since the late 1990s, the PLA has been an important factor in guiding defence S&T research and production activities for improving the performance of the defence economy.

Competition was brought into the R&D system by deviating from the traditional practice of spreading funds across a large number of projects (with little consideration for performance) and allocating research budgets on select high-priority projects. Efforts were also made to corporatise R&D institutes by allowing the major defence conglomerates to take them over.

Another noteworthy feature of the Chinese defence industrial innovation system is the close collaboration between the PLA, the defence industry R&D and the industrial entities throughout all stages of the product development process. In the present arrangement, feasibility studies are undertaken jointly by the PLA end-user units and the R&D entities while, R&D organisations are responsible for the project design and the engineering development. PLA organisations led by GAD review and approve the work done before it is allowed to progress to the next phase. Testing is also undertaken by defence endplay organisations.

In the Chinese defence innovation system, imitation (where there is no research constituent), is the primary focus of action, besides the effort to promote innovation, leadership and management are all top-down in nature. There is limited interaction with the outside world and the state plays a dominant role in setting priorities, providing strategic direction, and overseeing management of the system[37].

China is following two types of innovation development strategies[38]. The first is the "good enough" affordable approach to produce and field large quantities of arms that are the high-volume, low-cost version(s) of foreign products. Although their quality and performance are inferior but these are cheaper and meet the needs of the PLA. The second is the high-end, high-cost, "gold-plated" approach to develop sophisticated weapons that match those of advanced nations. This is a long-term strategy, as Chinese defence industry at present lacks scientific and technological capabilities to execute higher-end innovation. Notwithstanding, Chinese defence S&T institutes are attempting R&D in increasingly advanced emerging technologies and weapons which include directed energy laser weapons, robotic systems, and miniature nano-based systems.

PLA-run GAD established post the 1998 reforms acts as the primary purchasing agent for the PLA and oversees defence procurement and new weapons programmes. It leads the military's R&D system and manages the funding of defence programmes[39]. It's weapons and equipment development system is excessively based on the ground forces thereby, inhibiting comprehensive modernisation across China's armed forces. As a result, the air force and navy, has depended on the acquisition of foreign weapons from Ukraine, France, Israel, Germany, Switzerland, and the UK. GAD is the fourth general department for the PLA. It is the defence industry's main customer and actively engages with the industry as a regulator. In particular, the GAD ensures that local arms producers meet PLA requirements when it comes to capabilities, quality, costs and programme milestones. Its regulatory initiatives has implications for CMI and the current arrangements for licensing, R&D support through funding programmes and defence key laboratory accreditation, and collaboration with Civil–Military Integration Promotion Department (CMIPD) on military–civilian dual-use technical standards development, and all encourage this trend.

There is considerable interaction between the military and the government organisations managing defence science, technology, and industry. GAD and SASTIND jointly determine which enterprises may engage in weapons and equipment research and production. Both are involved in how the national defence key laboratories and defence industry advanced technology research and application centers are established. CMIPD works with GAD to prepare its civil–military integrated standards system. Since 2007 a series of regulations have liberalised the rules for civilian participation and investment in the defence industries. New GAD and SASTIND regulations for licensing weapons and equipment producers have opened up defence contracts to civilian enterprises, enabled private companies to provide R&D services directly to the military. The defence industry remains dominated by the ten defence conglomerates and their subsidiaries, but it is possible that in future the balance will shift more towards private actors, particularly if retired military personnel see increasing opportunities in a growing private sector contracting industry[40].

5.6 Exports

According to *Stockholm International Peace Research Institute (SIPRI)*, during the five-year period between 2009 and 2014, China has become the world's third-largest arms exporter, behind the US and Russia. China now represents five per cent of a global export market valued at more than US $ 300 billion a year. Although China is still a long way behind America's 31 per cent and Russia's 27 per cent, China's state-run companies have become increasingly popular names in defence weaponry, contributing to a 143 per cent rise in exports during the five-year period[41]. More than 68 per cent of Chinese exports are sold to three countries: Pakistan, Bangladesh and Myanmar. Further, China's exports are increasingly brokered in Africa, with major arms being exported to 18 African states during the time period. This includes armoured vehicles, transport and training aircrafts, and drones.

China has also been making strides in modernising and improving the quality of sales. "The equipment you get nowadays from China is much better than 10 to 15 year ago," Siemon Wezeman, a senior researcher at *SIPRI* said, China can produce some of the same equipment that the U.S. and Russia can, but at cheaper (sometimes at one third) prices. "*The factors attributed to China's success in exports include relatively cheap price of Chinese material, flexible repayment mechanisms, proven Soviet/Russian designs and technologies imbibed in many Chinese platforms, increased Chinese skills and capabilities in both indigenous development programmes and absorbing Western and Soviet/Russian technologies (some through CMI) and the fact that China's defence industry has not been majorly side tracked by its military programmes and compelling offset-like benefits that China offers to its military customer. China's drive to sell material to particularly developing nations across Asia, Africa and Middle East reflects a wider diplomatic policy to enhance relations with oil and gas producing countries and those deemed to be in strategic locations. China's export-offset strategy is supported by accepting flexible terms of payment of material, often through counter-trade linked to China's requirement of natural resources (oil and gas) and other commodities as agricultural products. Additionally, China offers customers military aid to purchase material and allow a government to purchase through soft loans or other financial deals with Chinese banks, such as the Export-Import (EXIM) of China*"[42].

5.7 Private Sector

The private sector has been in defence industrial activities since early 2000's. However, restrictions on what all the private sector can be exposed to has curtailed its participation to manufacturing components and auxiliary products. China recognised the need for increased private sector involvement to promote a more competitive DIB and thus introduced a number of measures to bolster its growth. "*In 2006 Beijing offered subsidies to private companies that enter the defence sector, next year it outlined plans to outsource some logistics services to the private sector, then in 2010 and 2011, announced plans to promote public-private R&D programmes and encourage private investment in listed state assets. Again in 2011 introduced guidelines towards reducing barriers for private companies entering defence and in 2012 allowed private sector to bid for unspecified selected military development and production programmes and the development of dual use technologies. In 2013, invited private sector to play a greater role in supplying MRO services and allowed greater access to SME's to government funds for R&D activities*"[43]. Notwithstanding the governments above initiatives, there are a number of reasons which limit the private sector's participation in defence. These include the "five per cent plus costs" rule on profits from defence contracts, lack of trusts and undue advantage to SOE's to win contracts and so on.

5.8 Major Reforms Programmes

China introduced two major ongoing reforms programmes in mid-2000. These were aimed at the restructuring and the capability development of the DIB. The first pertaining to restructuring involved the introduction of shareholding reforms in 2007. These included a continued focus of the DIB on Mergers and Acquisitions (M&A) (foreign acquisitions), disinvestments, increasing investments in defence enterprises and the listing of their subsidiaries on the domestic stock exchanges. The second CMI strategy intended to create a DIB wherein defence enterprises were also major manufacturers of commercial products.

The shareholding reforms were aimed to improve accountability, self-sufficiency, innovation, competitiveness and industrial capability by exposing the defence enterprises to market forces, improving financial capital through divestments, eliminating duplicity through consolidation, enhancing industrial efficiencies and forming large conglomerates to compete in the global market against large corporations from the West[44]. The reforms encouraged defence primes to list majority of their non-core subsidiaries on the Chinese stock exchanges and to establish internationally recognised business structures as forming boards of directors[45]. It also focused on Chinese companies benefiting from advances made in commercial and dual-use technologies. Beijing had hoped the shareholding exercise would be complete by 2012. However, "*by 2010 only 22 of AVIC's 200-plus* (military and commercial) *subsidiaries and 15 per cent of all defence companies subsidiaries were listed on Chinese stock exchanges*" following which, the Government in 2011 issued guidelines to accelerate completion of shareholding reforms by 2015 wherein, companies would be "*encouraged to list and restructure assets and increase M&A activity and provide opportunities for private capital to expand defence production capabilities*"[46]. Most industrial restructuring has happened in the aerospace and ordnance sectors while it has not led to much consolidation and restructuring in other sectors due to China's preference to maintain tight control of perceived sensitive programmes.

The CMI strategy intends integration of the commercial and defence industry capabilities to promote dual-use technologies and production processes and the use of personnel and facilities, to the extent possible, to undertake work in the two disciplines. CMI under the offset category is the acquisition of commercial technologies, production knowhow and research methods that can benefit Chinese military programmes and vice-versa. Impediments to CMI strategy include restrictions on private sector participation in defence projects, benefits accorded to SOE's, price control mechanism for private sector and the reduced profitability margins which will make them focus on commercial domains, and so on[47].

5.9 Foreign Investments

China is hoping to attract foreign investments in the SOE's and accordingly in 2010 published policy plans to reduce the barriers to market entry and provide guidance for potential investors. The document, primarily meant for Chinese private companies, also encouraged foreign investment in defence SOE's to assist them in penetrating export markets and participate in international competition. It also contained few details on how foreign and local private investors can meet the Chinese conditions for defence production and the areas that are excluded for investment as considered sensitive by the government. Foreign Investments in Chinese DIB is impacted adversely due to the sanctions imposed by the US and the EU. Yet companies like Boeing,

Euro copter and Sikorsky are investing in China's aviation industry, through JVs. "*Chinese defence industries are likely to benefit in the next few years from transfers of technology and skills from foreign JVs; increased government funding for R&D and procurement ; the acquisition of foreign military and dual-use technology; and increased partnerships with academic institutions which will improve student recruitment and technical training for existing staff*"[48].

5.10 Lessons for India

5.10.1 Rising Defence and Procurement Budget

The first and foremost factor that has led to the rapid progress in China's defence industrial capability is Beijing's sustained increase in its military spending in general and procurement spending in particular. From the defence industry point of view, this resulted in a growing portion of the defence budget to be allocated for procurement, thereby giving a push for sophistication in R&D, design and production capabilities.

5.10.2 Spin-on Benefits

Post-economic liberalisation, the rapid progress made in the Chinese civil industry and its integration with the global R&D and production chain largely contributed to the progress made in China's defence industry. In fact, this had been a deliberate decision of the Chinese leadership, as enshrined in the policy of *Yujun Yumin* meaning location of military potential in civilian capabilities. Accordingly, the Chinese President Hu Jintao in his report to the 17th National Congress of the CPC had noted that, "*We will establish sound systems of weapons and equipment research and manufacturing, military personnel training and logistics that integrate military with civilian purposes and combine military efforts with civilian support, build the armed forces through diligence and thrift, and blaze a path of development with Chinese characteristics featuring military and civilian integration*"[49].

5.10.3 Consistent R&D Investments

China's consistently high levels of R&D funding and Production/Maintenance contracts has enabled the defence sector to evolve from a reliance on Russia to higher levels of capabilities where most, but not all, platforms are designed and developed domestically. The massive and sustained R&D spending has enabled some of the "*innovative Chinese firms to develop a global brand and expand their operations abroad, in some cases with a view to tapping into the foreign pools of knowledge through M&A and the establishment of overseas R&D*"[50]. This has benefited its defence industry, in at least those sectors which are closely linked with global production and R&D. In particular two sectors —shipbuilding and defence electronics—have witnessed the 'greatest progress in recent years'.

5.10.4 Foreign Technology Acquisition

China's defence industry has historically been a beneficiary of foreign technological assistance, more prominently from the erstwhile Soviet Union. Since late 1980s, and especially consequent to the 1989 Tiananmen Square incident, which led to arms sales embargoes on Beijing by the US and EU, China resorted to Russia and Israel for weapons requirements and technical assistance. However the Israeli help was not as comprehensive and durable as that of Russia. Under pressure from the US Israel cancelled the transfer of Phalcon system in 2000. But, it provided crucial help for the development of China's J-10 fighter, which is widely believed to be based on the Israeli Lavi fighter project that Israel cancelled in 1987. As regards Russia, it is noteworthy that since 1990 China has received a host of state-of-the-art weapons from Russia, including Mi-17 helicopters, Il-76 transport aircrafts, Su-27 fighters, S-300 Surface-to-Air Missile (SAM) systems, Kilo submarines, Tor-M1 SAM systems, Sovremenny destroyers (with Sunburn Anti-Ship Cruise Missiles (ASCMs)), and Su-30 long-range fighters. For China's defence industry point of view, Russian assistance was significant for its shipbuilding and aero-space capability. Moscow provides crucial assistance in China's development of a range of submarines including Song-class diesel-electric submarine (SS), Type 093 nuclear-powered attack submarine (SSN), and Type 094 nuclear-powered ballistic missile submarine (SSBN)[51]. Russia also allowed production rights of its design and weapons to China for numerous weapons systems, notably Su-27. In many cases, China successfully used this assistance to copy produce weapon system, integrate technologies into production lines and raise the technical expertise of its personnel[52]. In addition to importing technical foreign technologies, China is also active in obtaining dual use technologies and diverting it to its military production facilities. China is also active in espionage activities to acquire some sensitive technologies—such as missile, imaging, semiconductor and submarine—vital for its 'informationisation' process[53].

5.10.5 Policy Reforms

When the PRC was founded in 1949, it inherited a "scattered and run-down assortment of arsenal and factories" (in the Manchurian region and the coastal cities of Tianjin and Shanghai) which barely constituted a credible base to build upon. In 1950, China had only 45-odd factories producing ordnance with an employee strength of about 1,00,000 employees. It was the Korean War in the early 1950s that provided early impetus for defence industrialisation. However, it was the Soviet material and technical assistance during the First Five Year Plan FFYP (1953-57) that led to a credible foundation of Chinese defence industry[54]. Under USSR's guidance, massive facilities were built to produce air craft, naval vessels, electronic equipment, land armaments, and a wide range of armaments. In addition, the Soviet Union also transferred know-how for thermonuclear weapons and trained a large number of Chinese engineers and designers, including those involved in Beijing's nuclear programme[55]. This expansion process was further accelerated following Chairman Mao's "Ten Great Relationships" speech in 1956, and especially his decision to create "Third Line" or "Third Front" wherein plants were set up in the interior cities such as Lanzhou, Chengdu, Kunming, Wuhan and so on. The "Third Front" decision—was motivated by Mao's belief to set up armament factories deep inside the interior region so as to reduce the risk to attack by the US and USSR—led to massive construction of plants in the mountainous and forested areas of Sichuan and Guangxi provinces between mid to late 1960s. (All together 483 factories and 92 institutes were established under the "Third Line" initiative)[56].

The huge expansion of defence industrial infrastructure led China to produce first generation of fighter aircrafts and transport aircrafts, tanks and Armoured Personnel Carriers (APCs), warships, including submarines and ordnance. However the momentum of production was hit by a series of set-backs. The first set back came in the form of the "Great Leap Forward" (1958-60) which drained valuable resources—capital, material and human—into the civil industry and the "mindless 'backyard' steel" production. The impact of the Great Leap decision was such that the growth rate of the machine-building industry – which represented defence production—fell from first to third position behind chemical fertiliser and petroleum industries. The deceleration in defence industry was again compounded in the wake of Sino-Soviet Split in early 1960s, and the onset of Cultural Revolution (1966-69). While the Soviet withdrawal in summer 1960 badly impacted, among others, the nuclear and aeronautic programmes, the Cultural Revolution impeded the growth of other sectors as "production was halted, factories came to a standstill, soldiers became involved in clashes with Red Guards, and scientists and bureaucrats were purged." (It is to be noted the nuclear and strategic submarines programmes were insulated during the Cultural Revolution)[57].

As the tension with the Soviet Union flared up, the defence industrial production showed some signs of revival between late 1960s and early 1970s. The revival however did not last long, with the eruption of a major controversy in mid-1971 surrounding the "electronics versus steel" debate. "*At issue was not civil versus military production (guns versus butter), but rather a more reûned argument as to budgetary allocation within the defence industries. It appeared that the ground forces were arguing for more "steel," while the air and nuclear forces made the case for more investment in high technology (i.e., "electronics")*[58]. Mao's doctrine of 'People's War' which was in sync with the 'steel' faction and not only ensured the defeat of 'electronics group', but pushed the defence industry to further backwardness and redundancy.

After succeeding Mao, Deng Xiaoping launched in late 1978 'Four Modernisations' programmes as a part of the broader economic liberalisation process. The 'Four Modernisations' programme included, in order of priority, Agriculture, Industry, Science and Technology and National Defence. The last priority for the defence coincided with Deng's 16-characteer principle of "combating the military and civil, combining peace and war and giving priority to military products, and making the civil support the Military" which in practical sense meant conversion of defence industrial infrastructure for civilian purpose[59]. At the same time, arms exports was vigorously promoted. In essence the new policy was a tacit admission of problems facing the defence industry, which Deng wanted to rectify. Particular focus was on the "third front' industries, which exhibited overcapacity and redundancy.

Deng's Conversion policy although led the defence industry to branch out to civilian production, the policy itself did not accrue much benefit to military production. This led to another policy shift around the mid-1990s, this time under Jiang Zemin. The policy focussed on promotion of integrated dual-use industrial systems[60]. The new strategy which was embodied in the 10th FYP (2001-05) continued to be in vogue in the 11th Plan (2006-1010). In fact, the policy was reinforced. The new policy, as Richard A Bitzinger puts it, emphasises on "the dual importance of both the transfer of military technologies to commercial use and the transfer of commercial technologies to military use". To make the policy successful in China's defence industry, he continues, "it is called for to not only develop dual-use technologies but to actively pursue joint civil-military technology cooperation"[61].

5.10.6 Structural Reforms

China's defence industry in past 60 years has undergone several rounds of structural reorganisation. The first major restructuring took place in 1952 under the Soviet tutelage, when two Ministries of Machine Building (MsMB) were established, one for civil and the other for military production. The Soviet withdrawal in 1960 however forced Beijing to relook at defence production, which resulted in creation of seven MsMB. Except for the first MMB, which was in charge of 'Civilian' each of others represented a major defence sector – (1) Atomic energy and nuclear weapons, (2) Aircraft and non-ballistic missiles, (3) Electronics and telecommunication, (4) Conventional ordnance, (5) Naval equipment and shipbuilding and (6) Ballistic missiles. In 1979, the eighth MMB was set up with of responsibility of space programme (rockets and satellites). However the newly created MMB was merged with the seventh MMB in a further re-organisational effort in 1981-82, which also saw the names of other MMBs being changed[62].

It is noteworthy that prior to 1981-82 reorganisation, China's defence industry, as represented by above mentioned MsMB were overseen by numerous organisations including the State Planning Commission, the Ministry of Finance (MoF), the PLA's National Defence Science and Technology Commission (NDSTC), the State Council's National Defence Industry Office (NDIO) and the Central Military Commission's Science and Technology Equipment Commission (STECO). However, these organisations were typified with "overlapping responsibilities and claim to ownerships." As part of broader reorganisation at the levels of State Council ministries and commission, decision was taken in 1982 to centralise decision-making, by merging NDSTC, NDIO and STECO to form a new organisation called COSTIND[63].

In 1988, and 1993 the defence industrial complex was again reorganised, as part of larger reform to reduce state support to the industry and force them to market-driven completion. In the 1988 restructuring, the number of ministries were brought down to four. In effect, this was done by merging the earlier ministries of Ordnance Industry, Electronics Industry and Machine Building, as well as combining Aviation Industry and Space Industry. The

Ministry of Energy was formed by merging Ministry of Nuclear Energy with Ministry of Coals and the Ministry of Electric Power Industry (MOEP).

5.10.7 Sustained Reforms

China has continuously tried to revitalise its moribund defence industry through a series of reforms. However the reform initiatives, carried out till late 1990s, were 'hesitant, piecemeal and incoherent'. As a result, the industry continued to "exhibit numerous weaknesses at all levels of the system, from government procurement to factory production." The peculiar problems facing the industry were: little incentive for quality production; hierarchical organisational structure; and excessive capacity, redundant personnel, lack of skilled labour, and poor management, among others[64]. To overcome these problems, the Chinese authorities took some radical steps beginning from 1998. The 1998 reform, which was initiated during the 9th meeting of the National People's Congress (NPC) sought, for the first time, to "genuinely transform the structure and operation of the system by streamlining them, by reducing corruption and inefficiency in the procurement process, and by forcing a degree of rationalisation and accountability at the enterprise level"[65]. The reform initiatives of the 1998 were again built upon by another round of reform initiatives undertaken in 1999, 2002 and 2008, which focussed on strengthening the concept of 'Four Mechanisms' of competition, evaluation, supervision and encouragement[66]. In the words of Tai Ming Cheung "*Reform measures included providing greater funding for research institutions, improving the management of research funds, introducing a competitive mechanism for defence research, adoption of a contract system for research projects, speeding up the application of research findings for production and improving the integration of military and civilian technologies*[67]. *Far-reaching organisational changes were also undertaken that led to a restructuring of the management hierarchy, a revamping of the country's military-industrial conglomerates, and a more influential and direct role for the People's Liberation Army (PLA) in the management of the defence S&T process*"[68].

The reform measures, particularly since late 1990s, have led to a dramatic transformation of the Chinese defence industry. As a consequence, the historical criticism that the Chinese defence industry is plagued with weakness is no more valid. There is visible progress in many sectors of the industry.

5.10.8 Consistent Progress of China's Defence Industry

The massive financial support and continued reforms measures, especially since the 1990s has led to significant progress in the Chinese defence industrial output and capability. After eight consecutive years of losses, the defence industry broke even in 2002. Since then the industry has kept the profit momentum, reaching 50 billion Yuan in 2009—a significant increase considering that in 1996 the industry's total loss was over five billion Yuan. As regards capability of the industry, the progress is evident across the sectors, although the degree of progress varies from one to other.

5.10.9 Nuclear and Missile

The sector comprising nuclear weapons and missiles has always enjoyed priority among the successive Chinese leadership. Even during the Cultural Revolution, which witnessed many conventional weapons programmes being atrophied, the nuclear along with strategic submarine programmes were insulated from chaos through passing of executive orders from Mao and other senior leaders. Because of the priority attached, the nuclear sector had always access to virtually unlimited resources. This combined with "an unusually capable cadre of Western-trained nuclear physicist", the sector has been a story of great success in Chinese defence industrialisation. Since the successful detonation of a nuclear bomb in 1964, China has increased in nuclear warhead significantly. In 2008, the *Bulletin of the Atomic Scientists* reported that China is the only member among the original nuclear weapons states, which is "believed to be increasing its nuclear arsenal, boosting roughly 25 per cent since 2005[69]. By January 2010, China's total stockpile of nuclear warheads was estimated to be around 240, of which nearly 200 were operational for delivery primarily by ballistic missiles and aircrafts[70]. More significantly, as China is "developing and testing [more] offensive missiles, forming additional missile units, [and] qualitatively upgrading certain missile systems, its nuclear warhead is bound to increase"[71]. For instance, China has already commissioned a JIN-Class (Type 094) nuclear powered ballistic missile submarine (SSBN) with four more are in the various states of construction. Each of these submarines can carry up to 12 JL-2 SLBM, requiring a minimum total of 60 warheads for five SSBNs[72].

Like the nuclear programme, China's missile industry has been a great success, primarily for the same reasons as in the nuclear sector: continued state support, significant investment and contribution from a group of remarkable scientists, most notably Qian Xuesen. After failures for six years, China in 1965 conducted its first successful ballistic missile test in the form of DF-2A, and an ICBM test in 1982[73]. Since then its capability, in terms of reach and sophistication has increased by leaps and bounds, with the present inventory comprising of "increasingly accurate Short-Range Ballistic Missiles (SRBM), new classes of IRBM to support anti-Kinetic Kill Vehicle (KKV) programmes and anti-carrier attack operations (e.g., DF-21), land attack cruise missiles, a revolutionary class of road-mobile ICBMs (e.g., DF-31 and DF-31A)"[74]. In addition, China has made great strides in the development and deployment of JL-2 SLBM, therefore achieving what is called the most credible strategic capability.

5.10.10 Aviation

Unlike the Nuclear and Missile sectors, China's aviation industry was historically a poor performer. The continuous reforms have narrowed the technology gap with the advanced counties. The launch of J-20 in January 2010 further narrowed the gap[75].

5.10.11 Diversification

The two ongoing reforms programmes of restructuring and CMI strategy for the DIB, introduced in 2007, has enabled the SOE's to diversify into a wide range of activities in the commercial sector and generate revenues for funding military programmes. Further, China has preferred to focus on building centres of excellence within the two corporations as opposed to diversifying capabilities across enterprises.

5.10.12 Acquisition of Defence Firms

Chinese cash-rich SOE's and private companies since 2009 are acquiring foreign aerospace and defence firms which have been based in Austria, US, Finland and France. These have been aerospace and shipbuilding firms which operate primarily in the commercial sector. For Beijing, these acquisitions facilitate activities under its CMI strategy and in future China will view Western companies operating in advanced technology sectors that could deliver modern technological capabilities and knowledge in Western management techniques (as related to project management and so on).

5.10.13 Acquisition of Dual-use High Technology

The arms embargo imposed by the US and Europe is unlikely to be lifted. However, a flexible interpretation of the embargo by the EU has resulted in the Chinese companies to gain access to some dual-use high technology, particularly from the UK and France. These technologies relate to networking and information-based warfare and could help Beijing's military modernisation drive.

5.10.14 Future Impetus

The focus of procurement policy is on strengthening basic and applied research and the research on key defence technologies related to networking and information – based warfare. Priority will be given to developing new types of advanced equipment and integrated electronic information systems[76].

NOTES

1. IHS "*Jane's World Defence Industry 2014* ", p.94.
2. Yitzhak Shichor (1997) "*Converting the Military-Aviation Industry to Civilian Use*" Chapter 6 of book "*Mixed Motives, Uncertain Outcomes. Defence Conversion in China*" edited by Jorn Brommelhorster and John Franksteinp.101 available at http://www. academia .edu/ 280913/Converting_the_Military-Aviation_Industry_to_Civilian_Use (Accessed July 10, 2015).
3. Paul H.B. Godwin, "*China's Defence Establishment: The Hard Lessons of Incomplete Modernisation*" Chapter 2 p.21 of book China's Defence Establishment available at kms2.isn.ethz.ch/serviceengine/Files/ESDP/...4cd5.../Chapter+2.pdf (Accessed July 13, 2015).
4. Richard A. Bitzinger and J. D. Kenneth Boutin "*China's defence industries: change and continuity*" Chapter 10 of book "*Rising China: Power and Reassurance*" p.129 available at http://press.anu.edu.au/wp-content/uploads/2011/05/ch1014.pdf (Accessed July 14, 2015.
5. Medeiros, Evan S., Cliff, Roger, Crane, Keith and Mulvenon, James C. 2005, "*A New Direction for China's Defence Industry*", RAND, Santa Monica, Califp. 162. available at http:/ /www.rand.org/content/ dam/rand/pubs/monographs/2005/ RAND_ MG334 .pdf (Accessed July 15, 2015).
6. Richard A. Bitzinger and J.D. Kenneth Boutin, "*China's defence industries: change and continuity*" Chapter 10 of book "*Rising China: Power and Reassurance*" p.130 available athttp:/ /press.anu.edu.au/wp-content/uploads/2011/05/ch1014.pdf (Accessed July 16, 2015).
7. Richard A. Bitzinger "*Reforming China's defence industries: Progress in spite of itself?*", p. 107 available at http://www. acad emia.edu/11905969/Reforming_China_s_Defense_ Industry_Progress_in_Spite_of_Itself (Accessed July 16, 2015).
8. Richard A. Bitzinger, "*Reforming China's defence industries: Progress in spite of itself?*", p. 108 available at http://www. acad emia.edu/11905969/Reforming_China_s_Defense_ Industry_Progress_in_Spite_of_Itself (Accessed July 17, 2015).
9. Medeiros, Evan S., Cliff, Roger, Crane, Keith and Mulvenon, James C. 2005, "*A New Direction for China's Defence Industry*", RAND, Santa Monica, Calif. pp. xvi-xviii available at http://www.rand.org/content/dam/rand/pubs/monographs/ 2005/ RAND _ MG334.pdf (Accessed July 17, 2015).
10. Medeiros, Evan S., Cliff, Roger, Crane, Keith and Mulvane, James C. 2005, "*A New Direction for China's Defence Industry*", RAND, Santa Monica, Calif., p. 28 available at http:// www.rand.org/content/dam/rand/pubs/ monographs/2005/RAND_MG334 .pdf (Accessed July 20, 2015).

11. Cheung, Tai Ming "*Innovation in China's Defence Research, Development, and Acquisition System* " pp. 3-4 available at https://escholarship.org/uc/item/43v5v0nt (Accessed July 20,2015).
12. Cheung, Tai Ming "*Innovation in China's Defence Research, Development, and Acquisition System*", p. 4 available at https:// escholarship.org/uc/item/43v5v0nt (Accessed July 21, 2015).
13. IHS, "*Jane's World Defence Industry 2014* ", p.95.
14. Richard A. Bitzinger, "*The PRC'S Defence Industry: Reform without Improvement*" p.1 The Jamestown Foundation China Brief 5 (6) available at http://www.jamestown.org/single/ ?no_cache=1&tx_ttnews%5Btt_ news%5D=3726# . Vd RmQLKqqko (Accessed July 23, 2015).
15. *Military Balance 2011* (International Institute of Strategic Studies) and "*ESI Signs a 5-Year Strategic Cooperation Agreement in R&D with AVIC, "Aviation Industry Corporation of China*" available at http://www.bloomberg.com/apps/news ?pid=news archive&sid=ae9p6QLlmC.M (Accessed July 23, 2015).
16. Official website of Aviation Industry Corporation of China, available at http:// www.avic.com.cn/EN/ (Accessed July 24, 2015).
17. IHS, *Jane's World Defence Industry*, February 2013, p.98.
18. Official website of China State Shipbuilding Corporation available at http://www.cssc.net.cn/ en/ (Accessed July 27, 2015).
19. Official website of China Shipbuilding Industry Corporation available at http:// www.csic.com.cn/en/ (Accessed July 28, 2015).
20. NORINCO (G) is different from NORINCO. The latter is an export-import entity.
21. "China North Industries Group (NORINCO (G))" available at GlobalSecurity.org, <http:/ /www.globalsecurity.org/military/world/ china/norinco.htm>. (Accessed July 29, 2015).
22. IHS, "*Jane's World Defence Industry 2014*", p.95.
23. Richard A. Bitzinger, "*China's Double-Digit Defence Growth - What It Means for a Peaceful Rise*" March 19, 2015 published in Foreign Affairs Magazine and available at https:// www.foreignaffairs.com/articles/china/2015-03-19/chinas-double-digit-defence-growth (Accessed July 30, 2015).
24. IHS, "*Jane's World Defence Industry 2013*", p.100.
25. Richard A. Bitzinger, "*China's Double-Digit Defence Growth - What It Means for a Peaceful Rise*" March 19, 2015 published in Foreign Affairs Magazine and available at https:// www.foreignaffairs.com/articles/china/2015-03-19/chinas-double-digit-defence-growth (Accessed July 31, 2015).
26. Evan S. Medeiros et al, "*A New Direction for China's Defence Industry (Santa Monica: RAND, 2005)*", p.22. available at http://www.rand.org/content/dam/rand/pubs/monographs/2005/ RAND_MG334.pdf (Accessed July 31, 2015).
27. IHS, "*Jane's World Defence Industry 2014,*" p.95.
28. IHS, "*Jane's World Defence Industry 2013*", p.100.
29. Cheung, Tai Ming "*The Role of Foreign Technology Transfers in China's Defence Research, Development, and Acquisition Process*", p.2 available at https://escholarship.org/uc/item/ 4dp213kd- (Accessed July 31, 2015).
30. Cheung, Tai Ming "*The Role of Foreign Technology Transfers in China's Defence Research, Development, and Acquisition Process*" p.4 available at https://escholarship.org/uc/item/ 4dp213kd(Accessed August 03,2015).
31. Cheung, Tai Ming "*The Role of Foreign Technology Transfers in China's Defence Research, Development, and Acquisition Process*" p.2 available at https://escholarship.org/uc/item/ 4dp213kd (Accessed August 03, 2015).

32. "*2014 R&D Magazine Global Funding Forecast*" December 2013, p. 14 available at http://www.battelle.org/docs/tpp/ 2014_ global_ rd_funding_forecast.pdf, (Accessed August 05, 2015).
33. "*2014 R&D Magazine Global Funding Forecast*", December 2013, p. 15 available at http://www.battelle.org/docs/tpp/2014_ global _ rd_funding_forecast.pdf , (Accessed August 06, 2015).
34. IHS, "*Jane's World Defence Industry 2014*", p.97.
35. Cheung, Tai Ming "*The Chinese Defence Economy's Long March from Imitation to Innovation*" p.2available at http://igcc. ucsd.edu/assets/001/500868.pdf- (Accessed August 07, 2015).
36. Walsh Kathleen A. "*China's Defence Technology Acquisition System, Processes, and Future as an Integrator and Supplier*" p.2 available at http://igcc.ucsd.edu/assets/001/505318.pdf- (Accessed August 10, 2015).
37. Cheung, Tai Ming "*The Role of Foreign Technology Transfers in China's Defence Research, Development, and Acquisition Process*", p.2 available at https://escholarship.org/uc/item/4dp213kd (Accessed August 11, 2015).
38. Tai Ming Cheung "*The Current State of Defence Innovation in China and Future Prospects*' p.5 IGCC Defence Innovation Briefs January 2014 available at http://igcc.ucsd.edu/assets/001/505243.pdf (Accessed August 12, 2015).
39. Francis Ed and Puska Susan M. *Contemporary Chinese Defence Industry Reforms and Civil–Military Integration in Three Key Organisations*, p.3 available at https://escholarship.org/uc/item/3dq7x6d2- (Accessed August 13, 2015).
40. Francis Ed and Puska Susan M., "*Contemporary Chinese Defence Industry Reforms and Civil–Military Integration in Three Key Organisations*", p.4 available at https://escholarship.org/uc/item/3dq7x6d2 (Accessed August 14, 2015).
41. "*China's Military Power: Now Third-Largest Arms Exporter, Unseating Germany*" by Michelle Flor Cruz *International Business Times* March 16, 2015 available at http://www.ibtimes.com/chinas-military-power-now-third-largest-arms-exporter-unseating-germany-1848320 (Accessed August 14, 2015).
42. IHS, "*Jane's World Defence Industry2014*", p.97.
43. IHS, "*Jane's World Defence Industry 2014*", p.96.
44. IHS, "*Jane's World Defence Industry 2014*", p.96.
45. IHS, "*Jane's World Defence Industry 2013*", p.99.
46. IHS, "*Jane's World Defence Industry 2014*", p.96.
47. IHS, "*Jane's World Defence Industry 2014*", p.97.
48. IHS, "*Jane's World Defence Industry 2013*", p.100.
49. "*Hold High the Great Banner of Socialism with Chinese Characteristics and Strive for New Victories in Building a Moderately Prosperous Society in all*", Hu Jintao's report at 17th Party Congress on October 15, 2007,available at http://www.china.org.cn/ english/congress/229611.htm (Accessed August 17, 2015).
50. Organisation for Economic Cooperation and Economic Development, *OECD* "*Reviews of Innovation Policy: China*", September 2008, p.17 available at http://www.oecd.org/sti/inno/41270116.pdf (Accessed August 18, 2015)
51. Shirley Kan et al, "*China's Foreign Conventional Arms Acquisitions: Background and Analysis*, Report for Congress (updated November 06, 2001), Congressional Research Service, RL30700 available athttps://www.fas.org/sgp/crs/row/RL30700.pdf (Accessed August 18, 2015).
52. Evan S. Medeiros et al, "A *New Direction for China's Defence Industry* (Santa Monica: RAND,

2005)," p. xvii. available at http://www.rand.org/content/dam/rand/pubs/monographs/2005/ RAND_MG334.pdf (Accessed August 18, 2015).

53. US DOD, "*Military Power of the People's Republic of China 2009*", Annual Report to Congress, pp.37-38 available at http://www.defense.gov/Portals/1/Documents/pubs/ China_Military_Power_Report_2009.pdf (Accessed August 18, 2015).

54. Godwin, Paul H.B., "*Development of the Chinese Armed Forces*" Air University Press: Alabama: June 1988 Chapter 11 Strategic Forces available athttps://fas.org/irp/dia/product/prc_ch-11.htm(Accessed August 19, 2015).

55. U.S. Congress, Office of Technology Assessment, *Other Approaches to Civil-Military Integration: The Chinese and Japanese Arms Industries* (Washington, DC: U.S. Government Printing Office), March 1995, pp.6-7 available at http://ota.fas.org/reports/9532.pdf (Accessed August 19, 2015).

56. David Shambaugh, "*Modernising China's Military: Progress, Problems, and Prospects* "(Berkeley, Los Angeles, London: University of California Press, 2002), pp.226-227 available at http:/ /www.scribd.com/doc/147138350/Modernizing-China-s-Military-David-Shambaugh#scribd (Accessed August 20, 2015).

57. Ibid

58. David Shambaugh, "*Modernizing China's Military: Progress, Problems, and Prospects* "(Berkeley, Los Angeles, London: University of California Press, 2002), pp.228-229 available at http:/ /www.scribd.com/doc/147138350/Modernising-China-s-Military-David-Shambaugh#scribd (Accessed August 21, 2015).

59. Richard A Bitzinger, "*Civil-Military Integration and Chinese Military Modernisation*", *Asia Pacific Security Studies*, 3 (9), December 2004, available at http://www.apcss.org/Publications/ APSSS/Civil-MilitaryIntegration.pdf (Accessed August 21, 2015).

60. Ibid.

61. Richard A. Bitzinger, "*Reforming China's Defence Industry: Progress in Spite of Itself?*",*The Korean Journal of Defence Analysis*,19 (3), Fall 2007, pp.98-118 available at http:// www.tandfonline.com/ doi/abs/10.1080/ 10163270709464143#. Vd2s PCWqqko (Accessed August 21, 2015).

62. David Shambaugh, "*Modernising China's Military: Progress, Problems, and Prospects* "(Berkeley, Los Angeles, London: University of California Press, 2002), p.231 available at http:// www.scribd.com/doc/147138350/Modernizing-China-s-Military-David-Shambaugh#scribd (Accessed August 21, 2015).

63. Evan S Medeiros et al, *A New Direction for China's Defence Industry*, p.14. available at http:/ /www.rand.org/content/dam/ rand/pubs/monographs/2005/RAND_MG334.pdf (Accessed August 24, 2015).

64. Evan S. Medeiros, *Analysing China's Defense Industries and the Implications for Chinese Military Modernisation*, Testimony presented to the U.S.-China Economic and Security Review Commission on February 6, 2004, and p.4.

65. Evan S. Medeiros et al, A *New Direction for China's Defence Industry* (Santa Monica: RAND, 2005), p.24. available at http: //www.rand.org/content/dam/rand/pubs/monographs/2005/ RAND_MG334.pdf (Accessed August 24, 2015).

66. Evan S. Medeiros et al, "A *New Direction for China's Defence Industry* "(Santa Monica: RAND, 2005), p24; James Mulvenon and Rebecca Samm Tyroler-Cooper, "*China's Defence Industry on the Path of Reform*", Report prepared for The US-China Economic and Security Review Commission, October 2009, pp.7-31. available at http://www.rand.org/content/dam/ rand/ pubs/monographs/2005/RAND_MG334.pdf (Accessed August 25, 2015).

67. Tai Ming Cheung, "Dragon on the Horizon: China's Defence Industrial Renaissance", *The*

Journal of Strategic Studies,32(1), February 2009, pp.29-66 available at http://www.tandfonline.com/doi/abs/10.1080/ 01402390802407418#. Vd71 PyWqqko (Accessed August 25, 2015.)

68. Tai Ming Cheung, "The Remaking of the Chinese Defense Industry and the Rise of the Dual-Use Economy", Testimony before the US-China Economic and Security Review Commission Hearing on China's Proliferation and the Impact of Trade Policy on Defence Industries in the United States and China, July 13, 2007, p. 2. (Accessed on August 25, 2015).
69. See Robert S Norris and Hans M Kristensen, "Chinese Nuclear Forces", *Bulletin of Atomic Scientists*, 64(3), July/August 2008, p.42 available at /menu/key-issues/nuclear-weapons/issues/capabilities/PDF%20files / Chinese%20Nuclear% 20Forces %202008.pdf (Accessed August 25, 2015.)
70. *SIPRI Yearbook 2010: Armaments, Disarmament and International Security* (Oxford University Press: Oxford, 2010), p.354 available at http://www.sipri.org/yearbook/2010 (Accessed August 26, 2015).
71. US Department of Defence, Office of the Secretary of Defence, Military Power of the People's Republic of China 2008, Annual Report to Congress,
72. SLBM is the abbreviation of submarine launched ballistic missiles. The JL-2 has a range of over 7,000 km.
73. David Shambaugh, *Modernising China's Military: Progress, Problems, and Prospects*, p.278.
74. James Mulvenon and Rebecca Samm Tyroler-Cooper, *China's Defence Industry on the Path of Reform*, p.33.
75. Tai Ming Cheung, "The J-20 Fighter Aircraft and the State of China's Defense Science, Technology, and Innovation Potential", Policy Brief 17, January 2011, available at http://igcc.ucsd.edu/research/security/SITC/ SITCpolicy brief 17 .pdf (Accessed August 26, 2015).
76. IHS, "*Jane's World Defence Industry 2013*", p.100.

CHAPTER 6

US Defence Industrialisation and Reforms: Lessons for India

6.1 Evolution and Growth

The US defence industry is of a significant size and is the world's largest and the most technologically advanced. US DIB is complex, multiple layered and globally connected. It emerged after World War II and is the result of two geopolitical developments. One, the Cold War that led to the formulation of a strategy to contain the Soviet power. Two, the invasion of South Korea by North Korea in June 1950, which led to a big increase in US defence spending. The "*National Security Council 68 (NSC-68), produced under Paul H. Nitze, in the spring of 1950, recommended a rapid build-up of US political, economic, and military strength to halt the spread of Soviet power*[1]. The consequent Military-Industrial Complex (MIC) that the two developments brought about is borne till date. The US defence industry's evolution and growth since 1945, in the context of this Cold War, can be divided into three periods: Pre-Cold War formation and early growth period i.e. after World War II (1945-60); During Cold War stabilisation period (1960-90); and Post-Cold War restructuring period (1990-to date).

Figure 6.1 shows US defence budget allocations called Total Obligation Authority (TOA) and includes the spending on Research Development Test and Evaluation (RDT&E) and on defence Procurements from Fiscal Year (FY) 1948 to FY 2007. The expenditures are in constant FY 2009 dollars. This means the effects of inflation over time have been eliminated. From 2001, the DOD's TOA subsumes the supplemental funding for the Global War on Terror (GWOT). The patterns in Figure 6.1 suggest the various aspects of the US defence industry. The Peaks in defence spending relate to major events as the 'Wars' or the 'Reagan administration's efforts to use defence spending to put pressure on Soviet Union during the final decade of the Cold War'. Such events were invariably followed by an immediate decline in the defence spending. The surges appear in the procurement graph too and there is steady, long-term growth in expenditure on military personnel and their operating costs. The latter due to the fact that a volunteer force today is much more expensive to pay and operate than the erstwhile military establishment where personnel could be drafted. Such additional costs in turn have put more pressure on procurement. Consequently, manufacturing has been subjected to swings in demand and affected the attractiveness of the industry to the companies. Notwithstanding, the RDT&E investment's from 1948 to 2007 has gradually increased to 42 per cent of DOD's cumulative procurement spending thereby implying, the government's intent to increasingly invest in technology.

Figure 6.1: US DOD TOA by Major Appropriations Categories 1948–2007 (Billions of Constant FY 2009 Dollars)

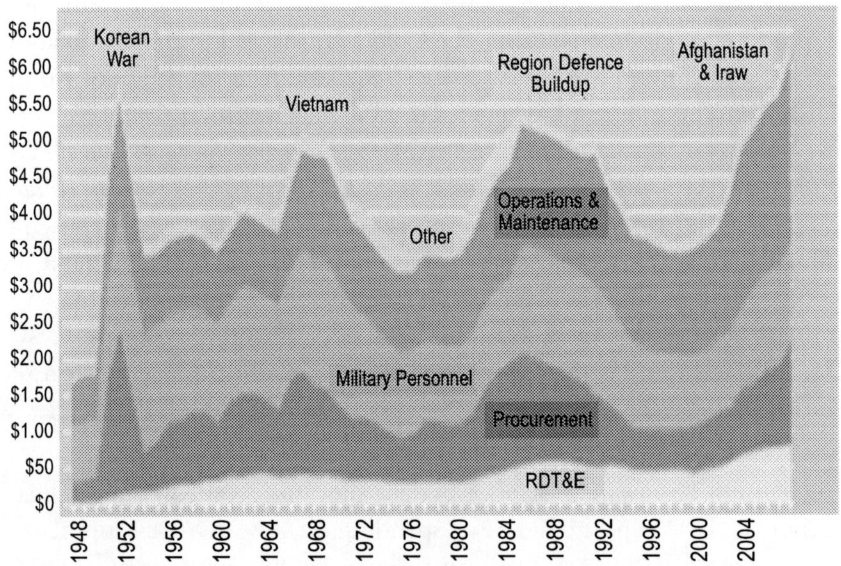

Source: 'US Defence Industrial Base Past, Present and Future' by Watts Barry.

Between 1948-60, the US for the first time established a massive peacetime military force. Accordingly, there were corresponding increases in the annual defence funding which led to investments in R&D and procurements to equip the armed forces. This encouraged many private-sector companies to support the US military. Most of the military's inventory was either to be replaced or redesigned. "*Entirely new technology approaches to weapons and systems appeared and new technology systems were tested as much by prototyping, procuring, and operating as by laboratory level work*"[2]. In case of military aircrafts, more new designs reached flight status in the 1950s than in all four subsequent decades combined. Individual systems were bought in large annual quantities. "*Before World War II almost all Army ordnance, most Navy ships and 10 per cent of Navy aircraft, were produced in arsenals. But by 1958 arsenals accounted for less than 10 per cent of US weapons production*"[3].

During the years 1948-60 investments in R&D and procurements occurred with the increase in the defence budgets. RDT&E saw an average annual growth rate of over 18 per cent while procurement increased by only 8.3 per cent[4]. "*From 1952 to 1960, the defence spending was between 9.3 per cent and 13.2 per cent of US GDP and by late 1950s the defence industry was one of the leading sectors in the nation's economy*, exceeding that of automobiles, steel or oil. *In 1960 government funded 58 per cent of the nation's industrial R&D*"[5]. Defence R&D focused on new hardware and systems while the majority of R&D in commercial firms was for product improvements. Even as defence spending has grown in real dollars since the 1950s, the pattern of the defence industry over the past half century has been of fewer competitors where companies have ultimately exited the business or reduced their capabilities. "*Relying on defence spending in the future as the major incentive to improving the participation of companies, therefore, would probably be ineffective*"[6].

The US DOD was created in 1947. Soon DOD started controlling the R&D and procurement activities of the military Services. The increasing size of the DOD led to a bureaucratic acquisition system having many organisations and individuals in the buying decisions. DOD started regulating procurement habits of the military, not just the numbers of systems to be bought but also which systems to choose and the degree of commonality and interoperability among them. "*By 1962, red-tape, slow decision-making and poor quality of government personnel were seen as disincentives to be in the business, but many firms simply accepted these impediments as facts of life*"[7]. "*For example, "Government personnel to oversee and manage projects have been insufficient in numbers and skills." "Several studies .... concluded the government's capabilities for planning and implementing advance weapons programs have been generally inadequate" (ibid., p. 86). The result is a pool of government engineers lacking a "close feel for the technology in their fields" (ibid., pp. 85–95). 30 years later a RAND study concluded that a key ingredient in program shortfalls was whether the government had "qualified technical staff, possessing sufficient flexibility (or slack) to respond to both unexpected or unanticipated difficulties in the programme, coupled with oversight that is qualified and that forces consideration of programme issues that are beyond the purview of programme managers"*

During the period 1945–60, firms often could not attain the initial goals for developing complex defence systems. "A study of twelve major programs showed that, on an average, the actual cost was 3.2 times the predicted cost, and the average development time was 1.36 times that originally predicted. By rough measures (e.g., speed, range or payload), performance also varied from initial goals by factors of 0.8 to 2.0. One 1957 report concluded that the lead time for full introduction of an advanced manned aircraft was 11 years[8]. The government used to progress payments to relieve firms of the burdens of financing new technology efforts[9].

From 1961-90, the US focused on retaining a military edge over the Soviet Union. This became the indicator of the adequacy of US military. The trend was for greater attention to improving connectivity, standardisation, interoperability, reliability, and maintainability which influenced many system development efforts. The growth of US economy during the period created new industrial sectors and reduced the dominance of the defence sector, diminishing defence industry's attractiveness as a new business opportunity for commercial firms. Private-sector technology investments increased post 1960 at such a rate that it eventually exceeded the government's levels in the 1970's. The defence budget grew at about 0.82 per cent per year, on an average, from 1961-90. Further, this period witnessed two cycles of much greater growth rates followed by contractions in the defence budget. The first cycle of rapid growth and subsequent contraction was associated with the Vietnam War in late sixties and the second with the Reagan defence build-up in mid-eighties. During this period some lasting changes were imposed on the defence industry and included the introduction of Planning, Programming and Budgeting System on the Pentagon's annual budget cycle, establishing an Office of Systems Analysis to use cost-effectiveness to make choices among alternative weapons programmes, and the government developed, increasingly comprehensive review and monitoring practices to control the award of contracts and their oversight. The impact of these on the companies was to lead them to expand their work forces and to implement special practices, and to become accustomed to providing the government with detailed cost and other proprietary data about their operations. As military procurement declined, DOD encouraged Foreign Military Sales (FMS) by the companies.

The 1980's initially saw major increases in defence spending by the Reagan administration. By 1985, more than two million industry jobs were added. However, events thereafter brought major changes in the industrial base. First, defence spending began declining in 1985, reducing the overall revenues of companies. The decline continued until 1998. Second, government instituted policy and legal changes that altered the ability of companies to make profits even as their sales declined. The changes included cuts in progress payments, changes in tax laws, and demands that companies fund investments that the government had previously funded. Third, parts of DOD—in violation of Defence Department's own policies—placed more and more of the risks of developing and producing systems on contractors, while reserving the right to change requirements or alter production quantities. Consequently, during 1985–1988 ten of DOD's top 60 prime defence contractors either acquired, or were acquired by others in the industry.

The Cold War's challenge of the Soviet power started receding from 1989 onwards. However, the US industry's restructuring effort got diverted towards dealing with the ever changing security environment that has been witnessed over the last two to three decades. The new, complex and varied challenges of terrorist groups, their state sponsors, powerful authoritarian regimes, a rising China, a resurgent Russia, and, the problem of proliferation of nuclear weapons have emerged and thus, it will be premature on part of the US to begin dismantling the defence industry. The US industrial base has been a source of strategic advantage in the past and with the progressive policies of the government is likely to continue to be so in the future.

The US DIB over the last seven decades witnessed large changes in their markets, product lines, industrial structure and the industry's relation's with the government's customers, especially, since the end of the Cold War. Beginning late-1980, the US defence industry started to contract and in early 1990's, entered a period of substantial industrial consolidation. In the early 1990's, Clinton Administration pursued a policy to encourage diversification of defence industry into civilian production and a policy to promote M&A and arms exports, which encouraged companies to consolidate and focus on defence markets"[10]. *The restructuring process created defence (military specialised) companies by undertaking M&A's of defence operations, divesting non-defence operations, exiting higher-cost urban locations and cutting employment.* In 1995

US government issued two policy briefs concerning exports: one stating industrial base concerns would be weighed in the arms export licensing process and the other introducing policies to increase subsidies for arms exports and eliminate fees on arms exports. In 1997 the merger policy was reversed as it became evident that mergers did not produce anticipated savings and only a few defence production lines were closed down. Consequently, 50 major defence firms at the beginning of 1990's had merged into only six large defence firms by the end of 1990's. The merger process also resulted in increased arms sales of the largest defence companies. Between 1990-99, six companies more than doubled their arms sales and three of these tripled their arms sales. Today, major surviving firms are larger than ever in the history of the US defence industry. Moreover, two to three decades ago the US Government for the next weapon platform could choose between the many companies but today, the number of firms that can viably offer "prime contractor" capabilities have shrunk. The shrinkage has altered the relationship between the companies and the government to that of a monopsony customer and oligopolies or monopolies supplier. Due to very few programmes being undertaken today the competition for major programmes has become more intense, with companies increasingly viewing new-start up programmes as "must-wins"[11].

During the first post-Cold War decade, 1989-98, US military expenditure declined continuously besides FY 1992 which witnessed a one year surge due to the 1991 Gulf War. Over this 10-year period, the outlay on defence fell by 29 per cent in real terms(from US $ 304 billion to 268 billion in nominal terms), procurement expenditure dropped by 41 per cent in nominal terms and expenditure on military RDT&E stayed roughly flat[12]. Since FY 1998, US defence outlays increased continuously and since 2001 increased rapidly. (By FY 2008, the US military expenditure had risen to US $ 607 billion while procurement spending increased to US $ 131 billion.) The post-Cold War era in the US continued to see rapid development of advanced, more complex and expensive weapon systems to stay in the forefront of technology and military capabilities. The developments in information and communication technologies were exploited to bring in changes in warfare and usher in new concepts of Revolution in Military Affairs (RMA), Information-Based Warfare (IBW) and Network-Centric Warfare (NCW) which resulted in a shift in the demand from traditional defence industry sectors producing weapon platforms to sectors producing a range of technologies and systems required for advanced Command Control

Communication Computers Intelligence Surveillance and Reconnaissance (C4ISR) capabilities and towards those companies to integrate interconnected and inter-communicative systems. Further, there was a shift in technological innovation and technological lead from the military to the civilian sector resulting in exploiting commercially developed technology for military applications (often referred to as 'spin-ins' or 'spin-ons') than the erstwhile 'spin-offs process of exploiting military technology for commercial applications. These factors led to post-Cold War restructuring of the US DIB.

Post 1990, the breakdown of the Soviet Union in December 1991 changed the international security environment in which the US defence industry had operated for more than 30 years. The US no longer faced a rival whose nuclear forces posed an existential threat to America. This sparked extensive debate within the US defence establishment about national security strategy and the types of military forces that would be needed in the coming decades. "*The debate led to numerous formal government efforts, including the NDP (1997) and five QDRs (1997, 2001 2005–06, 2009-10 and 2014-15). The Persian Gulf War of 1991 and its sequel in 2003, Operation Allied Force in the Balkans (1999) and Operation Enduring Freedom in Afghanistan (2002), and demonstrated the overwhelming power of the US military and its weaponry in conventional conflicts. However, the attacks of September 11, 2001 increased the focus on the threat of non-state actors, and combat in Iraq and Afghanistan was raised, once again, the challenges of counterinsurgency warfare (albeit with the addition of suicide bombers and improvised explosive devices). Building the post-Cold War national security strategy, therefore, has proven to be a difficult, complex process whose outcome continues to be in doubt. Meanwhile, the demands for goods and services by the American military have continued to evolve, as has the defence industrial base supplying those goods and services*"[13].

With the collapse of the Soviet Union, the decline in defence spending of mid-1980s continued through to FY 1998, with the exception of a 1.2 per cent increase in FY 1991. The Reagan build-up peaked in FY 1985. From then onwards, DOD TOA declined under Reagan, George W Bush and Bill Clinton's administration. Again RDT&E did not decline as sharply as procurement. Once it was obvious that the Cold War was receding, the DOD took steps to deal with the defence industry's overcapacity. In 1989, the Joint Staff began exploring substantial force-structure and personnel cuts to all military services over a five-year period. In April 1992 the Bush administration formed a Defence Conversion Commission (DCC) to assess how reductions in defence spending would affect the economy and suggest how to "*assist the transition of DOD personnel and those in the defence industry to non-defence work. The DCC recommended that "efforts to foster commercial-military integration be strengthened, expanded, and accelerated considerably. As first steps toward implementing this recommendation, the DCC recommended "a thorough revision of those procurement laws and regulations that constitute significant barriers to integrating military and commercial manufacturing," to include requiring that DoD use commercial specifications, standards, and buying practices except for those cases when there was a compelling need for military-unique practices*[14]. Thus besides cutting back on purchases of major weapon systems, cuts occurred in force structure and personnel across both military Services and the defence industry.

During the restructuring period (1991-till date) in the 1990s, few defence companies tried to follow the advise of US political leaders and defence industry analysts who had called for a single, integrated industrial base that would serve multiple customers. However, most had little success. This suggested how active a role the US federal government must play in structuring the DIB. Consequently, in 1993, a former Defence Secretary Les Aspin over supper told the leaders of 15 leading defence firms that around half of them needed to either exit the defence business or close down. How these firms were to respond was left to the industry leaders. "*The government's policy was to take a hands-off approach to the future structure of the industrial base, and the result was the emergence of supplier monopolies or duopolies in many defence product lines.* Aspin's meeting with industry executives sparked a period of intense consolidation and shrinkage throughout the US defence industry. To encourage consolidation, the government offered financial incentives as allowance for consolidation costs in overhead[15]. Boeing, Lockheed Martin (LM), Northrop Grumman (NG), General Dynamics (GD), and Raytheon are the five US giant firms that managed to survive the Last Supper period of industry contraction. *For example, the nation's six shipbuilding yards are now owned by two large defence firms, NG and GD, and LM is getting close to being the only prime contractor with a full capacity to design, develop, and produce advanced combat aircraft. Moreover, Boeing is now the only US supplier of the large transport aircraft that could be modified to replace the US Air Force's aging KC-135 fleet of aerial tankers. These developments, which erode healthy competition and limit the military's choice of suppliers, argue that the federal government should not continue with its laissez-faire approach to the structure of the defence industry*"[16]. "*Until 1998, mergers that reduced the supplier and component providers to just two firms were approved. For example, the government approved the mergers of Northrop and Grumman in 1994 and of Lockheed and Martin Marietta in 1995. But in 1998 the government stopped the merger of NG and LM. Evidently, the Last Supper set top-level goals for reducing the industry's overcapacity without having thought through what sort of industrial structure the defence department wanted or how best to achieve that structure*"[17].

The defence industries in Western Europe during this period underwent similar consolidation: "*The European Union (EU) sought to rationalise procurement strategies by allowing for the consolidation of national champions into supranational regional champions. Thus EADS, BAE Systems, Thales and Finmeccanica emerged as the big four producers of defence equipment in Europe .... [These] four firms are increasingly entangled in a complex web of partnerships, licensing agreements, JVs and other forms of collaborations. According to Mattis Axelson, EADS, BAE Systems, and Thales have "the sales and breadth of capabilities that are comparable to the leading US defence companies and each is based on a complex network of cross-border ownership structures and joint JV*"[18]. "*Nations have also been inclined to invest preferentially in domestic providers in order to build a defence industry, as has been the case in South Korea. These tendencies reflect a natural desire to ensure national security, protect local employment, and build technologically advanced domestic industrial capabilities*"[19].

DOD TOA finally rose in FY 1999 and received further augmentation by additional funding for the wars in Afghanistan and Iraq. Figure 6.1. includes the supplemental funding over FY's 2001–07. Consequently, from FY 1998 to FY 2007, DOD TOA rose at an average annual rate of over 7.4 percent. The average growth rate exceeded the 6.4 percent average annual growth in DOD TOA for FY's 1948–1960. Even after 9/11, government's acquisition practices have remained largely unaltered from those established decades earlier. "*These practices included altering programme funding from one year to next; awarding and evaluating programmes largely based on costs; creating very large programmes that would continue for decades, thereby reserving the revenues to the incumbent firms; making changes in requirements after development—or even production—had begun; and maintaining intricate oversight and control of defence firms' daily activities*"[20].

In 2004, the expenditure in real terms exceeded that at the height of the Cold War and the US defence budget has since then grown rapidly due to the wars in Iraq and Afghanistan. By end 2008 the budget reached US $ 689 billion—nearly 25 per cent higher in real terms than the previous peak in 1985, and equalled the levels seen during the Second World War[21].

The Operations and Maintenance (O&M) account of the defence budget pays for the fuel, spare parts and training exercises. In FY 90, the O&M spending and procurement represented nearly 28 to 29 per cent of the defence budget each while in 2007, the share of O&M had risen to 35 per cent and for procurement fell to 19 per cent. "*This, partly reflects an ageing fleet where Army's average medium truck is 21 years old, an M1 Abrams tank is 20 years old and the F-15 and F-16 fleet on average 17 years old*"[22]. With demand for sustainment rising, the DOD was looking for privatising the support services for weapon systems, although US law requires government depots to perform 50 per cent of all repair and upgrade work. Industry was reorganising and rapidly expanding the professional services industry.

Figure 6.2: US Defence Budget Allocations FY 2008 to FY 2015

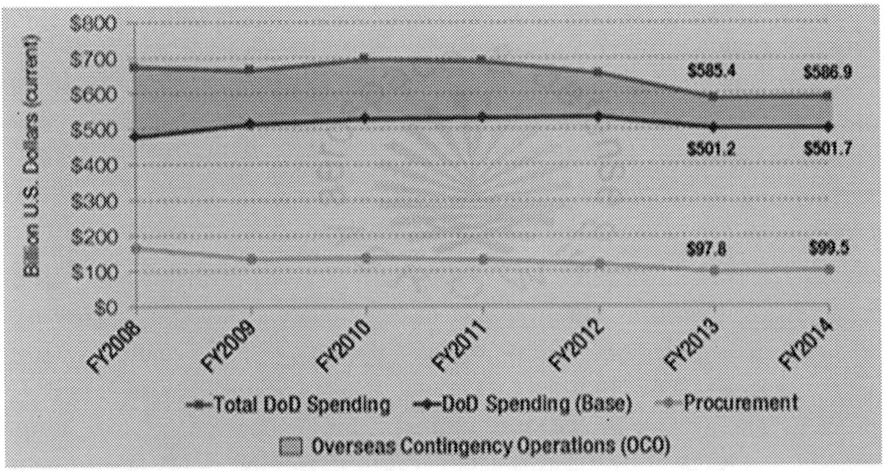

Source: Aerospace & Defence Intelligence Report 2014 Aero Web.

6.2 Overview and Trends

More recently, from FY 2008 to FY 2014, the US defence spending ranged between $ 560 billion to $ 700 billion (Figure 6.2). As per the President's budget of FY 2015 (fiscal year starting October 01, 2014), the DOD is to receive around US $ 569.3 billion[23] (a reduction of US $ 26.4 billion from FY 2014). Of this, an amount of US $ 501.7 billion is for base funding (discretionary + mandatory) while the remaining US $ 64.3 billion is for overseas contingency operations.

6.3 Defence Industrial Base

US military production, sustainment and research capabilities are endowed in both the public and private sectors with the DIB being capable of producing the full range of defence and security products and services and across all domains from bullets to nuclear and space systems. US perhaps is the only country that can claim true self sufficiency in defence production.

The US's major contractors include Boeing (for Aerospace and Defence), LM (for Defence Systems), NG (for Defence Electronics, IT and Space technologies), Raytheon (for Defence Electronics, Space, technical services and special mission aircrafts) and GD (for Land and Naval combat platforms, and systems, information communication and surveillance systems).

In the aircraft sector (manned, fixed wing, combat) LM is the leader in high-performance combat aircraft (F-22 and F-35 programmes), Boeing leads in large support aircraft (C 17 and KC/RC-135 series of tankers and surveillance aircraft, both rarely being produced now), NG the third supplier of advanced combat aircraft (B-2) today is the leading prime for DoD's unmanned air combat vehicle developments. In armoured vehicles, General Dynamics (GD) produces the M1 tank and leads in the development of the Army's Future Combat Systems (FCS), which includes a number of new land combat vehicles and accounts for nearly 40 per cent of the Army's RDT&E budget[24]. GD has also acquired foreign manufacturers of armoured fighting vehicles to build a worldwide presence in this product market. BAE produces the US Army's standard armoured personnel carrier, the M2 and M3 Bradley. "*Like GD, BAE has sought to build a worldwide presence in armoured vehicles, but has had some acquisitions blocked by local governments (e.g., UK refused to permit BAE to buy Alvis, which had already acquired Vickers). Thus, a duopoly appears to exist in this segment of the defence industry, although a number of companies have teamed to bid for the lighter weight armour vehicles to protect soldiers from IEDs in Iraq*"[25]. In ship building NG, produces all Nimitz-class aircraft carriers, NG and GD share the production of nuclear submarines, NG leads the development of next-generation surface combatant, and GD leads in the development and production of large amphibious ships.

The relationships among defence firms and between the firms and the government, have also changed. Earlier some were prime platform builders, some subsystem providers, and some component providers. Further, platform builders had some sub-system businesses, but went to other firms for most sub-systems. The DOD dealt with the platform providers, although, since the 1960s, dealt more directly with the sub-system builders for standardising sub-systems across platforms. Also, the institution of Large System Integrators (LSI) introduced opportunities for non-platform builders' to be an interface between the government and other companies, although many LSI's were also platform builders. "*With the consolidation, the structure of defence firms and how they compete has become more complex. Now major firms are often LSIs, platform builders, sub-system providers, and component providers in various mixes...Moreover, because of the post-Cold War industry consolidations, these major firms are teamed or linked across many programs and seldom fully separated.* The futures of the firms are inter-twined in complex alliances, teams, and prime or supplier contracts"[26].

6.4 Sequestration

The Congress in 2011 drafted a legislation requiring its members to agree to a US $ 1.2 trillion in savings across federal government accounts over 10 years, otherwise an additional US $ 500 to 600 billion in cuts against the Pentagon's base budget would be triggered until 2021[27]. The DOD had already budgeted to reduce the planned defence funding by about US $ 487 billion over 10 years. The deficit reduction agreement has not yet been reached. The Democrats prefer not to cut funding for entitlement programmes while Republicans prefer not to increase taxes. Both sides are averse to sequestration. In case full sequestration does occur, the DOD's base budget funding would first be reduced to US $ 470 billion and then grow with the inflation thereafter, thus the defence spending would be down to that of FY 2007. In the US there is a likelihood that the defence budget will no longer continue to grow and see significant reductions as the elimination of the large annual supplemental (of US $ 100 billion) in the future[28].

6.5 Procurements and Acquisition Process

The US DOD procures goods and services from contractors, federal arsenals, and shipyards. Acquisition is a term applied to more than just purchase of an item or service; the acquisition process encompasses design, engineering, construction, testing, deployment, sustainment, and disposal of weapons or related items purchased from a contractor. As per the US statutory regulation, a weapon system from concept formulation to deployment goes through a three-step process of identifying a required (needed) weapon system, establishing a budget, and acquiring the system. The three steps are organised as Joint Capabilities Integration and Development System (JCIDS)—for identifying requirements; Planning, Programming, Budgeting, and Execution System (PPBE)—for allocating resources and budgeting and, Defence Acquisition System (DAS)—for developing and/or buying the item.

The DAS uses "milestones" to oversee and manage acquisition programmes. At each milestone, a programme must meet specific statutory and regulatory requirements before the program can proceed to the next phase of the acquisition process[29]. There are three milestones:

- Milestone A—initiates technology maturation and risk reduction.
- Milestone B—initiates engineering and manufacturing development.
- Milestone C—initiates production and deployment.

The US armed forces spending power is expected to fall from FY 07 to FY 17 as per the 'Vision Conference' held in the US in 2006. The US Army, Airforce and Naval spending during the period is expected to dip by US $ 34.4 billion, 14 billion and 12 billion respectively[30]. Further, as per UK MOD's Defence Industrial Strategy (DIS) published in December 2005, less than 10 per cent of US procurement funds were spent with foreign owned firms in 2005; 90 per cent was spent with US-owned companies; seven per cent with foreign-owned companies trading within the US; and just two per cent on imported goods and services. Thus, the 75-year-old "Buy America" legislation continues to hold good.

6.6 Indigenous Innovation and Technology Development Strategy

The capability of the US to build complex systems and system-of-systems is a source of long-term advantage over other nations. "*For example, there is no design handbook of practices to guide engineers and managers in developing such complex systems as Fire Control System (FCS), or in implementing Network Centric Warfare (NCW). These are in many ways first-of-a-kind systems, and engineers and managers must learn from trial-and-error experience. Indeed, the difficulties that DOD and companies have had in developing systems is complex—and the large-scale integration experience gained from doing so—are seen as barriers to matching US military capabilities*"[31]. After the American rout in Vietnam, all US military Services committed themselves to long-term investments to improve the considered competence of their war fighters. The "revolution in training affairs" during the 1970s and the 1980s produced more improvement in the fighting power of the US forces than did any other development between the Vietnam War in the late sixties and Operation Desert Storm in 1991.

In the twenty-first century, majority of the R&D, innovative ideas, engineering skills, and technologically advanced products are with the commercial establishments. R&D in the US has progressively moved from the government-funded enterprises to the commercial firms. In 1954, US federal government funded about 54 percent of R&D which in 2006 dropped to less than 28 per cent. Further, DOD currently accounts for about half of federal government's R&D[32]. As time goes on, DOD will tap technology and capabilities from all sources—foreign as well as domestic, commercial as well as of defence related. In future, due to fast technological obsolescence, long production runs of military products will reduce, including for major platforms. Historically, however, long production runs have been most reliable and the largest source of profitability for defence firms.

6.7 R&D

"*US annual commitment to R&D has been two and half per cent to three per cent of GDP since the 1940's. This has laid the foundation of US technological innovation. In addition, public and private research has performed complementary roles. These researches have diversified to meet social and commercial/civil market requirements. This has ensured a continuous R&D support. R&D funds in the US are available from four sources; the federal government, industry, academia and non-profit organisations*"[33]. "*All these sources also perform R&D. Additional funding is available to academia from the state and local governments. R&D is also performed by government owned Federally Funded R&D Centres (FFRDCs), some of which are contracted to be operated by industrial firms, research institutes (of the non-profit kind) or universities*[34].

The RDT&E investments from 1940's to FY 2007 have gradually increased to 42 per cent of DOD's cumulative procurement spending implying, the government's intent to increasingly invest in technology[35]. The years 1948 to 1960 saw America establishing its first large-scale peacetime military force. Further, there was a need to increase defence spending commensurate to the requirement generated by the Cold War and the Korean War. This led to the development of a large defence industry post-World War II. Also, investments in R&D and procurement occurred with the increase in defence budgets. These developments led to the entry of the private companies in the defence sector. New technology systems were tested by prototyping, procuring and laboratory level work. From 1948-60 RDT&E saw an average annual growth rate of over 18 percent while procurement increased only by eight per cent[36]. The government persisted with its pre-

World War II practice of migrating more and more production of weapons and systems from the government-owned and operated facilities to the commercial suppliers (private firms). From 1952 to 1960, the high defence spending of nine per cent to 13 per cent of US GDP saw the defence industry correspondingly invest in R&D. In 1960, the government funded 58 per cent of the nation's industrial R&D. Also, the defence industry became the biggest industrial sector of the US economy, exceeding automobiles, steel and oil. Defence R&D regularly focused on new hardware and systems while the majority of R&D in commercial firms was for product improvements. Private-sector technology investments increased post 1960 at such a rate that it eventually exceeded the government's levels in the 1970's.

The RDT&E programme in FY 2015 is to grow to around US $ 65.2 billion (that is about 11.3 per cent of the defence budget)[37]. The total RDT&E budget at the DOD had earlier increased substantially after the September 11, 2001 attack (from 2001-11), exceeding the US $ 80 billion mark. (Figure 6.3) The trend reflected a new focus on national security in the last decade, as defence R&D spending till 2012 was more than twice of what it was in the early 1980s (low point) and more than 25 per cent than at the end of the Cold War that is 1986-87 (high point). Over 80 per cent of this goes towards the development or demonstration of specific military systems and components (called Weapon Development Activities - WDA's)[38]. The balance 20 per cent goes to primary R&D in sciences and technologies which are identified as vital for developing improved military capabilities and operations (called Science and Technology (S&T) activities).

Figure 6.3: Total DOD's RDT&E Budget Increase Post 9/11

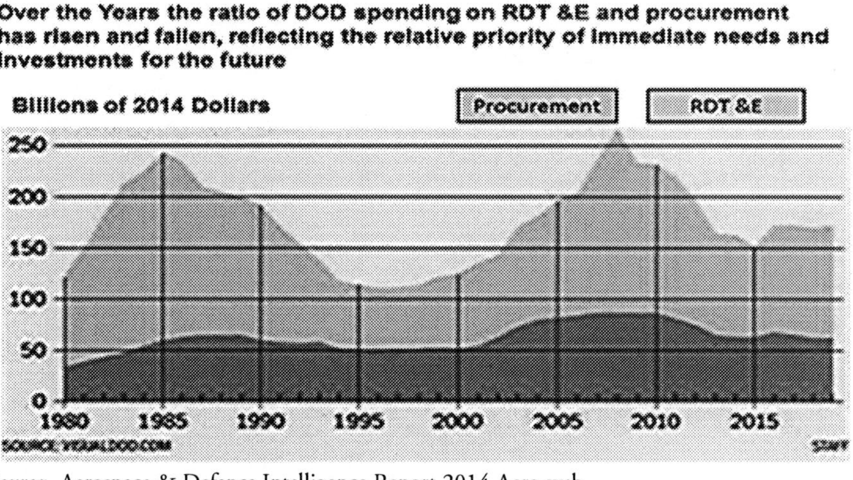

Source: Aerospace & Defence Intelligence Report 2014 Aero-web.

As per the Strategic Guidance 2014, the foundation of DOD's technological strength is its wide-ranging Research and Engineering (R&E) Enterprise which comprises of the military departments and their laboratories, all other DOD R&D product centres and laboratories, defence agencies as Defence Advanced Research Projects Agency (DARPA), Defence Threat Reduction Agency (DTRA), and the Missile Defence Agency (MDA), federal government laboratories, FFRDCs, university affiliated research centres, US and allied universities labs, US allied and partner government laboratories, and the US industrial base. Irrespective of the fiscal environment, the delivery of advanced technology remains a high priority, and requires the efforts of all the partners mentioned above.

"*DOD's Defence Technical Information Centre (DTIC) serves the DOD community as the largest central resource for DOD and government-funded scientific, technical, engineering, and business related information. DTIC and its Information Analysis Centres (IACs) are research and analysis organisations established by DOD to support researchers, scientists, engineers, and programme managers. With a broad imprint, DTIC allows the DOD to reduce duplication and build on previous research, development, and operational experience.*"[39]

"*DARPA is a non-hierarchical organisation whose primary role is to oversee creative research in short programmes that typically run for four to six years. Its role is to sponsor revolutionary, high-payoff research bridging the gap between fundamental discoveries and their military use.*" DARPA has six technology programme offices with about 140 programme managers and a small support staff totalling to a workforce of around 250 personnel. It has an investment strategy in which programme managers define the programmes that might lead to a revolutionary change. DARPA's overall objectives are to "demonstrate breakthrough capabilities for national security" and "catalyse a differentiated and highly capable US technology base." For this, DARPA solicits and reviews proposals with the military services and awards grants for basic and applied research with the most innovative potential.

DARPA serves as a catalyst for developing disruptive capabilities, with support from the upper echelon of the defence acquisition community. The DARPA-run programmes have the ability to reach into various sectors of industry by funding and the creation of new ideas—although some programmes can quickly become classified or 'black' because of the high pay-offs to the military. DARPA's success rests largely in its ability to steer high payoff research and convert new concepts and technology break-through to military programmes. Consequently, DARPA has been successful in several radical innovations including in the areas of stealth, internet, Global Positioning System (GPS) and Unmanned Aerial Vehicles (UAV). However, it does not have any of its own R&D labs. Rather, it identifies talent and ideas from the industry, academia, government laboratories and individuals, and awards R&D contracts that are to be executed. "DARPA's role is thus limited only to identify and shortlist projects and manage the programme"[40]. The private-sector defence industry is further supplemented by an extensive government funded defence R&D community.

A methodology that can be adopted to comprehend the performance required from a system is to "repeatedly experiment" with extensive user feed-back on prototypes—which will then evolve the "firm requirements "for the development of the first "block" of the system. "*Then, all weapons developments should utilise true "spiral development"—with a five year cycle for each block (from the time of commitment to system development, to its initial operational capability). This requires that each block of the system (beginning with block one) to utilise only fully-proven technologies; but that R&D is being funded, in parallel, for subsequent blocks. Thus, once the new technology is proven, it can be phased in to the next block. It is important that when properly implemented, such 'spiral development' will not only get higher-performance equipment more rapidly but (on an average) effect a savings of approximately 30 percent—and with much lower risk*"[41].

To encourage defence firms to continue to do more innovation, DOD plans to re-establish an allowable overhead expense for company-initiated Independent Research and Development (IR&D). "*This prior practice had deteriorated, because of a Congressional legislation that allowed a mixing of IR&D with Bid and Proposal (B&P) expenses. This encouraged companies to devote all of their resources to trying to win the next proposal (through elaborate B&P efforts) and ignore the longer term IR&D efforts. Returning to this separation of IR&D from B&P, and providing government visibility into the companies IR&D efforts, should stimulate the firms to focus on the importance of staying ahead*"[42].

6.8 Exports and Markets

US traditional arms-export policy envisages arms exports should not undermine long-term security and stability, weaken democratic movements, support military coups, escalate arms races, exacerbate ongoing conflicts, cause arms build-up in unstable regions, or be used to commit human rights abuses[43]. Post-9/11 the decisions on arms exports often gave precedence to other considerations of support for the US for combating terrorism or the wars in Afghanistan and Iraq. Consequently, during the period 2001-05 the total US arms sale to 25 countries that provided strategic services to the US were four-times higher than five years prior to 2001 and the countries received 18-times more US military assistance than during the previous five-year period. Such increase in arms sales were partly due to the lifting of sanctions by the US post-9/11 against countries like India, Pakistan, Armenia, Azerbaijan and Tajikistan.

US defence exports for the period 2010-14 accounted for about 31 per cent of the global arms exports market share[44]. The US Foreign Military Sales (FMS) reached US $ 31.2 billion in FY14 (i.e. ending September 30), and with additional exports handled through other mechanisms, the total sales announced by the Defence Security Cooperation Agency (DSCA) reached US $ 34.2 billion[45]. That's slightly above the previous years although back in FY 06 the US accounted for close to US $ 39.8 billion including FMS (government to government) and commercial sales (company to government). This was about 60 per cent of the global market share in 2006[46]. The global economic downturn has had a continuing negative effect on US defence exports and markets, though continuing global conflict, instability and competition for natural resources enable continuing demand for defence products although on a reduced scale.

6.9 Privatisation

The two wars in Afghanistan from 2001 and in Iraq from 2003 required a substantial increase in US defence spending which in turn led to a rapid increase in the outsourcing of the military functions to the private industry. Between FY 2000 and FY 2006 DOD contracts to the private industry increased from US $ 133 billion to 295 billion[47]. This attracted non-defence US companies who wanted access to the US defence markets through acquisition of defence companies located in the US. While the trend for privatisation and outsourcing of military services began in right earnest at the end of the Cold War, it was reinforced during the war in Iraq. During this period not only did the service specialised companies grow rapidly but also the more traditional defence companies were providing increasing number of military services.

6.10 Major Reforms Programmes

As per former US Defence Secretary Robert Gates who continued under the Obama Administration in 2009, there is no straight solution for a sweeping reform of Pentagon's weapons acquisition process and a number of steps are needed to be taken. These include avoiding inefficient extension of acquisition programmes which lead to cost over-runs; purchase weapon systems at efficient rates to promote economies of scales; focus buying larger quantities of 75 per cent solution systems than small quantities of 99 per cent solutions; choose future-oriented weapon system acquisition programmes to avoid redundancy; freeze requirements once contracts awarded to prevent cost hikes; encourage competition and prototyping between companies before contract is awarded and increase the size and quality of Pentagon's acquisition team[48].

The last US 'Weapon Systems Acquisition Reform Act of 2009' focused on improving the early stages of weapon system development and included certain Key provisions in the act pertaining to the appointment of a number of new functionaries as an Independent Director of Cost Assessment and Programme Evaluation (CAPE); a Director of Developmental Test and Evaluation; a Director of Systems Engineering; the requirement that the Director of Defence Research and Engineering periodically assess technological maturity of Major Defence Acquisition Programmes (MDAPs) and annually report findings to the Congress; and a requirement that combatant commanders have more influence in the joint military requirements generation process[49]. The policy reforms require greater consideration for trade-offs between system cost, time schedule and performance, besides assessing the products design prior to giving approval. The act hardens the 1982 Nunn-McCurdy law, which mandates that programmes be reviewed if they exhibit cost over-runs of 15 per cent and abandoned if cost over-runs reach 25 per cent unless essential to National security and no alternatives are available[50].

Prior to this the reform efforts that altered the process by which DOD procures goods and services included "*creating the Federal Acquisition Regulation (FAR) to develop uniform acquisition regulations across DOD and the federal government; establishing Defence Acquisition University to train and improve the performance of the acquisition workforce; instituting a streamlined management chain (Programme Manager, Programme Executive Office, Service Acquisition Executive, Under Secretary of Defence) to foster accountability and authority; implementing a milestone decision process to improve oversight; requiring independent cost estimates to improve budget forecasting; establishing a joint requirements board to improve requirements development and eliminate duplicative programs; moving away from the use of customised military standards and specifications to increased use of commercial technologies; and using multi-year procurements (with congressional approval) to lower costs*"[51].

6.11 Foreign Investments

The consolidation of the prime contractors in the US is now exhausted and nearly complete. The strategy of US defence industry is next to expand abroad through expansions or mergers with larger European companies—a step which is beyond the adhoc JV's and collaborations that were earlier evident. A number of US firms have accordingly invested across the Atlantic in Switzerland, Spain, Austria and Europe. US firms have also acquired foreign firms, established foreign subsidiaries and engaged in industrial participation programmes overseas in search for new markets leading to US defence industrial capabilities enmeshing in the global supply chain. For majority of the US acquisitions in Europe, the target has been a UK company (eight out of 17 European companies acquired in 2006-07 were based in the UK). This is because UK is Europe's largest defence market and the most open (32 per cent procurement funds are spent with foreign owned organisations and UK encourages foreign investment in the sector)[52].

US super primes are also moving into India which was forecasted to have an annual market of US $ 30 billion in 2012 with a number of deals on the horizon. LM has opened a subsidiary in New Delhi while Boeing planned a JV with Tata to produce parts for military aerospace sector. Raytheon signed with Precision Electronics Limited (PEL) in 2008 to jointly develop communications technology for the Indian military forces.

6.12 Lessons for India

The US $ 4.1 billion agreement to provide 10 Boeing C-17 Globe master III airlifters to India attracted a significant offset package wherein Boeing agreed to invest US $ 1.23 billion—30 per cent of contract value—in offset benefits which included establishing a high–altitude engine test facility[53]. Offsets are being applied by a combination of local suppliers and government controlled contractors for Boeing's supplier's works like wind tunnels etc. The Indian Air Force (IAF) plans to purchase additional six to 10 C-17's.

More countries are moving away from pure offset deals to long term partnerships and industrial footprint deals while many are shifting their non-defence focus into homeland security and counter terrorism, civil IT, services and air traffic management.

US on a number of occasions has not permitted the TOT of US equipment on board aircrafts, ships and land systems to former friendly countries or imposed military sales embargo on belligerent countries or nations displaying antagonism towards Washington.

The fast technological changes in the informational, biological and nanotechnology arenas are bound to have a profound impact on military operations and the warfighting equipment and, will eventually require a more responsive defence industry to keep up with the changes. In contrast to today's defence acquisition cycles of 15 to 20 years the technological cycles in the future will have to be measured in months and consequently most advanced critical technologies will be available globally as most of the commercial firms are now globalised[54]. The future weapons and defence systems needs that the defence industry will be required to fulfil is extremely difficult to predict as a result of the greatly uncertain security environment. The technologies and products coming from the defence industry in the next few years will be very different and will include emphasis on intelligence, unmanned systems, systems engineering, Advanced Information Systems (AIS) etc. This suggests a move away from the platform centric thinking to a much more network centric thinking—in terms of a system of systems thinking (with large number of sensors and shooters integrated with secure command, control and communication systems).

In a monopoly environment there is little incentive for achieving either lower cost or higher performance. Thus, it is important DOD undertakes "best value" competitions (i.e. competitions not based on the lowest cost or the maximum performance, but on the combination of these variables viz on a L1P1 criterion). The primary objective must be to achieve innovation and costs savings—at both the prime and the lower-tier elements. "*It is not necessary to have two firms in production at all times to maintain a competitive industry in every sector of the defence area. Rather, it is necessary to have at least two design teams in all critical areas, and to have each of them at least going through funded prototyping—so that they are addressing not only technical feasibility, but also affordability, productibility, and supportability. On the other hand, if quantities are sufficient, it makes sense to have continuous production competition (such as was held for the engines on the F-15 and F-16—where the presence of continuous production competition yielded higher performance and higher reliability, yet with significant cost reductions). Competition should not be a firm requirement—beyond the competitive prototype phase, where it always should be utilised—rather, as long as the current producer is continuously improving performance and lowering costs, they should be rewarded by a continuation of their contract. However, it is essential that a credible option must always be present. An inexpensive way to maintain this option (and to encourage continuous innovation) is to fund a second source for interchangeable, yet next generation, lower cost/higher performance prototypes (at either the system or subsystem level)*"[55].

For DOD to compete with the industry for the "best talent" there have to be revisions to the salary policies. "*The current 'pay for performance' initiatives are in the right direction, but further steps are required as increasing starting pay for engineers to compete with industry. In addition, DOD must develop, and implement, a personnel training and career development programme for the government civilian workforce; one that is comparable to the military programme (where funds, time, and additional positions, are allocated to provide for training and development). Another step that will be necessary due to the retirement of the senior people within the DOD acquisition core—is to increase the rotation from industry to government (and visa-versa). Additionally, for all functions which are not inherently governmental (many of which are currently being done by either civilian or military government personnel) should be subjected to 'competitive sourcing'—between the public and private sectors. This on an average can bring down the costs by over 30 per cent—no matter who wins (public or private sector)—while the performance can go up significantly (since the 'measurement' of performance now becomes an important consideration)*"[56].

NOTES

1. Watts Barry D. "*Strategy for the Long Haul: The US Defence Industrial Base Past, Present and Future*" p.12 available at www. dtic.mil/cgi-bin/GetTRDoc?AD=ADA490689 (Accessed September 01, 2015).
2. Jeffrey A. Drezner, Giles K. Smith, Lucille E. Hogan, Curt Rogers, and Rachel Schmidt, "*Maintaining Future Military Aircraft Design Capability*" (Santa Monica: CA: RAND, 1992), p. 28. available at http://www.rand.org/content/dam/rand/pubs/ reports/ 2006/R4199.pdf (Accessed September 03, 2015).
3. Scherer Fredric M. and Peck Merton J, "*The Weapons Acquisition Process: An Economic Analysis*", p. 98 available at http://www.amazon.com/Weapons-Acquisition-Process-Economic-Analysis/dp/0875840256. (Accessed September 03, 2015).
4. Watts Barry D., "*Strategy for the Long Haul: The US Defence Industrial Base Past, Present and Future*", p. 14 available at www.dtic.mil/cgi-bin/GetTRDoc?AD=ADA490689, (Accessed September 04, 2015).
5. Scherer Fredric M. and Peck Merton J, "*The Weapons Acquisition Process: An Economic Analysis*", pp. 99–107, 214–215. available at http://www.amazon.com/Weapons-Acquisition-Process-Economic-Analysis/dp/0875840256. (Accessed September 04, 2015).
6. Watts Barry D. "*Strategy for the Long Haul : The US Defence Industrial Base Past, Present and Future*" p.12 available at www.dtic.mil/cgi-bin/GetTRDoc?AD=ADA490689 (Accessed September 04, 2015).

7. Scherer Fredric M. and Peck Merton J, "*The Weapons Acquisition Process: An Economic Analysis*", pp.68–78, 85–95, 218–219 available at http://www.amazon.com/Weapons-Acquisition-Process-Economic-Analysis/dp/0875840256. (Accessed September 07, 2015).
8. Scherer Fredric M. and Peck Merton J, "*The Weapons Acquisition Process: An Economic Analysis*", pp. 19-45 available at http ://www.amazon.com/Weapons-Acquisition-Process-Economic-Analysis/dp/0875840256. (Accessed September 07, 2015)..
9. Scherer Fredric M. and Peck Merton J, "*The Weapons Acquisition Process: An Economic Analysis*", pp. 214-215 available at http://www.amazon.com/Weapons-Acquisition-Process-Economic-Analysis/dp/0875840256. (Accessed September 08, 2015).
10. Elisabeth Skons "*The US Defence Industry after the Cold War*" p.237 of a handbook "*The Global Arms Trade*" edited by Andrew T.H.Tan available at https://www.routledge.com/products/9781857437973 (Accessed September 09, 2015).
11. Watts Barry D. "*Strategy for the Long Haul : The US Defence Industrial Base Past, Present and Future*" p.2 available at www. dtic.mil/cgi-bin/GetTRDoc?AD=ADA490689 (Accessed September 10, 2015).
12. Elisabeth Skons "*The US Defence Industry after the Cold War*", p.235 of a handbook "*The Global Arms Trade*" edited by Andrew T.H.Tan available at https://www.routledge.com/products/9781857437973 (Accessed September 11, 2015).
13. Watts Barry D. "*Strategy for the Long Haul : The US Defence Industrial Base Past, Present and Future*" p.27 available at www.dtic.mil/cgi-bin/GetTRDoc?AD=ADA490689 (Accessed September 14, 2015).
14. Defence Conversion Commission (DCC), *Adjusting to Drawdown*, Washington, DC, December 1992, pp. 18 and 23-24. available at http://babel.hathitrust.org/cgi/pt?id=coo.31924062290501;view=1up;seq=18 (Accessed September 14, 2015).
15. Gansler Jacques S., "*US Defence Industrial Policy*", p.1 available at http://www.securitychallenges.org.au/ArticlePDFs/ vol3 no2Gansler.pdf (Accessed September 15, 2015).
16. Watts Barry D. "*Strategy for the Long Haul:The US Defence Industrial Base Past, Present and Future*" p.ix available at www.dtic.mil/cgi-bin/GetTRDoc?AD=ADA490689 (Accessed September 16, 2015).
17. Watts Barry D. "*Strategy for the Long Haul:The US Defence Industrial Base Past, Present and Future*" p.32 available at www.dtic.mil/cgi-bin/GetTRDoc?AD=ADA490689 (Accessed September 17, 2015).
18. Peter J. Dombrowski, Eugene Gholz, and Andrew L. Ross, *Military Transformation and the defence Industry after Next: The defence Industrial Implications of Network-Centric Warfare* (Newport, RI: Naval War College, Newport Paper Number 18, 2002, p. 25. available at https://www.usnwc.edu/Publications/Naval-War-College-Press/-Newport-Papers/Documents/18-pdf.aspx (Accessed September 18, 2015).
19. Watts Barry D. "*Strategy for the Long Haul:The US Defence Industrial Base Past, Present and Future*", p.35 available at www.dtic.mil/cgi-bin/GetTRDoc?AD=ADA490689 (Accessed September 21, 2015).
20. Watts Barry D. "*Strategy for the Long Haul:The US Defence Industrial Base Past, Present and Future*", p.29 Centre for Strategic and Budgetary Assessments Strategy for the Long Haul available at www.dtic.mil/cgi-bin/GetTRDoc?AD=ADA490689 (Accessed September 22, 2015).
21. IHS Jane's World Defence Industry 2013 p.559.
22. IHS Jane's World Defence Industry 2013, p.559.

23. "*U.S. DOD Defence Spending & Procurement I FY 2014-15*", p. 2 available at http://www.bga-aeroweb.com/Defence-Spending. html, (Accessed September 23, 2015).
24. IHS Jane's World Defence Industry 2013 p.558.
25. Watts Barry D. "*Strategy for the Long Haul:The US Defence Industrial Base Past, Present and Future*" p.37 available at www.dtic.mil/cgi-bin/GetTRDoc?AD=ADA490689 (Accessed September 24, 2015).
26. Watts Barry D. "*Strategy for the Long Haul:The US Defence Industrial Base Past, Present and Future*" pp.40-41 available at www.dtic.mil/cgi-bin/GetTRDoc?AD=ADA490689 (Accessed September 24, 2015).
27. IHS Jane's World Defence Industry 2013 p.559.
28. Gansler Jacques S., "*US Defence Industrial Policy*", p.3 available at http://www.securitychallenges.org.au/ ArticlePDFs/3(2) Gansler.pdf (Accessed September 24, 2015).
29. Moshe Schwartz, "*Defence Acquisitions: How DOD Acquires Weapon Systems* "Congressional Research Service Report May 23, 2014 available at https://www.fas.org/sgp/crs/natsec/RL34026.pdf (Accessed September 29, 2015).
30. IHS Jane's World Defence Industry 2013, p. 562.
31. Watts Barry D. "*Strategy for the Long Haul: The US Defence Industrial Base Past, Present and Future*", p.37 available at www.dtic.mil/cgi-bin/GetTRDoc?AD=ADA490689 (Accessed September 30, 2015).
32. National Science Board (NSB), *Science and Engineering Indicators 2008* (Arlington, VA: National Science Foundation, January 2008) NSB 08-01A, p. O-22 and data table O-33b, "National R&D by funding sector: 1953–2006." available at http: //www.nsf.gov/statistics/seind08/ (Accessed September 30, 2015).
33. "2014 *R&D Magazine*Global Funding Forecast", December 2013, p.8 available at http://www.battelle.org/docs/tpp/2014 _global_rd_funding_forecast.pdf , (Accessed September 30, 2015).
34. Ranjit Ghosh, "*Defence Research and Development: International Approaches For Analysing the Indian Programme*" p.11 available at http://www.idsa.in/occasionalpapers/OP_DefenceResearchandDevelopmen_RanjitGhosh_140815.html (Accessed October 01, 2015).
35. Watts Barry D., "*The US Defence Industrial Base Past, Present and Future*" available at www.dtic.mil/cgi-bin/GetTRDoc? AD=ADA490689 (Accessed October 01, 2015).
36. Watts Barry D., "*The US Defence Industrial Base Past, Present and Future*" available at www.dtic.mil/cgi-bin/Get TRDoc? AD=ADA490689, (Accessed October 01, 2015).
37. "*U.S.DOD Defence Spending & Procurement I FY 2014-15*", p. 4 available at http://www.bga-aeroweb.com/Defense-Spend ing.html (Accessed October 01, 2015).
38. "*IB10022: Defence Research: DOD's Research, Development, Test and Evaluation Programme*", p. 2, John D. Moteff, Resources, Science and Industry Division available at http://digital.library.unt.edu/ark:/67531/ metacrs939/m1/1/highresd/ IB 10022.html, (Accessed October 01, 2015).
39. Ranjit Ghosh "*Defence Research and Development: International Approaches For Analysing the Indian Programme*" p.19- available at http://www.idsa.in/occasionalpapers/OP_DefenceResearchandDevelopmen_RanjitGhosh_140815.html (Accessed October 05, 2015).
40. Ranjit Ghosh, "*Defence Research and Development: International Approaches For Analysing the Indian Programme*" pp.27-28 - available at http://www.idsa.in/occasionalpapers/

OP_DefenceResearchandDevelopmen_RanjitGhosh_140815.html (Accessed October 05, 2015).

41. Gansler Jacques S."*US Defence Industrial Policy*", p.8 available at http://www.securitychallenges.org.au/Article PDFs/vol3no2 Gansler.pdf (Accessed October 05, 2015).
42. Gansler Jacques S."*US Defence Industrial Policy*", p.9 available at http://www.securitychallenges.org.au/ArticlePDFs/vol3no2 Gansler.pdf (Accessed October 06, 2015).
43. Elisabeth Skons, "*The US Defence Industry after the Cold War*", p.246 of a handbook "*The Global Arms Trade*" edited by Andrew T.H.Tan available at https://www.routledge.com/products/9781857437973 (Accessed October 06,2015).
44. "*The United States leads upward trend in arms exports, Asian and Gulf states arms imports up*", *SIPRI* March 16,, 2015 available at http://www.sipri.org/media/pressreleases/2015/at-march-2015 (Accessed October 06,2015).
45. "*Russian, US 2014 Armament Exports* "*Defence Industry Daily*, October 28, 2014 available at http://www.defenceindustrydaily.com/american-russian-defense-exports-2014-028119/ (Accessed October 07, 2015)
46. IHS Jane's World Defence Industry 2013, p.561.
47. Elisabeth Skons "*The US Defence Industry after the Cold War*", p.242 of a handbook "*The Global Arms Trade*" edited by Andrew T.H.Tan available at https://www.routledge.com/products/9781857437973 (Accessed October 07, 2015)
48. IHS Jane's World Defence Industry 2013 p.563.
49. Moshe Schwartz, "*Defence Acquisitions: How DOD Acquires Weapon Systems*", p.6 Congressional Research Service Report May 23, 2014 available at https://www.fas.org/sgp/crs/natsec/RL34026.pdf (Accessed October 08, 2015).
50. IHS Jane's World Defence Industry 2013 p. 564.
51. Moshe Schwartz, "*Defence Acquisitions: How DOD Acquires Weapon Systems*", p.4, Congressional Research Service Report May 23, 2014 available at https://www.fas.org/sgp/crs/natsec/RL34026.pdf (Accessed October 08, 2015).
52. IHS Jane's World Defence Industry 2013, p. 560.
53. IHS Jane's World Defence Industry 2013, p. 561.
54. Gansler Jacques S., "*US Defence Industrial Policy*", p.3 available at http://www.securitychallenges.org.au/ArticlePDFs/vol3no2Gansler.pdf (Accessed October 08, 2015).
55. Gansler Jacques S., "*US Defence Industrial Policy*", pp.10-11 available a thttp://www.securitychallenges.org.au/ArticlePDFs/ vol3no2Gansler.pdf (Accessed October 08, 2015).
56. Gansler Jacques S., "*US Defence Industrial Policy*", p.12 available at http://www.securitychallenges .org.au/ArticlePDFs/ vol3 no2Gansler.pdf (Accessed October 08, 2015).

CHAPTER 7

Re-modeling Indian Defence Industry Apparatus for Accelerating Indigenisation, Self-Sufficiency and Strategic Capability

7.1 Introduction

It was brought out in the Introductory chapter that the best way to re-model the Indian DITB is probably to first carry out a study of the state of defence Industrialisation in India. This could be followed by analysing the defence industrialisation process that was adopted by the militarily developed and developing nations for driving indigenisation, with a view to adapt their best processes and practices to the Indian defence industry apparatus. The analysis was carried out in the next four chapters of the book wherein, the third and fourth chapters reviewed the fast-upcoming defence industries of Israel and South Korea to draw important takeaways for India while the fifth and sixth chapters analysed the international practices adopted by the defence industry of the top two leading military nations i.e. the US and China. The analysis brought out valuable defence industry experiences and vital lessons for the Indian defence planners. It also revealed that there is a requirement to re-assess, re-align & re-model the Indian defence industry apparatus in line with our vision of accelerating indigenisation, self-sufficiency and building the requisite strategic capability as pertaining to military systems. The book in its last chapter looks at three plausible options for remodeling the Indian programme, discusses in detail the most pragmatic and feasible model, recommends the way ahead for India before finally, suggesting an action plan for *MAKE IN INDIA* in the Defence Sector.

7.2 Options Available For Re-modeling the Indian DITB

The approaches that were adopted in the defence industrialisation process of the four countries studied earlier, reveal three plausible options that can be adopted for re-modeling the Indian DITB. These are discussed next.

7.2.1 The De-Novo Approach

De-novo in Latin means 'starting from the beginning' or 'anew' or 'afresh'. This approach is suggested in the backdrop of the developments in information and communication technologies that are being exploited by all nations to bring in changes in warfare and new concepts of Revolution in Military Affairs (RMA), Information-Based Warfare (IBW) and Network-Centric Operations (NCO). This in turn has led to transforming the demand from traditional defence industry sectors producing weapon platforms to sectors producing a range of technologies and systems required for advanced C4ISR capabilities and towards those companies to integrate inter-connected and inter-communicative systems. Further, there is a shift in technological innovation and technological lead from the military to the civilian sector resulting in exploiting Commercially Off The Shelf (COTS) developed technology for ruggedised Military OffThe Shelf (MOTS) applications (often referred to as 'spin-ins' or 'spin-ons') than the erstwhile 'spin-offs process of exploiting military technology for commercial applications.

In fact, the very same factors led to the post-Cold War restructuring of the US DIB, in 2006, the ROK implementing a DRP - 2020', in mid-2000 China introducing two major ongoing reforms programmes of 'restructuring through share-holding reforms' and 'capability building of DIB through CMI strategy where, defence enterprises manufacture commercial products' and lastly, Israel too, focusing on high technology systems and subsystems, and, their integration and upgrades to existing platforms besides the development and manufacture of unmanned systems.

These approaches hope to achieve a significant reduction in the size of the armed forces, intend equipping them with the state-of-the-art weapon systems that would provide qualitative improvements and enhance operational capabilities for the conduct of future network-centric and joint warfare operations. Accordingly, under the DRP - 2020, South Korea is to acquire new destroyers, submarines, fighter aircrafts and missile defence systems, to be sourced preferably through indigenous development and production. "*The ROK military thus expects to deploy its first units of next-generation MBTs, fighter aircraft, multiple-rocket launchers, surface-to-air missile systems, submarines and naval surface combatants within the set time frame of the defence reform plan*"[1].

In the RMA debate, the Indian defence analysts too have reiterated this requirement. One of the publications paper in 2008 had stated that "*Organisational structures for conventional wars/limited conflicts under nuclear over hang already exist but they need to be remodeled, reequipped & reoriented to conduct joint/integrated battles in digitised battle space and to have the necessary flexibility to undertake other types of operations which lie at the lower end of the spectrum of conflict, at short notice*"[2].

In the Indian context adopting this approach in its entirety (downsizing and simultaneously equipping the armed forces with all new RMA weapon platforms and systems) may be cost prohibitive today. Its implementation would affect the budget process, requirements process, acquisition process, and the organisations and management processes throughout the MOD. Although the Indian Armed Forces since the late 1990's have been advocating RMA, IBW and NCO, the conversion process towards these concepts have moved at a slow pace and in a piece meal manner. Thus, at this stage, the De-novo approach as a comprehensive option can only be a long term strategy.

7.2.2 The Optimisation Approach

Since, the Indian Government ever since Independence has conscientiously built up capabilities in defence R&D, OF's and DPSU's to provide the armed forces the equipment, armament, ammunition, weapons platforms and systems and similarly, constantly equipped the in-house MRO facilities of the Base Workshops of the Army, the Base Repair Depots of Air Force and the Dockyards of the Navy, it would only be prudent that these are not wasted out but re-oriented to optimise their efficiency and productivity levels. Such organisations, by all militarily developed nations are considered to be strategic military assets and thus nurtured and preserved. There is no reason as to why India should not consider them to be so. This is because such establishments over a period of time, due to the continuous government support tend to develop distinct capabilities in niche areas and become domain experts and centres of excellence in their respective arenas. They also become the repositories of knowledge and develop assets that need to be sustained and preserved.

The requirement then is that all such resources be suitably re-oriented and re-structured, through a well-directed strategy to address the numerous current problems of the indigenous defence industry. This calls for a far-sighted vision, a coherent strategy, streamlining organisational structures, the policy framework and guidelines. Thereafter, undertaking detailed planning, precise programming, accurate forecasting, budgeting and, working out the mechanics and modalities of execution. Implementation would involve making available the necessary resources in terms of the financial investments, incentives to raise loans, developing/acquiring the required technologies and facilitating the technical assistance, where required. A host of other issues would involve ease of doing business and, above all an integrated approach to achieve this. Notwithstanding, in case this option is to be adopted in a stand-alone mode, it could best be a short term approach or strategy as it will be unable meet the long term requirements of the Armed Forces.

7.2.3 The Simultaneous Two Pronged Combination Approach

As the name suggests, the approach will adopt a combination of the long-term de-novo plan and the short-term optimisation plan for India's DITB. This is the preferred option because if India's military-industrial acumen is to match the size of the US along with China by 2045, we need to take giant strides to bridge the gap. Further, the likely "*changes in the requirements of future warfare will need defence planners to (be dynamic and) focus on a broad range of research, development and acquisition activities, including force planning and re-structuring, articulation of requirements, integration of advanced technologies and systems, and changes in the defence budgets that in turn may change acquisition processes*"[3]. Conceptually, this approach would be analogous to parts of both, ROK's plan of DRP-2020 and China's long term and short term innovation development strategies.

The ROK's DRP-2020 envisages a reduction in force levels; mandates the acquisition of indigenously developed RMA-related military assets; shifts the administrative control over the force improvement budget and acquisition process to civil servants at the DAPA; reduces ADD's dominance in defence R&D sector by DAPA delegating defence R&D activities to contractors; the government designates defence contracts and contractors then by law are entitled benefits and subsidies ; once a contract is awarded the government provides guarantees that it will procure the products once manufactured and assembled[4]. Thus, defence industry enjoys major incentives to maintain production, as the supply and demand process is institutionally guaranteed by the Korean Government. For joint operation assets as C4IRS, the software is mostly acquired through domestic R&D, while the hardware as AWACS and high altitude UAVs were purchased from abroad.

China's strategic objective for its DIB since 1995, has been benchmarked in its defence White Paper(s). These have been released bi-annually since 1998, less the latest paper of 2015. These papers bring out China's defence planners intent to achieve the capability to develop and produce advanced military systems on par with those of major industrialised nations by 2020. The defence White Paper published in 2013 states the expectations out of its indigenous DIB. It states China's armed forces are looking for military preparedness for winning local wars under conditions of informationisation meaning, high intensity, information centric, regional military conflict of short duration, for which the PLA would work to strengthen the development of new and high-tech weaponry and equipment to build a modern military force structure with Chinese characteristics[5].

China's short term "good enough" approach is to produce large quantities of military systems that are the low-end cheaper version(s) of foreign products, whose quality and performance are inferior but meet the needs of the PLA. The long-term 'gold-plated' approach is to develop high-end, high-cost, sophisticated weapons that match those of the advanced nations. This is a long-term strategy, as Chinese defence industry is building scientific and technological capabilities to execute higher-end innovation.

7.3 Remodeling Indian Defence Industry Apparatus

Apparently, the sole reason for a sub-optimal Indian DITB seems to be the absence of a unified integrated approach of stake holders comprising of the User (primarily the three Services), Developer (R&D organisations), Production Agencies (Public/Private sector enterprises), Bureaucracy (those formulating and implementing policies and procedures pertaining to defence acquisition, procurement procedures for direct purchase and development projects, TOT, private sector participation, industrial licensing, FDI, JV's, offsets, taxation regimes, defence indigenisation and export strategies, long term product support, strategic partnerships with OEMs for sustenance and maintenance management that can bring down the overall life cycle costs, PBL, Public Private Partnership (PPP), and so on) and lastly the Political Leadership (enunciating the National vision and security strategy, military operational directive, approving defence capability planning, programming and budgeting to maintain specified operational readiness level of weapon platforms and systems and so on). All these actions need to be directed in unison for achieving a pragmatic and feasible model for a successful indigenous DITB. As brought out earlier in Chapter II, the growth of a country's DITB is the direct consequence of its Armed Forces defence capability plans which by themselves stem from the National security imperatives.

7.3.1 National Security and Military Capability Development

In order to facilitate defence planning, most developed countries like the US, China, Australia, Canada, UK and France have the concept of preparing a number of security documents like the NSS, Defence Planning Guidance (DPG), Defence Capability Plan (DCP), defence white/green papers etc. The findings of these are shared with their legislatures and citizens. The portion for general public is made available in the open domain while the classified portion of the plan(s) retained as an Annexure. The Parliaments of these countries are thus kept apprised about how their government would go about meeting the security challenges and what outcomes might be expected.

7.3.2 Defence Planning in India

In the Indian context "*The National Security Council (NSC) has been in existence since 1999. Yet, the government has not put out an official document outlining a NSS (document) for India*"[6]. This document is essential to achieve consensus of all political parties on national security issues and thus provide the inputs to formulate the military security strategy and the security objectives. The attainment of these military security objectives would determine the required national military capabilities and the consequent long and medium term defence plans.

The Indian defence planning process may (also) be adverely impacted by the absence of a Chief of Defence Staff (CDS). As suggested earlier by the GOM Report, there is a need to set up a Defence Planning Board (DPB) under the chairmanship of the Defence Minister. "*The Board could comprise of the NSA, the Cabinet Secretary, Secretaries of Planning Commission and Ministry of Finance, the Defence Secretary, Chairman Chiefs of Staff Committee (COSC) and two or three whole-time professional experts who are able to analyse and evaluate the services plans with relevant analytical tools. The Board's tasks would be to oversee planning on a regular basis in close collaboration with the services, other relevant ministries/agencies and the Ministry of Finance. Such a Board will have the requisite authority of Defence Minister; The members would be in a better position to take a holistic, integrated view, free from any service bias; the Board will be in a better position to ensure coordination between defence and other relevant sectors on the one hand and the NSC on the other*"[7].

7.3.3 Evolving a Defence Industrialisation Model

As highlighted earlier it is essential that India charts out a rapid defence industrialisation model to become self-reliant in a time frame of not more than 15 years after 2027 i.e. by 2042 or so, if India's military-industrial acumen is to match the size of the US and China by 2045. Further, the Indian DITB at the moment seems to be lacking a unified integrated approach of the stake holders. At the outset there is the need of constituting an institutionalised high powered body under the Defence Minister which can bring together senior reps of all the stakeholders including the private industry. Moreover, the two pronged approach selected should provide for the Indian DITB to deliver for both, the ongoing comparatively short-term (15 years) requirements under LTIPP 2012-27 and simultaneously build the capabilities required for meeting a long term (30 years) requirements of up to 2042. For this to happen the long term 30 years requirements of the services up to 2042 (17th plan period) need to be worked out by the three services. The requirements could emanate from the probable timelines of the replacements that would be due in respect of the platforms, weapons, systems and equipment. The new technology that is desired to be incorporated in new systems could next be spelt out. A detailed net-scan of the world's current and future military system hardwares and softwares which are globally available or likely to be available and are on the anvil, would help formulate the system architectural requirement while a deliberate net-scan for technology could identify where the desired new technology can be obtained from. Considering, the wide differential in the weapon development cycle and the technology development cycle of the militarily developed nations vis-à-vis of India today, the long term order book with the tentative Provisional Services Qualification Requirements (PSQR's) could thus be worked out with a fair degree of accuracy. This next could be made known to all stakeholders including the private sector.

Thereafter, the private sector or their associations could be invited with all other stakeholders to come together on a common platform and discuss each of these future requirements, clarify queries and mis-perceptions if any, as pertaining to the design, R&D, engineering, fielding of prototype, manufacturing, system integration, production processes, technology sharing or technology acquisition requirements, systems performance requirements, sustenance engineering and logistics management aspects, specific *MAKE IN INDIA* policy and procedural frame-work to identify, whether each serial of the 30 years requirements can be met indigenously in the time frames stipulated. Accordingly, the forum could decide the initial categorisation of each of the requirements, for the stakeholders to know the probable order book. Lastly, the forum, could also help identify the agencies/consortiums which are likely to participate and compete for each order. The long term requirements of the armed forces could thus be known to all including the private sector in advance and would give them adequate time to look for foreign tie-ups or establish the necessary facilities. The government on its part needs to provide an assured commitment to the 30 year long term acquisition plan. This needs to be legislated in the Parliament and thereafter honoured by successive governments.

The GOM Report in 2001 had also recommended a somewhat similar institutional mechanism through the creation of a Defence Minister's Council on Production (DMCP) under the Defence Minister with members who could be drawn from the defence establishment, departments of space, atomic energy and science and technology, as well as eminent industrialists from the private sector. The DMCP was to '*lay down the broad objectives of the long term equipment policies and planning on production, simplification of procedures, and so on*[8]. Such an institutional body needs to be expanded to include the development and procurement functions as well. What is thus needed, is a combined Defence Development Production and Procurement Council (DDPPC) which should be overarching in its stature, all-embracing in its constituents and holistic in its approach. It could evolve a framework that would consider all long-term equipment development, production and procurement requirements of the armed forces and to which the entire DIB could relate to. As analysed earlier in the book, these were the very same reasons for the structural and organisational deficiencies in China and South Korea which had impeded the design, development and manufacture of advanced conventional arms and necessitated the requirement of introducing reforms.

The apex level DDPPC could be presided over by the Defence Minister to provide the necessary vision and strategy for the attainment of the defence industrialsation strategy, policy, goals and targets. The council could have representation of the three Industry associations and also from the defence Medium Small Micro Establishments (MSMEs) who can envision their stakes in the Defence business, the associated secretaries in the MOD (defence secretary, secretaries defence production, R&D, defence finance), DG (acquisition) and the three Service Chiefs. The council could meet periodically and review the progress in implementation of specific long-term equipment development, production and procurement policies and programmes as earlier approved by the council and identify the measures to overcome the inadequacies, if any.

A rapid defence industrialisation model to become self-reliant in a time frame of about 30 years would require specific initiatives and respective road maps in the areas of defence R&D, OF's, DPSUs, the Private Sector, T&E facilities, Quality Assurance (QA), sustenance engineering and maintenance management as well as the specific policy and procedural frame-works pertaining to these. Each of these costituents are discussed next.

7.3.4 Defence Research and Development (R&D)

7.3.4.1 Defence R&D Apparatus and Budget

The investment in R&D by the DITB, i.e. by the DRDO, DPSU's, OF's and the private sector, in absolute terms, is relatively small by world standards. Compared to the US and China, which spend in excess of 10 per cent of their defence budget on R&D, India's spending has been less than six per cent[9]. Even this percentage share was allocated only after 1980s before which the share was about one per cent of the defence budget in 1960s, rising to about two per cent in the early eighties[10]. This trivial share of the defence budget, along with India's relatively small defence budget has meant that defence R&D budget in absolute terms is minuscule when compared to the consistently high allocations made by other advanced countries. Further, for the optimum utilisation of this meagre budget, there is a need for the DRDO to shed off all non-core activities and focus on developing core technologies that are not available to the country from around the world. Most other defence R&D efforts of systems engineering and integration, in the ROK and elsewhere in the world are being increasingly outsourced to the domestic private defence research institutions/centres and the industries. A similar approach needs to be adopted in India as well.

7.3.4.2 Long Term Planning of Technologies – A Defence Technology Road Map

The 15 year LTIPP of the three Services (or the 30 year Very Long Term Integrated Perspective Plan (VLTIPP) suggested in this book) forms the basis of the immediate defence technology requirements of the armed forces. This, followed by an extensive technology scan of the available state of the art existing and emerging defence technologies world-wide and an assessment of the technologies which may be denied to the country, can help formulate India's defence technology road map which could list and bring out the sources of how each of these technologies are to be acquired i.e. either:

- By collaboration for joint research, design, development and production
- or through the 'Buy & Make' route based on TOT
- or through the offset route
- or for a time bound indigenous R&D effort that is required due to the restrictions imposed by the export control regimes.

DRDO's Long Term Technology Perspective Plan (LTTPP) prepared in FY 2014-15 has endeavored to align its technology development plans to the Services systems acquisition plans of 12th, 13th and 14th FYP periods spanning from 2012-27[11]. This has been done based on the documented Services 15 year LTIPP. The DRDO's LTTPP details out the technology projects that need to be taken up and the resources that would be required in respect of the test facilities infrastructure, test ranges and the centers of research excellence. It also covers new technologies that are not mentioned in the LTIPP but would be of use and of potential interest to the Services and covers the period beyond 2027.

After that, there is a need to prioritise all key technology gaps envisaged in the execution of India's ongoing and further identified long term technology requirements up to 2042 and, work out the specific strategies to address and overcome each of these gaps in a time bound manner. The DRDO within each defence technological field, has to also identify and formulate specific Defence Technology Objectives (DTO's), the technological assistance that would be required to either develop or acquire these technology objectives in terms of the research agencies/institutions/countries to outsource to or collaborate with, in India and abroad, or whether the technology is to be developed in-house, in case so, the desired talent, know-how and know-why, infrastructure, detailed methodology to be adopted to ensure complete technology development/transfer, assimilation, absorption and adoption in defence products and systems, their financial investment requirements, the roadmap for timelines to be met and plotting the desired rate of progress of each technology development plan with phase lines and milestones as done by the US, identify alternate options in case the planned progress is slow or scuttled due to technology embargo, controls or sanctions and so on[12]. The Sisodia Committee too in 2007 had recommended to the defence planners and the private industry to jointly finalise a "*Long Term Defence Capability Plan*". Each DRDO technology cluster could also hereafter make it a practice to periodically identify their future technology development areas and the associated resource requirement for each technology development plan.

7.3.4.3 Collaborative R&D for a TOT Base with Full Know How and Know Why.

The collaborative TOT should cover all aspects of data packages, engineering drawings and designs, R&D, engineering, manufacturing know-how, complete technical information for PA to manufacture, assemble, integrate, T&E, install, undertake Quality Checks (QC) and QA tests, commissioning, usage, MRO support etc for the product. Design data would include all engineering drawings and specification details that may be needed to undertake modification/upgrade of the product and give production agencies deviations/ concessions for import substitution of parts and systems of the product, as required by the PA. By involving the Indian Industries during the collaborative TOT and the development cycle, many of the Indian private sector industries can improve and move up the value chain i.e. from Build to Print (B2P) to Build to Specification (B2S) to Build to Design (B2D) and finally onto Build to Requirements (B2R) successively.

7.3.4.4 DRDO Developed Systems/Technologies

DRDO and PA's need to take on the responsibility of up gradation, modification and product improvement of systems developed by the DRDO/ specific PA. Only when this responsibility is assigned to them, will their R&D centres take on the ownership and provide the best solutions for exploiting the systems optimally over their extended service life.

DRDO developed technologies could also be offered for production, both in the private and the public sectors (including the OFB, all PSU's and Services MRO agencies). An appropriate amount could be worked out by the DRDO and charged for it. Moreover, the costly government T&E facilities developed for the DRDO labs and projects need to be offered on an appropriate fee, for their optimum utilisation by other emerging defence R&D entities both, in the private and public sectors.

7.3.4.5 Technology Acquisition through the Buy and Make (with TOT) Route

The key technologies for TOT need to be identified jointly by the designated PA, DRDO, the User Service and the MOD, prior to the issue of the RFP. Also, there is a requirement for the DDP to associate the DRDO and the User in all stages of a major defence acquisition under the 'Buy and Make route' of defence procurement to include, the vetting of TOT proposals offered by OEMs, technical evaluation of the offered bids, the contractual negotiations and in final contract formulation. This would help ascertain and ensure the comprehensiveness of a TOT proposal and enable formulating a near full proof contract. The depth of TOT offered could be studied by the DRDO and the User Service and due to their prior experience on similar contracts would assist in overcoming the associated nuances of such a proposal. At the technical evaluation stage, the DRDO and the User's involvement can help draw comparisons between the TOT offered by the various OEMs and also provide an assessment of the depth of technology being transferred. Once a vendor is selected after the technical & commercial evaluation stage, the DRDO and the User could assist in the contractual negotiations on the various aspects of the TOT.

In order to ensure optimum utilisation of the technology acquired from licensed production or through collaborative R&D arrangements, there is a need to discuss contractual ingredients during the contract formulation stage and ensure that adequate contractual safeguards are built in to overcome the Intellectual Property Rights (IPR) restrictions. Since the IPR for the technology being transferred is paid for by the country, the endeavor should be to extract the permission of the seller for exploitation of these technologies for indigenous applications and exports.

The DRDO could also assist the PA's in absorbing, assimilating and imbibing the state of the art technologies acquired through these technology transfers. The technologies being contemporary in nature can best be understood by the DRDO and not the PAs.

7.3.4.6 TOT Acquisition through the Offset Route

The technology that is being sought for the DRDO or other R&D agencies through the offsets purchase route must be stated upfront in the RFP. This could be done only after carrying out prior consultations with regards to their availability with the probable vendors/OEMs during the pre-bid meeting held prior to the issue of the RFP, with a view to clear any mis-perceptions that may arise later.

7.3.4.7 Risk Analysis and Short Closing of Projects

The steering committee adopted for close monitoring R&D projects should mandatorily be headed by a senior level officer of the User Service. Moreover, all R&D projects must be subjected to annual reviews. The reviews need to become half-yearly whenever the risks, costs and time frames are found to be unacceptably beyond the originally stated aims. The reviews need to undertake a risk analysis by evaluating the costs incurred vis-a-vis the results attained. Further, effort should be to short-close long drawn development projects. DRDO's project-wise details, regarding the original and revised date of completion and the sanctioned cost of a few major projects up to June 30, 2014 are listed in Table 7.1[13]. The last US 'Weapon Systems Acquisition Reform Act of 2009' focused on periodically assessing the technological maturity of Major Defence Acquisition Programmes (MDAPs). The policy reforms require greater consideration for trade-offs between the system cost, time schedule and performance besides assessing the products design prior to giving approval and the act also hardened the 1982 Nunn-McCurdy law,

Table 7.1: DRDO Major Projects Original and Revised Date of Completion and Sanctioned Cost up to June 30, 2014

Ser No	*Project*	*Probable Date of Completion (PDC)*			*Sanctioned Cost (INR in Cr)*
		Original	*Revised*	*Time Over-run (Years)*	
1.	Light Combat Aircraft (LCA), Phase-II	Dec 2008	Mar 2015	06	5777.56
2.	Aero Engine Kaveri	Dec 1996	Dec 2009	13	2839.00
3.	Air Borne Early Warning & Control (AEW&C) System	Oct 2011	Oct 2014	03	2275.00
4.	EW Suite for Fighter Aircraft (EWSFA)—Tejas	Mar 2011	Dec 2014	04	154.74
5.	Long Range Surface-to-Air Missile (LR-SAM)	May 2011	Dec 2015	05	2606.02
6.	Helicopter Version Third Generation Anti-Tank Guided Missile, Helina	Dec 2010	Dec 2015	05	72.00
7.	Air-to-Air Missile, Astra	Aug 2012	Dec 2016	04	955.00

Source: Lok Sabha starred question number 161 answered on 18.07.2014.

which mandates that programmes be reviewed if they exhibit cost over-runs of 15 per cent and abandoned if cost over-runs reach 25 per cent unless essential to national security and no alternatives are available[14]. Similar yardsticks need to be applied to the DRDO and other developmental agencies in India to ensure efficiency, accountability and the timely delivery of military systems.

7.3.4.8 Long-Term Civil-Military Dual-Use R&D Strategy – 2042

There is a need to constitute a joint task force which would comprise of the representatives of all stakeholders, i.e., to include representation from universities, academia, research centres, research institutions, various ministries, defence public and private sector, DRDO, Services and so on for formulating a comprehensive long term civil-military dual-use R&D strategy – 2042. This document could provide the necessary direction, impetus and a unity of effort and purpose for all stakeholders to pursue a joint civil-military dual-use R&D strategy as done by China and other developed countries.

7.3.5 Ordnance Factories (OF's)

7.3.5.1 OF Apparatus

The OF's are an integrated base for the indigenous production of defence equipment and ammunition. The massive investments made in the past in the OF's necessitate that these continue to perform their role albeit their effectiveness and efficiency needs to be improved. Optimisation would pertain to their functioning and would require a re-look at their structure, capacity utilisation, orders given by the Services, delays in execution of orders, quality issues, product support, modernisation, in-house R&D effort, interface for DRDO transferred technologies, offset absorption roadmap and, exports and so on.

7.3.5.2 OF Management

The factories are more or less independent in their functioning in terms of certain financial powers delegated to them and are also not fully accountable to the board or its chairman. To allow greater autonomy to the organisation in running its own affairs while, at the same time, be accountable for its performance, the factories need to be corporatised. It involves restructuring a government organisation into a joint-stock, publicly listed company to introduce corporate and business management techniques in their administration. It results in the creation of state-owned corporations where the government retains the majority ownership of the corporation's stock. The Chinese SOE's in 1990 were transformed into corporations wherein the state companies remained to be owned by the central government but were managed in a semi-autonomous fashion to improve efficiency and performance.

However, in many cases, corporatisation leads to partial or full privatisation, which involves a process where the public enterprises are sold to private business entities by listing their shares on publicly traded stock exchanges. "*In early 1990's, in order to 'corporatise' the DIB, the Chinese transformed the Military Industrial Complex (MIC) from a series of machine-building ministries into large SOE's*"[15]. At the same time, control of individual production facilities, research units and trading companies was transferred to these new corporations. The apprehension of a strong opposition from the labour unions of these factories is not unfounded and would need to be overcome through a strong political will, as was done by the US during the restructuring of its DIB after the cold war had ended.

7.3.5.3 OF's Transfer of Technology and Self-Reliance

In the period 1999-2005, the OFB entered into a TOT agreement with four OEM's and since 2005, there has been no further TOT agreements in OFB. The non-transfer of designs on critical assemblies by the OEM's and the inability to develop a strong vendor base for the components, were the principal causes for setbacks in the TOT[16]. This pushed the OFB to rely on perennial import of critical components. While the planned date of indigenisation ranged between 2002-03-09-10 for these TOT products, the absorption of technology has till date not fully realised as shown in Table 7.2.

Since until now the OF's and the DPSU's were nominated to absorb the production and maintenance TOT of defence procurements under the 'Buy and Make' route, these establishments could have maintained a compendium listing out the major lessons that were learnt in each of the previous major contracts with regards to the contractual or procedural inadequacies pertaining to the technology transfer, its assimilation and absorption as also the measures required to be taken in the contract formulation to obviate the same in future.

Table 7.2: OFB TOT Agreements 1999-2005 and Status of Indigenisation

Year	*Item*	*OEM*	*Cost (Rs. in crore)*	*Planned period for indigenisation*	*Status of indigenisation*
May 2004	AK-630 Guns	Rosoboronexport Russia	96	2007-08	48 per cent
February 2005	84 mm Rocket Launcher Mark-III	FFV Ordnance, Sweden	460	2009-10	47 per cent
June 2000	155 mm Screening Smoke Blue Emission Ammunition	M/s Denel Swartklip, South Africa	-	March 2003	25 per cent
October 2003	130 mm cargo Ammunition	IMI Sirael	40	2008-09	Nil progress because of ban On IMI
Februrary 2001	T-90 tanks	Rosoboronexport	2424	2006-07	59 of 78 codes (main assemblies)
	Total		3020		

Source: Report No. 35 of 2014 - Union Government (Defence Services).

7.3.5.4 OF's Role in Product Support

The principal concern of the OFB till now has been to meet the production targets only. They have thus not paid much attention to maintaining a high state of serviceability of the weapon systems supplied by them. The OFB needs to initiate action to set up separate structures that can take on the responsibility of providing life time product support for the range of weapon systems that is supplied by them to the Services as done by the SOE's of Israel, ROK, China and the US. This could encompass reliable and timely supply of spares besides in-situ equipment repairs or defect rectification during the warranty periods. The key gaps need to be urgently bridged through appropriate restructuring. The concept of PBL (as discussed earlier in the book) could be enforced in respect of the OFB as well.

7.3.5.5 OF's Offset Absorption Roadmap

The OFB needs to task all it's OF's to identify key deficiencies and requirements as pertaining to their current and contemporary technology requirements, know-how and know-why's of the present and future critical systems and sub-systems for planning and directing offset investments that are envisaged as inflows into the OF's.

7.3.5.6 OF's Exports

The MOD allowed the OFB to venture into direct exports business since

investment in capability and access to unutilised naval capacity in the private sector"[24] as being attempted by the government today.

With the *MAKE IN INDIA* initiative gaining grounds, it is the opportune time for getting the major Indian defence sector private players to take on the overflow of the manufacturing orders of the major defence systems. This will bring in competition and force the DPSU's to improve their efficiencies and productivity. To provide a level playing field to private players, the DPSUs infrastructural facilities like that of the DRDO and OFs, constructed at huge government costs, could be made available to the selected Indian defence industry on payment. The DPSU's while holding the advantage of being in the defence business for much longer than the private players will thus be forced due to competition to improve upon their performance.

Table 7.3: DPSUs Order Book Position and Order Book to Turnover Multiple

Company	*Turnover F11 (US$ Bn)*	*Turnover FY10 (US$ Bn)*	*Order book position (US$ Bn)*	*Order book to Turnover (Year $)*	*Turnover Per employee (US$)*
HAL	2.47	2.16	18	6-7	70,000-80,000
MDL	0.50	0.55	19	35-40	60,000-80,000
GRSE	0.20	0.16	1.3	6-7	40,000-50,000
HSL	0.11	0.12	0.30	3-4	30,000-40,000
GSL	0.19	0.18	0.43	2-3	0.1-0.3 Mn
MIDHANI	0.08	0.07	2.8	35-36	70,000-80,000

Source: Aviotech Research.

7.3.6.5 DPSU's Voids in Transfer of Technology and Self-Reliance

The DPSUs, like the OF's, have been unable to optimise the indigenisation model envisaged through licensed production. This was due to the contractual and procedural inadequacies as formulated and implemented by the OF's and DPSU's. The voids and lessons learnt in the previous contracts need to be incorporated and plugged in all future contracts which in turn, would essentially imply a comprehensive capture of the know-how and know-why of a licensed production programme. The contractual provisions need to be so worded that the intent initially needs to be to absorb the broad scope of production TOT based on SKD/CKD kits and subsequently to completely absorb the full scope of production TOT including the manufacturing capabilities during the Indigenous Manufacture (IM) stage (based on the raw material route). For this to happen, it will have to be ensured that the raw material route caters to about 65 per cent of the total licensed manufacture programme and no more than 35 per cent is obtained through the SKD/ CKD route which provides very low 'value addition'.

7.3.6.6 DPSU's In-house R&D Effort

The lack of in-house R&D reiterates the need for India to consider issuing a policy to regulate its DPSU's and OF's to spend at least 10 per cent of their annual revenues/value of sales on R&D as done by China. In-house R&D in each of the DPSUs is a must to ensure the goal of a vibrant DIB in the country. This needs to cater for potential upgrades/modernisation of the systems delivered earlier by DPSUs and endeavour to bring in new versions or altogether new products through intensive in-house R&D activity and constant interface with the user Service.

7.3.6.7 DPSU's Role in Product Support

DPSU's, as earlier suggested for the OF's too, need to set up their separate divisions to meet the life time product support requirements of the Armed Forces for all future products supplied by them. These divisions will have to maintain continuous contact with the Service Headquarters for all future products supplied to the Services to provide effective service cover on a real time basis in order to ensure higher levels of serviceability. The first and second line maintenance capabilities have to be retained by the Services in-house agencies due to operational constraints. Further, the DPSUs could start the process of getting into Performance Based Life-cycle product support (PBL), which like in the other developed countries, is likely to be adopted in the coming years whereby, the OEM/PA will be responsible for ensuring a guaranteed level of serviceability/uptime and payments will be released accordingly. The User Service will thus be absolved of the responsibility of third and fourth line maintenance support where-ever feasible.

7.3.7 Private Sector Participation

7.3.7.1 Foreign Direct Investment (FDI) in Private Sector in Defence Production

The Indian Government from January 2002 onwards allowed 100 per cent private equity with 26 per cent FDI in the defence sector. The FDI provision besides the financial considerations, was to attract technology into India due to the private sector's lack of experience in defence production and the low R&D base in India. "*Also, with the cap of 26 per cent, the private sector was expected to form partnerships with foreign companies while retaining ownership. .... (However), given the strategic and technology-intensive nature of investment, no foreign vendor (was) interested in parting with technology to an Indian partner over which it (had) little control*"[25].

The FDI policy has thereafter been reviewed twice in August 2014 and November 2015. In the first instance, a composite foreign investment of up to 49 per cent was allowed through the government route (Foreign Investment Promotion Board - FIPB) and beyond 49 per cent was allowed with the approval of the Cabinet Committee on Security (CCS) on a case-to-case basis wherever, it was likely to result in access to modern and state-of-the art technology in the country. Besides, the restrictions as, the single largest Indian shareholder to hold at least 51 per cent equity and the complete restriction on Foreign Institutional Investor (FII) in the earlier policy was removed to facilitate investment in the sector. In the second instance, the government further relaxed and permitted foreign investment up to 49 per cent under the automatic route instead of the earlier government approval route. Further, Investments over 49 per cent are to be cleared by the FIPB instead of the CCS. Moreover, portfolio investors and foreign venture capital firms can also invest up to 49 per cent as against 24 per cent earlier[26]. The government's decision to lift the overseas investment ceilings for the defence sector is an apparent move to turn India into a preferred destination for foreign investors and is in line with the aim to turn India into a manufacturing powerhouse through the government's *MAKE IN INDIA* initiative. The crux of these reforms is to further ease, rationalise and simplify the process of foreign investments into the country and to put more and more FDI proposals on the automatic route instead of the government route where, the time and energy of the investors are wasted.

Consequent to the opening up of the defence industry sector to the Indian private sector in 2001, and with the FDI participation as per current policies from time to time, as on Jul 15, 2014, 33 FDI proposals/JVs have been approved in defence sector for manufacture of various defence equipment's, both in the public and private sector. FDI amounting to INR 24.84 crores (US $ 5.02 million) has been received in the defence industry sector from April 2000 to June 2015[27].

It is worthwhile to encourage India as an investment destination for defence production both, because of its own sustained and long term needs for defence goods and services as well as for nurturing the capabilities to exploit strategic exports to countries of interest which include countries in Africa, Asia and Latin America. In this context, a consortium approach covering a few entities in the public and private sectors in India and a foreign strategic partner has already been adopted and can prove to be useful in future as well as seen in the case of Pinaka and the Brahmos programmes.

7.3.7.2 Indian Private Sector in Defence Production and Embargo/Export Control Regimes of Large Foreign Manufacturers

Although, since 2006, the government has permitted 100 per cent FDI in defence on a "case-by-case basis" for the OEMs who bring in high-end technology to build military systems in India, no foreign OEM has so far responded. This is because a foreign OEM has to obtain the explicit sanction of its government to export or transfer proprietary information and technology to India. This requirement is legislated over the defence exporters by most of the countries who implement export control regimes in order to protect their technological competitive advantage in weapon systems. Governments which fund the invention and development of complex weapon systems have an inherent interest in restraining the transfer of cutting edge weapon systems and thus create export barriers or control regimes for some systems. "One example of an exporting barrier is the USA's International Traffic in Arms Regulations (ITARS)[28]. The ITARS is a set of regulations that controls defence related equipment and services which are on the United States Munitions List."

7.3.7.3 Export Profile of Indian Defence Industry including Private Sector in Defence Production

As per No Objection Certificate (NOC) issued by the DDP, the value of exports of Indian defence industry, including that of the nine DPSUs and OFB, grew from INR 460.97 crore in FY 2013 to INR 686.27 crore in FY 2014[29]. The trend in exports indicates a growth of the defence industry. The exports by private defence industry has also accelerated. About 12 to 14 companies in the private sector have contributed to defence exports. Some of government's recent initiatives include, the Standard Operating Procedure (SOP) for the issue of NOC for export of military stores has been revised and put on the website. As per the revised SOP, the requirement of End User Certificate (EUC) to be countersigned/stamped by the government authorities has been done away with for export of parts, components, sub-systems etc. The list of military stores have been finalised and put in the public domain. The process of receiving applications for NOC for export of military stores and for the issuing of NOC has been made online to reduce the delay and to remove human interface in the process. Defence Exports Strategy outlining the various steps to be taken, has been formulated and put up in the public domain.

7.3.7.4 Private Sectors Perspective of Entering Defence Production

The private sector CEO's in India when asked as to why they are not venturing into defence production state that there are primarily four aspects which merit attention. Firstly, there should be a clear business case i.e. the ability for a private firm to make profit on getting into the production of a defence item, secondly, there should be a clear long-term order book and assured continuous orders, thirdly, the parameters for the equipment to be developed should be firmed up after prior consultations for permitting minor changes in parametres, if acceptable to the Services, to reduce costs with a lower QR vis-à-vis higher specification while achieving a near par performance, overcome design, engineering, manufacturing technology or process limitations and so on, and lastly, the evaluation criterion should be pre-decided and not changed after a product is developed as it only leads to an increase in costs.

Unfortunately, the present procurement system does not permit divulging the envisaged total requirement over a longer period of time and the procurements are undertaken based on the annual reviews undertaken by the stocking echelons. Thus piecemeal quantities are procured which is contrary to making it a business case based on the economies of scales. Further, there is no long term commitment by the MOD for a regular flow of orders. Both these reasons are stated to discourage Indian companies from committing resources for establishing production facilities as the venture can prove both expensive and risky. The other side of this view is that, provision for repeat order exists in the DPP and a private company must bring down its initial cost to become the L1 and win the initial order. Thereafter, it could amortise its costs over subsequent repeat orders. Notwithstanding, for the Indian companies to make a decision regarding investment of their resources, the RFP can indicate the envisaged total requirement over the years without making any firm commitment and stating as such to avoid future legal problems.

7.3.7.5 Suggested Methodology to Enhance Private Sector Participation in Defence Production

Despite nearly 15 years having passed since the time the private sector was allowed an entry into defence production, the private industry has been unable to make major inroads into defence production and consequently remained to be an outsourcing base for the public sector. The primary reason for this is that unlike the public sector, the private sector has been deliberately or otherwise kept out of the defence acquisition planning process. To start with, as earlier brought out, the long term requirements of the services for the next 30 years (based on the replacements due of the various systems) need to be worked out by the three services, tentative PSQR's formulated (could be based on the current systems available and known futuristic systems likely to be available world over). Next, this could be made known to all stakeholders who must include the private sector. The private sector or their associations need to be invited with all other stakeholders to come together on a common platform and discuss each of these future requirements, clarify queries and mis-perceptions if any, as pertaining to design, R&D, engineering, fielding of prototype, manufacturing, production processes, technology sharing or acquisition requirements, systems performance requirements, sustenance and maintenance management aspects and specific *MAKE IN INDIA* policy and procedural frame-work to identify whether, each serial of the 30 years requirement can be met indigenously in the time frames stipulated. Accordingly, the forum could decide the initial categorisation of each requirement and the probable order book for the stakeholders to know the same. Lastly, the forum could also help identify the agencies/consortiums which are likely to participate and compete for each order.

Once all this is made known to all including the private sector, well in advance, will give them adequate time to look for foreign tie-ups or to establish the necessary facilities. The government on its part has to give an assured commitment to the 30 year long term acquisition plan. This next needs to be legislated in the Parliament and thereafter honoured by all successive governments. The apprehensions of acquisition managers that once the private players enter the defence sector and make a foothold in defence procurement and sustenance activities, will hike up their costs and hold the government to a ransom can be offset by imposing the 'five per cent plus costs' rule on profits from defence contracts as done by China.

7.3.7.6 The Department of Private Sector (DPS)

There is a need for a separate department, other than the DDP, which should address the needs and concerns of both the domestic private sector and the foreign companies participating in defence production. This could be called the Department of Private Sector (DPS). The representative of this department should then form an essential part of all the inter-agency defence procurement interaction forums starting from the SCAP CC/SCAP CHC, DPB/DAC, DDPPC (as suggested earlier in this book) or the existing 'Defence Production Board', 'Defence Development Board' and so on. Thus, valuable inputs pertaining to the capabilities and competency levels of the domestic and global private sector companies can be known and considered while deciding whether to import a system and technology or not. Their presence will also help in confirming and firming up the parametres for the equipment to be developed, produced or procured as these are mostly formulated keeping the foreign equipment in mind. Also, in order to encourage the domestic players, minor changes in parametres, if acceptable to the Services, can be introduced early during deliberations, which may in turn make the Indian firms eligible for their consideration.

7.3.7.7 "Make" and "Buy and Make (Indian)" Categorisation are Non-starters

Under the DPP provisions, the "Make" and "Buy and Make (Indian)" categorisation involve at least one more additional step each vis-à-vis the other two categorisations of "Buy" and "Buy and Make" which makes the former categorisations virtually un-operational[30]. In the case of "Make", HQ IDS is mandated to undertake a feasibility study of all projects under the LTIPP and in the case of "Buy and Make (Indian)", SHQ is required to prepare a Capability Definition Document (CDD), outlining the "requirement in operational terms" and describing the "present capabilities determined on the basis of the existing equipment, manpower, etc." The additional steps of doing a feasibility study and preparing a capability definition document could naturally be avoided by the Services because they have an easy option under the "Buy" and/or "Buy and Make" routes to procure nearly all the items of "contemporary technology", with the Qualitative Requirements (QRs) modified to encompass all "essential parameters". The objective of a feasibility study is to ascertain domestic capability with respect to design and development of a system. The new 'Make Procedure' under formulation with the MOD for nearly four years now should try and address this issue.

7.3.7.8 Comprehensive Updated Data Bank of Indian Defence Industries

There is also a need for the MOD to maintain an updated data bank of all Indian defence industries along with their essential information pertaining to their product range, competency and capability levels, foreign tie-ups, turnover, supplies made to MOD and so on. It is presumed the Acquisition Wing must be having the information but the same needs to be comprehensive and regularly updated to be useful for the issue of RFI, RFP, Evaluation of bids, benchmarking, contract formulation, payment terms, repeat orders and so on.

7.3.7.9 Purchase and Price Preference Support to Indigenous Producers

Most countries support indigenous producers by giving them purchase and price preference (as buy Indian/buy Korean/buy American etc.). In ROK, the emphasis is on procuring equipment that is based on domestic R&D and production within the country is also mandated by the Defence Reform 2020 Plan. Preference is given to Israeli products over imported ones provided the cost of the former does not exceed more than 15 per cent of the latter[31]. An Israeli product is one whose Israeli content exceeds 35 per cent. Further, there has to be some incentive for the foreign companies to increase their collaborations with the Indian companies. As earlier brought out, Israel's new 'mandatory industrial cooperation' regulation or rules impose a mandatory requirement for government corporations and public agencies to ask for industrial cooperation when their purchase of foreign goods or services exceeds the threshold of Israeli Shekels (ILS) 25 million (or $ 5 million) and includes provisions for offset investment in Israel worth 50 per cent of the contract value as an 'Industrial Cooperation Undertaking'[32]. This also applies to related follow-on contracts worth $5, 00,000 or more[33]. Further, in Israel, the Industrial Cooperation Authority (ICA) requires a minimum of 20 per cent subcontracting for any foreign project/product purchased. Such aspects could be made mandatory in India, as done by Great Britain too under its Industrial Participation Policy (IPP).

7.3.7.10 Offset Policy to Enhance Domestic Industrial Capability

For the offset policy to enhance domestic industrial capability and technological prowess, the policy needs to guide the off-set inflows into desired areas, which are to meet the country's long-term requirements. This requires a comprehensive technology roadmap, formulated in consultation with the Services and the Industry, among others, to leverage the cause of off-sets.

Further, there is a need to rapidly develop the Tier 2 & Tier 3 Companies in India through the offset obligations as this in future can help absorb the PBL arrangements in case ever made mandatory as per acquisition guidelines.

7.3.7.11 Level Playing Field in Taxation Regime

The economies of scale and the capacities already created or in the process of augmentation in the DPSUs/OFs, may not always allow the private sector in defence production of all the major platforms. However, in a large number of cases, it would be possible to get the private sector companies to take on the overflow and thus supplement the effort. This will also bring in competition in meeting the requirements of the Indian Armed Forces. For true competition between the Private Sector and the DPSUs/OFB as also between procurements ex-imports and domestic production, it will be necessary to ensure a level playing field which has to span across all financial comparisons undertaken to decide the lowest bidder 'L1'. Similarly, deliverables, in terms of costs, efficiency and quality, must be comparable.

7.3.7.12 Forge Strategic Partnership with Domestic Private Companies

It would be useful for the Armed Forces to get into long term arrangements with the private sector for meeting the product support (sustenance engineering and maintenance management) requirements of the military systems subject to the partnership remaining competitive in terms of its pricing, reliability and timely delivery of supplies.

Considering that the involvement of the Indian private sector in defence has been nearly non-existent and that there is now the need for a radical transformation of India's DITB, it would be desirable that India's defence industrialisation is targeted for a much larger number of entities for each of the tiers. For this purpose, the evaluation criteria norms concerning the turn over, profitability, availability of technical and managerial manpower, net assets etc. could be prescribed as the qualification criterion to ensure that the competition for each of the tiers is restricted to the best.

7.3.8 Sustenance Engineering and Maintenance Management Aspects for Self-Sufficiency in Imported and Indigenous Systems

7.3.8.1 Improving the Serviceability of Combat Systems at time of Acquisition

At the time of capital acquisition of a major weapon system or equipment, especially if procured from foreign sources, endeavour should be to either make provisions for receiving the lifelong product support needs of the system or in the case of licensed production, to acquire all components of both Production and Maintenance TOT. In order to ensure self-sufficiency with respect to imported systems there is a need to leverage future capital acquisitions with a view to make the OEM's follow internationally recognised business practices and fulfil their life time product support obligations in a more responsive manner. This will assist in optimising the serviceability levels and minimising the overall life cycle costs of military systems.

7.3.8.2 Shift Emphasis in the Absorption of TOT

DPSUs/OFs/SHQs and the MOD in all future acquisitions need to emphasise and insist on acquiring the TOT relating to the manufacture of critical parts, fast moving items and Automatic Replenishment Stores (ARS) than just acquiring the one time activities like that relating to the fabrication of frames etc. so that, the lifetime product support of these frequently required items can be ensured indigenously. If necessary, the OEM be asked to set up JV for these as a part of the offset obligation.

7.3.8.3 JV as Part of Offset Obligation

In fulfilment of the offset obligation, OEM's could be directed to create JV's for the following:

- Manufacture of ARS and fast moving spares.
- Warehousing of spares in India.
- Training infrastructure in India comprising CBT packages for class room training and simulators.
- Data mining and storage facilities for life cycle monitoring, documentation and life extension.
- MRO of aggregates and systems.

7.3.8.4 Long Term Pricing Policy Agreements for Supply of Spares by OEM's and Seeking Illustrated Spare Parts Price List (ISPPL) at Time of Acquisition

It has been experienced in the past that on a number of occasions both, the foreign and Indian OEM's, after supplying the Manufacturers Recommended List of Spares (MRLS) at prices negotiated during the finalisation of the initial contract, tend to subsequently arbitrarily increase the prices when the spares are procured during the life-time of the equipment. For ensuring long term product support to In-service imported systems that are to be retained and sustained over longer periods of time, there is a need to conclude pricing policy agreements in respect of spares, sub-assemblies and assemblies of major equipment and weapon systems. This can be done by entering into long term business agreements with the OEM's and then contract for three to five years consumption with a staggered delivery schedule. Tendency of piecemeal procurement must be curbed. Contracts for spares should be in usable batches for improvement in serviceability to the defined levels.

It is further suggested, that the complete catalogue of the Illustrated Spare Parts Price List (ISPPL) along with the price escalation formulae for the guaranteed calendar life be sought initially itself from the OEM. This can be done by mentioning the requirement upfront in the RFPs of all acquisitions of major defence equipment and weapon systems. The pricing mechanism finalised initially will go a long way in reducing the negotiation period of maintenance procurements undertaken subsequently and will also provide some kind of assurance with regards to their prices.

7.3.8.5 Performance Based Life-Cycle Product Support (PBL)

The concept of PBL ensures the sustenance of weapon systems at user defined levels of performance and operational readiness through its service life. This needs to be specified at the time of acquisition itself. For introducing PBL in India, the costs for a defined usage in terms of life cycle, operational readiness and exploitation will have to be stated upfront in the RFP's and made the selection criterion for the acquisition of major systems. The MMRCA case is one such instance. PBL also involves the payment of higher incentives for beyond the specified performance level as well as fines for any under-performance. The system has the benefit of ensuring a specified level of availability of the weapon system and reduces the sustenance and the maintenance infrastructure that is required to be set up for it by the Services, thus, reducing the organisational responsibilities and costs. It also creates a single point accountability of the OEM.

The PBL system can be progressively introduced in India. To begin with, it could be entered into with one of the Indian PA's like the HAL for the entire Indian Armed Forces. This could start with the next tri-services acquisition of a HAL produced aircraft or helicopter order. HAL could be asked to carry out the entire sustenance engineering and maintenance management activities from first line to fourth line and sustain the pre-defined level of serviceability. An evaluation of its success and cost effectiveness (cost-benefit analysis) vis-à-vis by in-house sustenance engineering and maintenance management agencies could be carried out. In case found to be successful, a similar arrangement could then be entered into with other DPSUs (BEL, BEML etc.) and other Indian OEMs for future contracts. Offset obligations could be leveraged for ensuring PBL or an assured life time product support.

7.3.9 Defence Exports

It is in the interest of the indigenous DITB to encourage defence exports. This will help the industry to optimise its capacity utilisation and lower the costs of its domestic supplies. The export competition could bring in quality and timely deliveries. If pursued seriously, like that done by the US, China, ROK, Israel and others, defence exports can help India build long term strategic ties with countries of interests located in South East Asia, West Asia, Africa, Latin America and so on. Exports, require building a long term relationship with the importing countries and ensuring a reliable lifetime product support.

The measures that need to be initiated by the government for export of defence products include the creation of an apex body with the RM as its Chairman for enunciating the defence exports strategy and consequent policy direction, a Defence Export Council (DEC) under the apex body which can act as a single window for granting export clearances.

7.4 Way Ahead for India

In the case of India, like that in the Republic of Korea (ROK) and China, the ability to develop both advanced weapons systems and the capabilities required for essential technologies have continued to remain at comparatively lower levels, due to three main reasons. Firstly, the country's constant dependence on foreign nations for advanced weapon systems, secondly, the country's defence research activity being heavily focused on systems development as against developing technologies, and lastly, the separation, between the agency which managed the R&D and the defence industry which finally undertook the assembly and production of defence systems. Also, the communication between the R&D institutes (designing the weapons), the factories (producing them), the defence enterprises collaborating on weapons development projects as also between the defence industry and the User Services, on the requirements and specifications was limited. Thus, India like Israel, ROK, China and the other militarily developed nations has to now pursue a dual-policy approach towards defence procurement. India needs to progressively reduce its dependency on weapons procurement from abroad and concurrently increase its investment in establishing a sophisticated DITB. This investment must be directed towards creating advanced defence oriented R&D facilities that will be in a position to adapt the new weapons systems to its doctrinal requirements and develop those new ones which are cost intensive, required in large numbers and not easily available from elsewhere.

A comprehensive restructuring of India's DITB will call for closing or downsizing organisations, laying off workers to make industry—leaner, efficient and prepared to compete in the global arms market. Their management's focus has to shift to profitability and mobilsing cash flows which can improve their financial situation and allow for diversification and expansion into new areas and products, besides increasing partnerships with the foreign defence companies. The Indian defence companies will have to form permanent JV's with foreign firms to deliver for their own requirements as also enhance output for sales to the third parties world-wide.

India, like the ROK, needs to designate certain industries as defence contractors and provide them financial incentives and other economic benefits. The defence contractors could be major subsidiaries of large Indian business houses engaged in the civil sector. For defence production, the identified defence contractors, besides besides being allowed to diversify their defence business, could be asked by the Government to specialise in specific weapons systems as combat vehicles, aircrafts, surface combatants, guided munitions and so on[34]. While, it may not be possible, as in the case of South Korea, to ensure that the selected industries are mandatorily made to engage in defence production in parallel with their activities in the civilian sector or required by law to devote 70 per cent of their industrial capacity to production of defence material[35], these may be provided suitable incentives in the form of soft loans, low cost land allotment, tax holidays/tax concessions, government subsidies and bailout packages, when required and so on. There can also be a system of state subsidy to existing defence industries wherein, a large contract for a specific weapons system is given to one contractor while it is complemented by a smaller contract in the same technical area to another defence industry. In this way multiple and parallel competencies can be upheld in the defence sector. As followed by South Korea, the government, after awarding a contract, should provide necessary guarantees that it will procure the products once it is manufactured and assembled[36]. The defence industry would thus enjoy major incentives to maintain production, as the supply and demand will be institutionally guaranteed by the government.

China's defence reform of July 1999 of creating 10 new Defence Industry Enterprise Groups (DIEGs) is worth emulating by India and is the next logical step after the designation of contractors as done by the ROK. These DIEGs functioned as true conglomerates, integrating R&D, production and marketing. It also encouraged new industry enterprise groups to compete with each other for procurement contracts, which would pressurise them to be more efficient and technologically innovative. These new enterprise groups were given authority to manage their own operations and take on the responsibility for their own profits and losses. Before the 1998 reforms, the defence enterprise groups were all state-owned, bureaucratic, monopolies with little independence from the central government[37]. The reforms transformed the conglomerates into profit-oriented, shareholding entities with operational autonomy while remaining entirely state owned. Moreover, each defence conglomerate was divided into two entities to promote limited competition within their industrial sectors. The arrangement ensured cooperation between the firms and the armed forces through realistic commitments and extensive information sharing. Accordingly, revenues and profits for the entire defence industry has grown strongly since the early 2000's. The cooperation between the Users and the defence industry is at multiple levels ranging from high-level strategic and doctrinal planning and policy-making at the center to the factory floors around the country. Users, civilian defence industry officials, and S&T experts have been cooperating on long-range S&T development plans since the early 2000's. This includes the drafting of the S&T development plans. Further, China's 10 defence conglomerates own a large part of the R&D apparatus and invest heavily in innovation activities. Their collaboration with foreign firms and accessing of foreign markets has helped bring in external knowl-edge and technology.

India's industrialisation approach like the ROK, China and other militarily developed nations has to go beyond licensed production and onto product development through modification, redesign, and reproduction via reverse engineering as also, enhance indigenisation activities by accelerating the pace of domestic R&D for developing and producing its own weapons systems. The acquisition process encompasses design, engineering, construction, testing, deployment, sustainment, and disposal of weapons or related items purchased from a contractor. The US Defence Acquisition System (DAS)—for developing and/or buying the item uses "milestones" to oversee and manage acquisition programmes. At each milestone, a programme must meet specific statutory and regulatory requirements before the programme can proceed to the next phase of the acquisition process[38]. There are three milestones which minimise risks and optimise system development and production and include the following:

- Milestone A—initiates technology maturation and risk reduction.
- Milestone B—initiates engineering and manufacturing development.
- Milestone C—initiates production and deployment.

The methodology that can be adopted to comprehend the performance required from a new system that is to be developed could be similar to that of the US to "repeatedly experiment" with extensive user feed-back on prototypes—which will then evolve the "firm requirements "for the development of the first "block" of the system. "*Then, all weapons developments should utilise true "spiral development"—with a five year cycle for each block (from the time of commitment to system development, to its initial operational capability). This requires that each block of the system (beginning with block one) to utilise only fully-proven technologies; but that R&D is being funded, in parallel, for subsequent blocks. Thus, once the new technology is proven, it can be phased in to the next block. It is important that when properly implemented, such "spiral development" will not only get higher-performance equipment more rapidly but (on an average) effect a savings of approximately 30 per cent—and with much lower risk*"[39].

The statement in 2009 by the former US Defence Secretary, Robert Gates that a number of steps are needed to be taken for a sweeping reform of Pentagon's weapons acquisition process is true for India as well. These include avoiding inefficient extension of acquisition programmes which lead to cost over-runs; purchase weapon systems at efficient rates to promote economies of scales; focus buying larger quantities of 75 per cent solution systems than small quantities of 99 per cent solutions; choose future-oriented weapon system acquisition programmes to avoid redundancy; freeze requirements once contracts awarded to prevent cost hikes; encourage competition and prototyping between companies before contract is awarded and increase the size and quality of Pentagons acquisition team[40].

India too needs a new organisation like the ROK's DAPA which will be responsible for managing and executing both, the defence acquisitions of foreign as well as of domestic material. It could streamline and consolidate various organisations responsible for equipment procurement and development of technology and systems. To ensure long-term continuity of the acquisition staff, the organisation should be manned by a permanent cadre of civilian and military officers fully trained and experienced in defence equipment and technologies, their acquisition process activities, development process activities of engineering drawings designs and development, manufacture technologies and production processes, sustenance engineering and maintenance management aspects and so on. Due to the very nature of the job and since the organisation will be dealing with equipment and technologies, the staff must have a sound engineering background. They should be trained specialists who have gained adequate experience of weapon system induction and exploitation in the field. As far as the Services are concerned, their in-house MRO organisation officers will probably be best suited for the job as equipment management has always remained their responsibility and forte. Thus, as far as the military goes, there should be a separate permanent acquisition cadre raised from the selected officers of the in-house MRO organisations having more than 15 years of military service and initially coming on deputation for a tenure of three to five years. In case found suitable and selected, they could be permanently absorbed to form the new cadre and granted assured growth opportunities based on their performance in the organisation. A similar process could be adopted for the civilian engineering officers forming a part of this cadre who could initially come on deputation for a tenure of three to five years from the DRDO, OF's and DPSUs. In case found suitable and selected, they could also be permanently absorbed to form the new cadre and granted assured growth opportunities based on their performance in the new organisation

This organisation's head could report to the Defence Minister, discuss and control the decision-making process by its Executive Committee—which in turn could also have the User and external expert's participation. The local agents to supply their products and services to the MOD could be asked to register and be certified by this organisation. This agency could play a major role in the acquisition process. It could be the government's only institution conducting formal negotiations on the issues pertaining to the price, technology transfers, local production and offset packages. It could exercise authority over the budget allocations for acquisitions and whether a weapons system is to be procured domestically or from the foreign market. It could also promote the domestic industry and R&D whereby it can naturally favour the procurement of defence material developed and produced within the country. The domestic competition for R&D and production contracts should also be handled by this organisation. It could select the prime contractor based on the bidders' level of both, technological advancement and the estimated cost of production (L1T1) rather than the cost of production (L1) only as is being done today. R&D contracts could be increasingly awarded to industries other than the DRDO to improve the capabilities of the industry and reduce the dominance of DRDO in the defence R&D sector. India could reserve the right to select the local companies as Indian Offset Partners (IOP's) who in ROK are known as Korean Industry Participants (KIP's), who would partner foreign companies for the discharge of offset obligations. In cases where the foreign vendors are allowed to suggest IOP's, this dedicated agency could have the final say. By reserving the right to select IOP's, the agency could ensure that the right kind of domestic industry players get the opportunity which is in the interest of the industry. The 'Defence Technology Innovation Centre' (DTIC) could be a new department established within the agency for planning and delegating R&D programmes either to industries or to the DRDO. The Defence Technology and Quality (DTaQ) Centre need not be a part of the agency but can be practically directed by it, as also the DRDO. By exercising control over domestic defence acquisitions while at the same time having both, export promotion and regulatory authorities situated under the same roof, the agency can be a special, if not unique, kind of organisation as ROKs DAPA.

India, like the US, should consider setting up the DOD's DTIC which could serve the MOD community as the largest central resource for MOD and government-funded scientific, technical, engineering, and business related information. "*DTIC and its Information Analysis Centres (IACs) are research and analysis organisations established by US DOD to support researchers, scientists, engineers, and programme managers*"[41]. With a broad imprint, India's DTIC like that of the US, can allow the MOD to reduce duplication and build on previous research, development, and operational experience.

The fast technological changes in the informational, biological and nanotechnology arenas will eventually require a more responsive defence industry to keep up with the changes. In contrast to today's defence acquisition cycles of 15 to 20 years (or the 30 to 40 years development cycle in India today) the technological cycles in the future may have to be measured in months and consequently most of the advanced critical technologies will be available globally since most of the commercial firms are now globalised[42]. The technologies and products coming from the defence industry in the next few years will be very different and will include emphasis on intelligence, unmanned systems, systems engineering, advanced information systems etc. This suggests a move away from the platform centric thinking to a much more network centric thinking—in terms of a systems of systems thinking (with large number of sensors and shooters integrated with secure command, control and communication systems).

In a monopoly environment there is little incentive for achieving either a lower cost or a higher performance. Thus, it is important, Indian MOD, like the US, undertakes "best value" competitions (i.e. competitions not based on the lowest cost or the maximum performance, but on the combination of these variables). The primary objective must be to achieve innovation and costs savings—at both the prime and the lower-tier elements. "*It is not necessary to have two firms in production at all times to maintain a competitive industry in every sector of the defence area. Rather, it is necessary to have at least two design teams in all critical areas, and to have each of them at least going through funded prototyping* (unlike the Indian system of 80:20 for MAKE projects with 20 per cent funds to be invested by the development firm without being assured of a subsequent order)—*so that they are addressing not only technical feasibility, but also affordability, producibility, and supportability. On the other hand, if quantities are sufficient, it makes sense to have continuous production competition (such as was held for the engines on the F-15 and F-16—where the presence of continuous production competition yielded higher performance and higher reliability, yet with significant cost reductions). Competition should not be a firm requirement—beyond the competitive prototype phase, where it always should be utilised—rather, as long as the current producer is continuously improving performance and lowering costs, they should be rewarded by a continuation of their contract. However, it is essential that a credible option must always be present. An inexpensive way to maintain this option (and to encourage continuous innovation) is to fund a second source for interchangeable, yet next generation, lower cost/higher performance prototypes (at either the system or subsystem level)*"[43].

Lastly, for MOD to compete with the industry for the "best talent" there have to be revisions to the salary policies as done in the US. "*The current "pay for performance" initiatives are in the right direction, but further steps are required as increasing starting pay for engineers to compete with industry. In addition, DOD must develop, and implement, a personnel training and career development programme for the government civilian workforce; one that is comparable to the military programme (where funds, time, and additional positions, are allocated to provide for training and development). Another step that will be necessary due to the retirement of the senior people within the DOD acquisition core—is to increase the rotation from industry to government (and visa-versa). Additionally, for all functions which are not inherently governmental (many of which are currently being done by either civilian or military government personnel) should be subjected to 'competitive sourcing;'—between the public and private sectors. This on an average can bring down the costs by over 30 per cent—no matter who wins (public or private sector)—while the performance can go up significantly (since the "measurement" of performance now becomes an important consideration)*"[44].

7.5 Suggested Action Plan For *MAKE IN INDIA* in Defence Sector

The *MAKE IN INDIA* campaign of the Indian government was announced in 2014. It envisaged an increase in the contribution of the manufacturing sector to 25 per cent of India's GDP. The defence sector was one of the 25 sectors listed under the scheme. However, unlike the other manufacturing sectors in India which have witnessed a noticeable growth in the past, the Indian defence sector has lagged in innovation, productivity and exports. This is because there is a lack of clarity as to how the *MAKE IN INDIA* exercise is to be progressed in the case of defence manufacturing. The public sector, i.e. the DRDO, the OF's and the DPSU's perceive this to be a capability building exercise for them and want it to be re-phrased as a *MADE IN INDIA* defence manufacturing initiative. To the contrary, the private sector perceives it to be a *MAKE IN INDIA* initiative which in effect need not necessarily lead to full self-reliance as could have been made possible from a true 'Make-by-India' initiative. Accordingly, the private sector envisages it to be an opportune time to forge tie up's with foreign OEM's to bring in cutting edge technology for the manufacture of various defence systems in India. Such like defence manufacturing could be undertaken either independently or as a JV with a foreign partner/partners. Notwithstanding the perceptional differences, it can be safely assumed that in case the Government's aim is to acquire and develop in-house research, design, development and production capabilities to enhance the self-reliance of the existing Indian DITB, then the public sectors views are correct. However, if the aim is to invite the foreign manufacturers to set up defence manufacturing bases and produce their products in India and, in turn get an incidental access to the critical technologies and systems, then the private sector's viewpoint may not be correct in its entirety as it does not fully benefit the Indian cause. The reason for this is that, there could always be the risk that such a *MAKE IN INDIA* campaign could finally end up becoming a programme of 'Make in the Private sector through TOT from Foreign OEM's.' As a result, what happened in the Indian defence public sector in the last 70 years could very well get replicated in the private sector, with virtually no knowledge creation and technology incubation as was experienced by the public sector earlier. Therefore, this time there is a need to adopt a result oriented, if need be a graduated approach for the private sector to achieve true self-reliance.

Moreover, the public sector over the years has built considerable infrastructure, acquired the state of the art manufacturing facilities and trained an experienced work force. Duplicating all these essentials in the private sector will only lead to redundancies and drain the national resources. Also, the private sector has mastered different business models and adopted varied managerial practices and marketing skills which need to be tapped to bring in the latest technology that is available globally. Therefore, synergising the strengths of these public and private sectors could be a win-win situation. The government should realise that both the sectors are national assets and there is a need to devise methods to harness their full potentials to achieve self-reliance in defence production. For that reason, it should treat both the sectors as equal partners in our persuit for self-reliance.

Yet, probably what is important to understand is that there is very little knowledge that is available in the Indian private sector as pertaining to 'weapons systems engineering'. Thus, almost all the Indian prime players involved in the defence business have signed MOU's with leading manufacturers abroad for the transfer of technology of specific major defence systems. However, with their poor knowledge of 'weapons systems engineering' we could very well end up getting either, old generation systems assembled in India which had earlier been developed for the foreign armies or alternately, end up paying a much higher cost for the 'Through-Life Capability Management' of the military systems under acquisition.

As far as the Knowledge Centres are concerned, part of this 'weapons systems engineering' resides with the DRDO, OF's and DPSU's, which absorbed the production TOT of the major defence systems under licenced production. Unfortunately, this knowledge is only limited to the assembling of the equipment and consequently their understanding of systems engineering is very poor. Moreover, more often than not, these agencies have been found to be lacking the Users perspective. To the contrary, in this regard, the Army's Base Workshops (ABW's), the Naval Dockyards and the Air Force's Base Repair Depots (BRD's) are the leading engineering resources which possess a comprehensive knowledge cache of systems engineering of major weapons systems. This knowledge has been built over the years through the maintenance TOT that was obtained for undertaking the base level reset of tanks, armaments, engineering and bridging equipment, rocket systems, missiles, radars, small arms, aviation, avionics, sensor and communication systems and their sub-systems.

The aim of such base-level reset is to re-store the full mission capability of a major weapon system which degrades over a period of time, due to the effects of vintage, usage and deployment. For e.g., a new Bofors gun, at the time of induction, is capable of firing 800-900 rounds before a critical failure occurs. However, the very same gun after an exploitation of 25-30 years would , due to the effects of vintage, usage and deployment, degrade in its capability to such an extent, that the same critical failure would now occur on firing only 180-200 rounds. A comprehensive base-level reset programme when executed, can re-store the gun to its near full mission capability status of 800-900 rounds before the same critical failure occurs (i.e. to a Like New Condition). This is the operational significance of the Base level repair infrastructure which the advanced armies of the world possess, preserve and modernise. Thus, these base level agencies are aptly suited to participate in the *MAKE IN INDIA* programme, as they alone possess the comprehensive engineering Know-How and Know-Why of the in-service weapon systems. They are the actual knowledge leaders who know how these systems are wired, architected and what are their technological leads and shortcomings.

The above aspect also reiterates the fact that at this juncture the complexities of systems engineering of military systems precludes the Indian private sector to translate the Governments *MAKE IN INDIA* dream into a reality all by themselves. The private companies accordingly need to be inducted into defence manufacturing in a graduated and caliberated manner to obviate the inevitable pitfalls experienced earlier by the Public sector. Moreover, for manufacturing major defence systems like tanks/armaments/rockets/missiles/radar systems/aviation or ship-building assets, and so on, there will be a need to form national defence clusters possessing the knowledge cache for each type of major defence system's. Such defence clusters would need to integrate the specialist elements/entities which at present are providing the desired effort for a specific major defence system, be it the associated R&D lab/establishment(s) of the DRDO or any other associated S&T/R&D agency; the OF/DPSU currently providing the production effort for such a defence system; the ABW/BRD/Naval Dockyard providing the base level reset for a similar system; the Private vendor and its foreign JV partner selected as the agency for manufacturing that major defence system in India (the proposal to designate such private vendors has recently been termed as 'Strategic Partners' as well) and so on.

The induction of the designated private industry or the selected Strategic Partner into defence production of a specific major defence system needs to be undertaken in a graduated manner. The aim should be to progressively introduce the designated private vendor into the nuances and complexities of the specific class of weapon system wherein, it learns from the various elements of the defence cluster that is being proposed to be formed for each major defence system. The following approach for the smooth induction of the private vendor could be adopted:

- **Initial Induction Phase** The designated private industry could initially be made to execute a sub-system level upgrade programme on the allocated weapon system. The upgrade to be inserted could either be readily available indigenously or could be required to be developed in the private sector. An example of such an upgrade could be the installation of a new advanced Fire Control System (FCS) in a batch of MBTs/ICVs. The upgrade once executed could either meet a technology upgrade requirement or an operational upgrade requirement wherein, the concerned ABW/Naval Dockyard/BRD could assist the private sector by providing them with invaluable domain know how of the technologies incorporated in the existing in-service system as also as to what all need to be technically achieved to provide for the enhanced performance of the technology insertion programme. These agencies could also assist them in understanding the various FCS parameters, the inter-se inter-play between such parameters and their impact on the designing of the sub-system, the different FCS configurations that are possible for a specific class of MBT/ICV/Armament System for a Naval Platform or a combat aircraft, what could be the specific architecture for the shortlisted configuration, its inter-se spatial requirements besides its impact on any future system level upgrade and so on.
- **Interim Induction Phase** The designated private industry could next be made to execute a major system level upgrade programme on an in-service weapon platform. An example of this could be to upgrade the Powerpack in a batch of MBTs/ICVs/a class of ships or aircrafts. A single system level power pack upgrade programme, can provide invaluable insight and a large amount of knowledge to the private vendors, as to how the entire

power train of a tracked vehicle/ship/aircraft is engineered and in turn could generate adequate interest for the creation of design houses in India. These design houses could later, take on the power pack development as their core competency for future programmes like the Future Infantry Combat Vehicle (FICV)/Future Ready Combat Vehicle (FRCV) etc. Like wise, another private vendor could venture into the field of turret manufacturing for the FICV/FRCV by carrying out an armament upgrade to an existing wheeled or tracked ICV/MBT. Again here, the concerned ABW could assist the private vendors in comprehending the system engineering aspects pertaining to the complicated power train of a tracked vehicle which would essentially comprise of the power pack (engine and gearbox) and the running gear drive line (intermediate/transmission gear box, side gear boxes, final drives, sprocket/idler, tracks, suspension and the road wheels). Similarly, the manufacturing of a turret would require the ABW to make the private vendors understand the system engineering intricacies of the turret structure, turret armour, the race ring, mounting of the missile and guns (main, co-axial and top mount guns), sighting system (for Commander, Gunner and Driver, by day and by night, by direct viewing optics and by thermal observation, gun control system, ammunition stowages, auto loading gear and so on.

- **Final Induction Phase** The designated private industry could lastly graduate to undertake the performance optimisation programme for an in-service variant of the specific major weapon system that it has been designated for, such as a MBT. An example of this could be to carry out the weight and performance optimisation of MBT Arjun. Alternately, this could also be performed by a DARPA like special force comprising of a group of technical/engineering experts from the designated private sector, academia, DRDO and the Army that could be formed for a fixed term with total accountability. Such an effort, besides facilitating the designated private vendor to learn from the exercise, will also accelerate the optimisation process and may also obviate the need for the FRCV programme. A similar team can be employed to give a positive push to the National Engine Mission—an attempt to develop a range of high horsepower military engines.

The above initiatives could also be run simultaneously rather than sequentially to compress the time lines, especially in cases wherein some of the Indian vendors over the years have already acquired the sub-system level integration capabilities, for e.g. L&T and Tata Power in the Pinaka Programme of the Indian Army or L&T and TCS in the Advance Technology Vessel (ATV) programme of the Indian Navy.

Simultaneously, would also be the requirement to carry out an effective mission engineering exercise of all military systems held with the Armed Forces to arrive at a reality check and ascertain as to which all defence systems can meet the futuristic operational requirements through a system of upgrade programmes and where-all is there the real need for inducting or developing new systems. This could be followed by the commissioning of those system's that are identified for the upgrade programme(s) as also, commissioning a few flagship programmes that are identified for induction or development as new systems. The explicit aim in both the categories could be to incubate and develop the 'Generation Next' technologies as the military systems are being upgraded/developed. The strategy could be to acquire the technological capability of design, system integration and testing of the proposed upgraded systems or in the acquisition of a tank, gun, UAV, missile or any other military system.

Finally, what is needed is 'Wise Knowledge Leadership' to drive this initiative. The general management approach, as adopted in the past, would only end up delivering half baked results of yester years. In case persisted upon, India, could yet again find itself left with no other option but to take the recourse to imports, to plug its operational capability voids. This ongoing practice is required to be averted and can only be possible by replacing the 'Generalists' in the system by the 'Domain Experts' who understand the 'Systems Engineering of Military Systems'.

This can be done by introducing an Apex-level Body, say a 'Defence Systems Engineering and Technology Management Centre (DSETMC)'. The Centre could be assigned the full charge of the *MAKE IN INDIA* initiative for the defence sector. This technology management outfit must have a sound engineering knowledge of the major defence systems, should be able to understand and appreciate the complexities involved in either developing a new system de-novo or undertaking an operational or technological upgrade to an existing system and their associated logistics requirements. Thus, it has to be an organisation comprising of 'Domain Experts' who have a systems view of the operational, engineering and logistics aspects of the military systems. The inhouse MRO engineering officers of all the three Services are perhaps the only ones who have this systems view and meet all the criterion of such a requirement. These officers could thus be deputed for staffing such an organisation. In today's world, which is more and more giving way to increasing specialisation in order to enhance the efficiency levels, this is perhaps the opportune time to introduce the concept of 'Domain Experts'. The proposed Apex Body thus needs to comprise of individuals who possess the desired specialist skill sets of understanding and configuring the 'Systems Engineering Technology Trees' as pertaining to the different major defence systems that are either held or required to be developed for the Indian Armed Forces. The DSETMC would also be required to carry out a technology gap analysis of the indigenous DITB with respect to the 'Systems Engineering Technology Tree' of each major weapon platform and initiate the proactive steps required to fill the voids, albeit using MOD funding, where required.

The configuring of these 'Technology Tree's of Major Defence Systems' would also point towards the need of creating new 'System Houses' having the abilities to architect systems and integrating them. The DSETMC could also provide the insights into the need to create a web of sub and partial system manufacturers who could provide robust and high quality sub systems to the 'System Houses' and also contribute immensely in pushing their research into the development pipeline. It could prevent unwarranted competition amongst the 'System Houses' thereby, controlling the wastage of the scarce national resource. It could also vet all future TOT agreements with foreign suppliers and use the lever of the main acquisition to get in new technologies and set up the 'Technology Towers' that are not yet available indigenously.

A start could be made by gifting a set of obsolete and obsolescent major defence systems to the private sector and IITs for reverse engineering and technology incubation through MOD funding. In all these initiatives, a strong 'Engineering Knowledge Base' is critical and be it the ABWs, the Naval Dockyards, the BRD's, the DPSU's and the OF's have these in abundance and in many forms—be it explicit, tacit or pragmatic to assist the academia or the industry to understand the systems engineering principles, skills and training needs. Once this 'Defence Technology Knowledge Base' is established, then the creativity and innovation of the Indian Universities and the Indian Defence Industry in the emerging technologies will follow and find their expression. This will then put the Governments *MAKE IN INDIA* initiative in an overdrive to deliver the desired outcome that is envisaged out of the *MAKE IN INDIA* scheme for the defence sector.

NOTES

1. Kaan Korkmaz and John Rydqvist, "*The Republic of Korea: A Defence and Security Primer*", p. 53 available at http://foi.se/ Report Files/foir_3427.pdf (Accessed October 22, 2015).
2. VK Kapoor, "*RMA and India's Military Transformation*" p. 1, *IDSA Journal of Defence Studies* available at http://www.idsa.in / jds/ 2_2_2008_RMAandIndiaMilitary Transformation_VKKapoor (Accessed October 23, 2015).
3. Maggie Marcum and Aliaksandr Milshyn, "*Changing trends in global research ,development and acquisition processes*", p. 2 of Institute on Global Conflict and Cooperation Policy Brief 2014 January 01, 2014 available at https://escholaship.org/uc/item/ 75z4632q?query= Maggie%20 Marcum% 20and%20 Aliaksandr%20Milshyn%20%E2%80%9 CChanging%20trends%20in%20global%20research%20,development%20and%20acquisition %20% 20processes%E2%80%9D,#page-1 (Accessed October 26, 2015).
4. Moon and Paek, "*Defence Innovation and Industrialisation in South Korea*", p. 5 available at https://escholarship.org/uc/item/ 29n4c3jv (Accessed October 26, 2015).
5. IHS, "*Jane's World Defence Industry2014*", p.95.
6. Arvind Gupta, "*A National Security Strategy Document for India*", IDSA Comment October 20, 2011 available at http://www.idsa.in/idsacomments/ANationalSecurityStrategy DocumentforIndia_arvindgupta_201011 (Accessed October 27, 2015).
7. Narendra Singh Sisodia and Amit Cowshish, "*Defence Planning, Programming and Budgeting*", p.109 of IDSA book titled "*Core Concerns in Indian Defence and the Imperatives for Reforms*" available at http://www.idsa.in/book/CoreConcerns inIndian Defence _vmisra (Accessed October 29, 2015).
8. "*Report* of the *Group of Ministers* on National Security", p.109 available at http:// www.vifindia.org/sites/default/files/ GoM%20Report %20on%20National%20Security.pdf (Accessed October 29, 2015).
9. International Institute for Strategic Studies, "*Military Balance 2013*", p. 262 and Ministry of Defence MoD, Government of India, "*Defence Services Estimates 2013-14*" *available at* http://www.mod.nic.in/forms/Default.aspx (Accessed November 02, 2015).
10. Standing Committee on Defence, 10th Lok Sabha, "*Defence Research and Development: Major Projects, 5th Report (Lok Sabha Secretariat: New Delhi, 1995),*" p. 4. available at http:/ /www.worldcat.org/title/eighth-report-standing-committee-on-defence-1995-96-tenth-lok-sabha-ministry-of-defence/oclc/51379274 (Accessed November 02, 2015).
11. "*Government of India MOD Annual Report 2014-15*", p.87 available at http://mod.nic.in/ writereaddata/AR1415.pdf. (Accessed November 03, 2015).
12. Ranjit Ghosh "*Defence Research and Development: International Approaches for Analysing the Indian Programme*", p. 23 IDSA Occasional Paper No. 41 available at http://www.idsa.in/ occasionalpapers/OP_Defence Research and Development_Ranjit Ghosh_140815 (Accessed November 04, 2015).
13. Reply to Lok Sabha starred question no 161 answered on July 18,2014 and available at http://164.100.47.132/Annexture _New/ lsq16/2/ as161.htm (Accessed November 07, 2015).
14. IHS Jane's World Defence Industry 2013, p.564.
15. Richard A. Bitzinger, "*Reforming China's defence industries: Progress in spite of itself?*", p. 108 available at http://www. academia.edu/11905969/Reforming_China_s_Defense _Industry_Progress_in_Spite_of_Itself (Accessed November 10, 2015).
16. "Report No. 35 of 2014- Union Government (Defence Services)" Performance of Ordnance Factory Board (OFB) pp.127-128 available at http://www.saiindia.gov.in/english/ home/

our_products/Audit_Report/ Government_Wise/union_audit/ recent_ reports/ union_ compliance/2014/Defence/Report_35/chap_8.pdf (Accessed November 11, 2015).

17. Laxman Kumar Behera, "*India's Ordnance Factories: A Performance Analysis*" pp.74-75 *IDSA Journal of Defence Studies available at* http://www.idsa.in/journalofdefencestudies (Accessed November 14, 2015).
18. Report No. 35 of 2014- Union Government (Defence Services)" Performance of Ordnance Factory Board pp. 126 available at http://www.saiindia.gov.in/english/ home/ our_products/ Audit_Report/Government_Wise/union_audit/recent_reports/ union_ compliance/2014/ Defence/Report_35/chap_8.pdf (Accessed November 14, 2015).
19. Laxman Kumar Behera, "India's Defence Public Sector Undertakings: A Performance Analysis" p.118 *IDSA Journal of Defence Studies*l 3(4). October 2009 *available at*www.idsa.in/ sites/default/files/jds_3_4_lkbehera.pdf (Accessed November 14, 2015).
20. Department of Public Enterprises, Public Enterprises Survey 2009-10 I-Chapter 7 "Delegation of Enhanced Financial Powers to CPSEs" pp.112-116 available at http:// dpe.nic.in/sites/upload_files/dpe/files/sur0910/survey01/volume1/vol1ch7.pdf (Accessed November 15, 2015).
21. Laxman Kumar Behera, "*India's Ordnance Factories: A Performance Analysis*" p.65 *IDSA Journal of Defence Studies available at* http://www.idsa.in/journalofdefencestudies (Accessed November 15, 2015).
22. "Arun Jaitley seeks detailed review of defence PSUs", DNA Analysis, Thursday, July 24, 2014 available at http://www. dnaindia.com/india/report-arun-jaitley-seeks-detailed-review-of-defence-psus-2004771(Accessed November 15, 2015).
23. Aviotech Defense Advisory & Investments, "Summary of Performance of Unlisted Defence Public Sector Undertakings (DPSUs) for FY11 and FY10", p. 8 available at http:// www.aviotech.com/pdf/Summaryof_performanceof_unlisted_DPSUs.pdf (Accessed November 15, 2015).
24. Aviotech Defense Advisory & Investments, "Summary of Performance of Unlisted Defense Public Sector Undertakings (DPSUs) for FY11 and FY10", p. 5 available at http:// www.aviotech.com/pdf/Summaryof_performanceof_unlisted_DPSUs.pdf (Accessed November 15, 2015).
25. Laxman Kumar Behera, "*Enhancing Private Sector Participation In India's Defence Production*" Defence & Security Analysis 27 (3), p. 258, September 2011 *available at* http://www.idsa.in/ journalofdefencestudies (Accessed November 17, 2015).
26. "*Government eases FDI norms in 15 major sectors, including defence, civil aviation*" *Indian Express* Nov 11, 2015, available at http://indianexpress.com/article/india/india-news-india/ govt-eases-fdi-norms-fipb-limit-raised-from-rs-3000-crore-to-rs-5000-crore/ (Accessed November 17, 2015).
27. "*Fact Sheet on Foreign Direct Investment (FDI) Annex-B Statement on Sector-Wise FDI Equity Inflows from April 2000 To June 2015*" http://dipp.nic.in/English/Publications/ FDI_Statistics/2015/india_FDI_June2015.pdf (Accessed November 16, 2015).
28. Arindam Bhattacharya and Navneet Vashisht, "*Creating a Vibrant Domestic Defence Manufacturing Sector*", p.23 available at http://www.bcgindia.com/documents/file102698.pdf (Accessed November 17, 2015).
29. Government of India Ministry of Defence "*Annual Report 2014-15*", p. 57 available at http:/ /mod.nic.in/writereaddata/AR1415.pdf (Accessed November 17, 2015).
30. Laxman Kumar Behera, "*Enhancing Private Sector Participation In India's Defence Production*", Defence & Security Analysis 27 (3), p. 256, September 2011 *available at* http://www.idsa.in/ journalofdefencestudies (Accessed November 18, 2015).

31. "*Israel – Defence Industry*" IHS Jane's World Defence Industry 2013 p.18.
32. "*Israel – Defence Industry*" IHS Jane's World Defence Industry 2013 p.18.
33. "The Israeli arms industry" SIPRI Yearbook 2011 Armaments, Disarmaments and International Security p.239 available at http://www.sipri.org/yearbook/2011/files/SIPRIYB11summary.pdf. (Accessed November 18, 2015).
34. Kaan Korkmaz and John Rydqvist, "The Republic of Korea: A Defence and Security Primer" pp. 13-14 available at http:// foi.se/ReportFiles/foir_3427.pdf (Accessed November 19,, 2015).
35. Moon and Paek, "*Defence Innovation and Industrialisation in South Korea*", p. 2 available at https://escholarship.org/ uc/ item/29n4c3jv (Accessed November 19,, 2015).
36. Moon and Paek, "*Defence Innovation and Industrialisation in South Korea*", p. 5 available at https://escholarship.org/uc/ item/29n4c3jv (Accessed November 20, 2015).
37. Cheung, Tai Ming, "*Innovation in China's Defense Research, Development, and Acquisition System*", p. 4 available at https: //escholarship.org/uc/item/43v5v0nt (Accessed November 20, 2015).
38. Moshe Schwartz, "*Defence Acquisitions: How DOD Acquires Weapon Systems*", Congressional Research Service Report May 23, 2014 available at https://www.fas.org/sgp/crs/natsec/RL34026.pdf (Accessed November 21, 2015).
39. Gansler Jacques S., "*US Defence Industrial Policy*", p.8 available at http://www.securitychallenges.org.au/ ArticlePDFs/3(2) Gansler.pdf (Accessed November 23, 2015).
40. IHS Jane's World Defence Industry 2013 p.563.
41. Ranjit Ghosh, "*Defence Research and Development: International Approaches for Analysing the Indian Programme*", p.19 available at http://www.idsa.in/occasionalpapers/OP_DefenceResearchandDevelopmen_RanjitGhosh_140815.html (Accessed November 23, 2015).
42. Gansler Jacques S., *US Defence Industrial Policy*", p.3 available at http://www.securitychallenges. org.au/ArticlePDFs/l3(2) Gansler.pdf (Accessed November 23, 2015).
43. Gansler Jacques S., "*US Defence Industrial Policy*", pp.10-11 available at http://www.securitychallenges.org.au/ ArticlePDFs/ 3(2) Gansler.pdf (Accessed November 24, 2015).
44. Gansler Jacques S., "*US Defence Industrial Policy*", p.12 available at http://www.securitychallenges.org.au/ArticlePDFs/ 3 (2 Gansler.pdf (Accessed November 24, 2015).

Index

Advance Technology Vessel, 165
Advanced Information Systems, 119
Aeronautics and Space Industries of Israel (ASII), 44
Afghanistan, 107, 116
Africa, 153
Agency for Defence Development (ADD), 52, 58
Agni V, 7
Air Force's Base Repair Depots, 161
Annual Maintenance Contract (AMC), 3
Anti-Ship Cruise Missiles (ASCMs), 87
Anti-Submarine Warfare (ASW), 24
Anti-Tank Guided Missiles (ATGMs), 23
Armenia, 116
Armoured Personnel Carriers, 88
Army's Base Workshops (ABW's), 161, 164, 166
Aspin, Les, 106
Australia, 2, 8, 9, 129
Automatic Replenishment Stores, 151
Aviation Industries of China, 71
Aviation Industry Corporation, 74
Aviation Industry, 90
Azerbaijan, 43, 116

Bangladesh, 83
Base Repair Depots of Air Force, 126
Base Workshops of the Army, 126
Bharat Dynamics Limited, 23, 26
Bharat Earthmovers Limited, 22
Bharat Electronics Limited (BEL), 22, 26, 27, 141
Bill Clinton's administration, 105
Board of Research in Advanced Defence Sciences, 16
Brazil, 43
Build to Design (B2D), 134
Build to Print (B2P), 134
Build to Requirements (B2R), 134
Build to Specification (B2S), 134
Bureaucracy, 128
Bush administration, 105
Buy & Make (Indian), 31, 133, 148
Buy (Global), 31
Buy (Indian), 31

Cabinet Committee on Economic Affairs (CCEA), 141
Cabinet Committee on Security (CCS), 144
Canada, 2, 129
Capability Definition Document (CDD), 148
Central Government Expenditure (CGE), 8
Centre for Scientific and Industrial Research (CSIR), 16
China Aerospace Corporation (CASC), 71
China Aerospace Science and Industry Corporation (CASIC), 76
China Aerospace Science and Technology Corporation, 76
China Defence S&T Information Centre (CDSTIC), 78

China Electronics Technology Enterprise (CETC), 76
China National Nuclear Corporation (CNNC), 71, 75
China North Industries Group Corporation (CNGC), 75
China Nuclear Engineering and Construction Corporation (CNECC), 75-76
China Shipbuilding Industry Corporation (CSIC), 75
China South Industries Group Corporation (CSGC), 75
China State Shipbuilding Corporation (CSSC), 74
China, 8, 9, 10, 44, 69, 70, 72, 74, 78, 79, 80, 83, 84, 86, 90, 91, 93, 125, 127, 128, 129, 130, 132, 139, 147, 153, 155
China's
    aviation industry, 86, 93
    defence industry, 87
        modernisation, 71
    missile industry, 92
China's Civil-Military Integration (CMI), 25, 85
China's Military Industrial Complex (MIC), 25
China's Politbureau Standing Committee (PSC), 79
Civil-Military Integration Promotion Department (CMIPD), 82
Cold War, 99, 103, 104, 107, 112, 116
Command Control Communication Computers Intelligence Surveillance and Reconnaissance (C4ISR), 43, 105
Commercially Off The Shelf (COTS), 125
Commission of Science, Technology, and Industry for National Defence (COSTIND), 72
Completely Knock Down (CKD), 28
Compulsory Tender Law, 45
Cost Assessment and Programme Evaluation (CAPE), 117
Defence Acquisition Programme Administration (DAPA), 55, 57, 61, 62
Defence Acquisition System (DAS), 111, 155
Defence Advanced Research Projects Agency (DARPA), 114-15
Defence Capability Plan (DCP), 129
Defence Conversion Commission (DCC), 105
Defence Development Board, 148
Defence Development Production and Procurement Council (DDPPC), 131
Defence Export Council (DEC), 153
Defence Industrial Base (DIB), 40, 109
Defence Industrial Strategy (DIS), 111
Defence Industry and Technological Base (DITB), 1, 7, 9, 10, 12, 13, 129, 130, 154
Defence Industry Enterprise Groups (DIEGs), 73, 155
Defence Minister's Council on Production (DMCP), 131
Defence Planning Board (DPB), 13, 129
Defence Planning Guidance (DPG), 129
Defence Procurement Agency (DPA), 52
Defence Procurement Procedure (DPP), 6, 32
Defence Production Board, 148
Defence Production Policy (DPrP), 5
Defence Public Sector Undertakings (DPSU's), 5, 9, 13, 27, 126, 132, 140, 142, 143, 157, 161
Defence Security Cooperation Agency (DSCA), 116
Defence Systems Engineering and Technology Management Centre (DSETMC), 165
Defence Technology and Quality (DTaQ), 60, 158
Defence Technology Commission (DTC), 15
Defence Technology Innovation Centre (DTIC), 60, 158

Defence Technology Objectives (DTO's), 133
Defence Threat Reduction Agency (DTRA), 114
Delhi Metro Rail Corporation (DMRC), 24
Deng Xiaoping, 89
De-Novo, 125
Department of Defence Production (DDP), 17
Department of Industrial Policy and Promotion (DIP, 29
Department of Private Sector (DPS), 148
Department of Science and Technology (DST), 16
Developer, 128
Development of an operational weapon system, 4
Development of lab prototypes, 4
Development of operational weapon components, 4
Directorate General of Quality Assurance (DGQA), 21
Disinvestment, 25
Dockyards of the Navy, 126
Domain Experts, 165, 166
DRDO, 13-16, 19, 22, 23, 27, 28, 132-35, 137, 142, 157, 158, 161, 164

Economic Support Fund (ESF), 47
Egypt, 40
Elbit, 43
Electronics Industry, 90
Elisra, 43
End User Certificate (EUC), 145
European Union (EU), 44, 85, 87, 107
Exchange Rate Variation (ERV), 31

Federal Acquisition Regulation (FAR), 117
Federally Funded R&D Centres (FFRDCs), 112, 114
Finland, 44
Fire Control System (FCS), 111, 163
Foreign Direct Investment (FDI), 29, 143, 144, 145
Foreign Institutional Investor (FII), 144
Foreign Investment Promotion Board (FIPB), 144
Foreign Military Sales (FMS), 103, 116
Four Mechanisms, 72
France, 4, 8, 38, 39, 82, 93, 129
Future Combat Systems (FCS), 109
Future Infantry Combat Vehicle (FICV), 164
Future Ready Combat Vehicle (FRCV), 164

Garden Reach Shipbuilders and Engineers Ltd (GRSE), 24, 26, 142
Gates, Robert, 117, 156
General Armament Department (GAD), 72, 82
General Dynamics (GD), 106, 109
Generalists, 165
Germany, 8, 82
Global Positioning System (GPS), 115
Global War on Terror (GWOT), 99
Goa Shipyard Ltd. (GSL), 24, 26, 142
Group of Ministers (GOM), 13
Gulf War, 104

Heavy Vehicle Factory (HVF), 20
High Mobility Vehicle (HMV), 23
Hindustan Aeronautics Limited (HAL), 22, 24, 26, 42, 141, 142, 152
Hindustan Shipyard Ltd. (HSL), 24, 26, 142
Hu Jintao, 86

Illustrated Spare Parts Price List (ISPPL), 152
Independent Research and Development (IR&D), 115
India, 8, 9, 43, 116, 118, 153, 155, 156
Indian Air Force (IAF), 118
Indian Navy, 23, 24
Indian Offset Partners (IOP's), 32, 158

Indian Space Research Organisation (ISRO), 16, 24
Indigenisation, 1, 3, 7, 23
Indigenous innovation, 77
Indigenous Manufacture (IM), 4, 142
Industrial Cooperation Authority (ICA), 41, 149
Industrial Cooperation Undertaking (ICU), 41
Industrial Licenses (ILs), 29
Industrial Participation Policy (IPP), 149
Infantry Fighting Vehicle (IFV), 53
Information Analysis and Dissemination (IAD), 78
Information Analysis Centres (IACs), 158
Information Technology (IT), 7
Information-Based Warfare (IBW), 104, 125
INS Kamorta, 24
Integrated Defence Staff (IDS), 6
Integrated Project Team's (IPT), 56
Intellectual Property Rights (IPR), 135
Inter Continental Ballistic Missile (ICBM), 7
Inter-Factory Demands (IFD's), 18
International Traffic in Arms Regulations (ITARS), 145
Introduce, Digest, Absorb, and Re-innovate (IDAR), 78
Iraq, 107, 116
Israel Aircraft Industries (IAI), 23, 39, 42, 43
Israel Military Industries (IMI), 38, 39, 43, 45
Israel, 8, 40, 42, 43, 82, 139, 153
  defence budget, 40
  defence industry, 40, 48
Israeli Defence Force (IDF), 39
Israeli Shekels (ILS), 149
Italy, 8

Japan, 9
Jiang Zemin, 89
Joint Capabilities Integration and Development System (JCIDS), 110
Joint Ventures (JV's), 5, 118, 128, 154
Joint Warfare (JW), 54

Kinetic Kill Vehicle, 93
Kolar Gold Fields, 23
Korea Institute for Defence Analyses, 53, 62
Korean Industry Participant, 58, 158
Korean War, 51, 112

Large System Integrators (LSI), 110
Latin America, 153
Letters of Intents (LOIs), 29
Life Cycle Costs (LCC), 15
Limited Series Production (LSP), 4
Lockheed Martin (LM), 106, 109, 118
Long Range Surface-to-Air Missile (LR SAM), 23
Long Term Defence Capability Plan, 134
Long Term Integrated Perspective Plan (LTIPP), 6, 19, 130, 132
Long Term Perspective Plans (LTPP), 5
Long Term Product Support Agreement (LTPSA), 3
Long term product support, 4
Long Term Technology Perspective Plan (LTTPP), 133
Low-cost Guided Imaging Rocket (LOGIR), 63

M/s Rotem of South Korea, 24
Machine Building, 90
Main Battle Tank (MBT), 20, 53
Maintenance Transfer of Technology (MTOT), 6
Maintenance, Repair and Overhaul (MRO), 2, 157
Major Defence Acquisition Programmes (MDAPs), 117, 136
Major Unit Assemblies (MUA's), 15
Make in India, 10, 14, 124, 131, 142, 144, 147, 160, 162, 165, 166

Make, 31, 148
Mandatory Industrial Cooperation (MIC), 41
Manufacturers Recommended List of Spares (MRLS), 151
Mao, 88, 89
Marine Design and Research Institute of China (MARIC), 74
Massachusetts Institute of Technology (MIT), 43
Mazagon Dock Limited (MDL), 23, 24, 26, 142
Medium Range Surface-to-Air Missile (MRSAM), 23
Medium Small Micro Establishments (MSMEs), 9, 131
Mergers and Acquisitions (M&A), 84
Military Industrial Complex (MIC), 71, 138
Military Off The Shelf (MOTS), 125
Military-Industrial Complex (MIC), 99
Ministries of Machine Building (MsMB), 90
Ministry of Defence (MoD), 6, 17, 21, 22, 31, 32, 41, 126, 146, 159
Ministry of External Affairs (MEA), 140
Ministry of Finance (MoF), 90
Ministry of Home Affairs (MHA), 29
Ministry of National Defence (MND), 52, 54
Mishra Dhatu Nigam Limited (MIDHANI), 23, 26, 27, 142
Missile Defence Agency (MDA), 114
Myanmar, 83

National Defence Industry Office (NDIO), 90
National Defence Panel (NDP), 13
National Defence Science and Technology Commission (NDSTC), 90
National People's Congress (NPC), 91
National Security Council (NSC), 129
National Security Strategy (NSS), 12, 129
Naval Dockyards, 161, 166
Netherland, 44
Network-Centric Operations (NCO), 125
Network-Centric Warfare (NCW), 104, 111
No Objection Certificate (NOC), 145
North Atlantic Treaty Organisation (NATO), 140
Northrop Grumman (NG), 106, 109
Nuclear-powered attack submarine (SSN), 70, 87
Nuclear-powered ballistic missile submarine (SSBN), 70, 87

On-board Patrol Vehicle (OPV), 24
Operation Desert Storm, 111
Operations and Maintenance (O&M), 108
Ordnance Development Centres (ODCs), 19
Ordnance Factories (OF's), 5, 9, 13, 16-22, 26, 126, 132, 137-40, 142-43, 160-61, 166
Ordnance Industry, 90
Organisation for Economic Co-operation and Development (OECD), 47
Original Equipment Manufacturer (OEM), 2, 21, 152

Pakistan, 8, 83, 116
People's Liberation Army (PLA), 69, 71, 72, 73, 74, 76, 80, 81, 82, 91, 128
Performance Based Life-Cycle Product Support, 152
Performance Based Logistics (PBL), 3, 33
Performance-Based Life-Cycle Product Support (PBL), 2
PLA Air Force (PLAAF), 70
PLA Navy (PLAN), 70, 74
Planning, Programming, Budgeting, and Execution System (PPBE), 111
Poland, 43, 44
Post-9/11, 116
post-Cold War, 125

Precision Electronics Limited (PEL), 118
Press Information Bureau (PIB), 7
Procurement and Production Directorate (PPD), 41
Production Agency (PA), 2, 128, 135
Production Board, 5
Production, 4
Profit after Tax (PAT), 26
Provisional Services Qualification Requirements (PSQR's), 130, 147
Public Private Partnership (PPP), 128

Qian Xuesen, 92
Qing Dynasty, 69
Quadrennial Defence Reviews (QDR), 13
Qualitative Requirements (QRs), 148
Quality Assurance (QA), 132
Quality Certification, 4
Quality Checks (QC), 134

R&D Board, 5
Rafael, 39, 42, 43, 44
Raksha Udyog Ratnas (RUR) , 31-32
Raytheon, 106, 109
Red Guards, 89
Republic of Korea's (ROK's), 51, 53, 125, 139, 149, 153, 154, 155, 158
  Defence industries, 63
  Defence policy, 53
  Defence private sector, 61
  Reorganised Defence Acquisition Process, 56, 57
Request For Proposal (RFP), 2
Required Operational Capabilities (ROCs), 56
Research Development Test and Evaluation (RDT&E), 99, 112-13
Research, 4
Revolution in Military Affairs (RMA), 65, 104, 125-26
Romania, 44
Russia, 8, 80, 87

Saudi Arabia, 8
Science and Technology Equipment Commission (STECO), 90
Scindia Shipyard Limited, 24
Second World War, 107
Self-Propelled Howitzer, 53
Semi Knock Down (SKD), 28
Short-Range Ballistic Missiles (SRBM), 93
Sinai War, 38
Singapore, 8
Small and Medium Enterprises (SMEs), 31
South East Asia, 153
South Korea, 8, 9, 52, 53, 54, 57, 58, 59, 61, 64, 65, 154
South Korea's defence industrial strategy, 62
South Korea's defence industry, 55
Space Industry, 90
Spain, 8
Standard Operating Procedure (SOP), 145
State Administration for Science, Technology and Industry for National Defence (SASTIND), 72, 80, 82
State Owned Enterprises (SOE's), 25, 69, 85
Stockholm International Peace Research Institute (SIPRI), 83
Strategic Business Units (SBUs), 22
Submarine (SS), 87
Surface to Air Missile (SAM), 23, 87
Sweden, 4
Switzerland, 82
System Houses, 166
Systems Engineering of Military Systems, 165

Tai Ming Cheung, 91
Tajikistan, 116
talpiot, 42
Technology Perspective and Capability Roadmap (TPCR), 6
Technology Tree's of Major Defence Systems, 166
Test and Evaluation (T&E), 4, 16

Through-Life Capability Management, 161
Total Obligation Authority (TOA), 99
Transfer of Technology (TOT), 5, 119, 133, 135, 138, 151, 162, 166
Turkey, 8

UAE, 8
UK, 2, 4, 8, 38, 77, 82, 93, 129
Ukraine, 8, 82
Unmanned Aerial Vehicles (UAVs), 6, 65, 74, 115, 128
US, 2, 3, 8-10, 38, 40, 42, 43, 51, 53, 54, 61, 65, 85, 87, 88, 93, 102, 119, 125, 127, 129, 130, 132, 133, 139, 153, 159
  Department of Defence (DOD), 2, 99-101, 103, 105-17, 119-20
  Aid to Israel, 40
  Air Force, 106
  Defence budget, 99
  Defence exports, 116
  Military, 102
    expenditure, 104
User, 128

Value Of Issues (VOI), 19
Value Of Production (VOP), 18, 26, 140
Very Long Term Integrated Perspective Plan (VLTIPP), 132
Vietnam, 43

Welding Research Institute (WRI), 27
West Asia, 153
Wise Knowledge Leadership, 165
World War II, 99, 112, 113

Xinhua, 77